D0922313

SHAMBHALA CLASSICS

The Way of a Pilgrim

AND

The Pilgrim Continues His Way

TRANSLATED FROM THE RUSSIAN BY
Olga Savin

FOREWORD BY
Father Thomas Hopko

SHAMBHALA
Boulder
2001

Shambhala Publications, Inc.
2129 13th Street
Boulder, Colorado 80302
www.shambhala.com

16 15 14 13 12

PRINTED IN THE UNITED STATES OF AMERICA

Shambhala Publications makes every effort to print on acid-free, recycled paper.

Shambhala Publications is distributed worldwide by
Penguin Random House, Inc., and its subsidiaries.

LIBRARY OF CONGRESS CATALOGING-IN-PUBLICATION DATA

Otkrovennye rasskazy strannika dukhovnomu svoemu ottsu. English.
The way of a pilgrim; and, The pilgrim continues his way / translated from the Russian
by Olga Savin; foreword by Thomas Hopko.
p cm. — (Shambhala classics)
ISBN 978-1-57062-807-8 (pbk.)
1. Spiritual Life—Orthodox Eastern Church. 2. Jesus Prayer. I. Savin, Olga.
II. Iz rasskazov strannika o blagodatnom deistvii molitvy Iisusovoi. English.
III. Title. IV. Series.
BX382.O8513 2001
248.4'819—dc21 2001042048

CONTENTS

FOREWORD

THE ORIGIN OF this little spiritual classic is in many ways a mystery. No one knows for certain if it is a literally true story written by the narrator, or an account cast in the first person *about* a particular pilgrim (or perhaps based on several), or even a marvelously creative piece of spiritual fiction intended to propagate a certain understanding of the practice of the Orthodox Christian faith, and the prayer of the heart, particularly the Jesus Prayer.

Whatever the origin and intention of the anonymous author's fascinating story, it makes several things clear to spiritual seekers. It affirms first of all that the source, goal and content of human life is not spirituality or religion, liturgical ritual or ascetical regimes, but the living God Himself. It tells us that life is communion with God: personal, direct, immediate, real, painful, peaceful, and joyful. It tells us that ceaseless prayer in pursuit of God and communion with Him is not simply life's meaning or goal, the one thing worth living for, but it is life itself. It tells us that Jesus Christ is this life, and that constant, continual, ceaseless prayer in His name opens the door to Divine reality and puts us in immediate contact with the One who is the source, substance, and goal of our life, and our very life itself.

The pilgrim learns these things in the context of the Orthodox Church. His inspiration comes in the liturgical worship, which he faithfully follows and never abandons, and through the Bible, which he constantly carries with him as his greatest treasure. He searches for someone to help him to understand prayer and to practice it without ceasing. He finds people and writings that help him, often in the most unexpected places. He discovers the collection of writings of Christian spiritual masters, mostly Eastern and all Orthodox, called the *Philokalia* (which literally means love of the good and beautiful), with his whole life testifying to its teachings with disarming directness and awesome simplicity. What does he say about its message and teaching?

He says that one cannot practice ceaseless prayer in the name of Jesus outside the doctrinal and liturgical framework of the Christian Church and without the guidance and help of experienced teachers. He says that attempts to do this will be futile and fruitless and will inevitably lead to the spiritual delusion that is the perpetual risk of the spiritual seeker. While insisting on personal responsibility in the spiritual quest and on the radically personal character of prayer, the pilgrim insists equally on the need for participation in the community of faith with free and grateful obedience to its teachers and guides. He stresses the confession of sins and the need for perpetual repentance and moral conversion.

The pilgrim also stresses that the practice of prayer, which is the "art of arts" and "science of sciences" that proves everything else in a person's life, is a ceaseless labor whose fruit is always the result of God's grace. It is a disinterested activity—characterized by an interest only in God's glory and the salvation of souls, first of all one's own. It provokes the demons to relentless and ruthless attack. It invites the ridicule and rejection of the world. It excites the passions of mind and flesh before it cures their misuse and heals their abuse, and directs them to their proper end. It is practiced not to gain extraordinary experiences or unique consolations. It teaches us to fear visions and voices and every such thing as the source of great temptation, confusion, and pain. It is always accompanied by the peace that passes understanding and the joy that no one can take away, yet it inevitably involves suffering, of which the pilgrim is the first witness. For the purpose of ceaseless prayer is not to remove the crosses of pain and difficulty, but to empower the praying person to endure them and even to embrace them with enthusiasm and joy as the sole source of happiness in this sad sinful world in which we find ourselves wandering as pilgrims in pursuit of our homeland.

The pilgrim also tells us that the constant repetition of the Jesus Prayer, or any other such prayer of the heart, is not a magical or mechanical means to spiritual peace and perfection. The prayer is not an incantation or a talisman. It is a personal calling upon the personal God. It is a petition for the Lord to act as He knows and wills for our purification, enlightenment, and deification in an unending life of growth and perfection.

Both *The Way of a Pilgrim* and *The Pilgrim Continues His Way* remind us that we are all pilgrims on a journey to God. Like a safe and hospitable inn along the way, this book provides protection and nourishment for the trip, pointing to its perils and demonstrating its rewards. We greet Olga Savin's fresh new translation with gratitude and joy.

Father Thomas Hopko
Saint Vladimir's Seminary
Crestwood, New York

The Way of a Pilgrim

First Narrative

By the grace of God I am a Christian man, by my own actions a great sinner, and by calling a homeless wanderer of the humblest origins, roaming from place to place. My worldly belongings consist of a knapsack on my back, containing some dried bread, and a Holy Bible in my breast pocket. That is all.

On the twenty-fourth Sunday after Pentecost I went to church to worship at the Liturgy. During the reading of the Epistle of Saint Paul to the Thessalonians [1 Thess. 5:17] I heard the following words: "Pray without ceasing." This verse especially fixed itself in my mind, and I began to wonder how one could pray unceasingly, since each man must occupy himself with other matters as well, in order to make a living. I checked in the Bible and read with my own eyes that which I had already heard: namely, that one should "pray without ceasing," "pray at all times in the Spirit" [Eph. 6:18], and "in all places pray with uplifted hands" [1 Tim. 2:8]. I thought about this for some time but was unable to understand it.

"What should I do?" I thought to myself. "Where will I find someone who would be able to explain this to me? I will visit some of the churches that are renowned for their excellent preachers, and perhaps there I will be enlightened." So I went and I heard many fine sermons on prayer. However, they all dealt with prayer in general: what prayer is, the need to pray, and what are the fruits of prayer. Yet nothing was said about how to succeed in prayer. There was a sermon on praying in the Spirit and on unceasing prayer, but no mention was made about how to attain to such prayer.

Having had my fill of listening, without acquiring any understanding of how to pray unceasingly, I gave up on such sermons that were geared to the general public. I then resolved, with the help of God, to seek an experienced and knowledgeable guide who would explain unceasing prayer to me, for I now found myself so irresistibly drawn to learning about it.

I set out and wandered for a long time through different places and faithfully continued to read the Bible. Everywhere I went I inquired as to the local whereabouts of a spiritual director or a devout spiritual guide. Eventually I was told that in a certain village there was a landowner who had lived there for a long time and who spent all his time working out his salvation. He had a chapel in his own house and never went out, but continually prayed to God and read spiritual literature. When I heard this I gave up walking and took to my heels to get to this village. When I arrived there, I found the gentleman in question. "What is it that you require of me?" he asked.

"I have heard that you are a man of prayer and wisdom. In the name of God, would you please explain to me the meaning of the Apostle's words, 'Pray unceasingly,' and how one is to pray in this manner? I want to know this, yet I cannot understand it at all!"

He was silent for some moments. Then he looked closely at me and said, "Unceasing interior prayer is the continual striving of man's spirit toward God. To succeed in this delightful exercise, you must beseech the Lord more frequently that He teach you how to pray unceasingly. Pray more and ever more earnestly, and the prayer itself will reveal to you how it can become unceasing. This effort will take its own time."

Having said this, he offered me refreshment, gave me money for my journey, and let me go on my way. He did not, after all, provide me with an explanation.

So I set off again. I continued to think and read and wonder about what that man had told me, and still I could not understand it. Yet my longing for comprehension was so intense that it kept me awake at night.

When I had covered about 125 miles I came to a large provincial capital, where I saw a monastery. I stopped at the inn and happened to hear that in this monastery there was an exceptionally kind abbot, a prayerful and most hospitable man. I went to see him, and he welcomed me joyfully, sat me down, and offered me refreshment.

"Holy Father," I said, "I do not need food, but I seek your spiritual guidance on what I must do to save myself."

"Well, now—what must you do to save yourself? Live according to the commandments, pray to God—and you will be saved!"

"I have heard that one should pray unceasingly, but I do not know how to do this. I do not even understand what unceasing prayer is. My father, please explain this to me."

"I don't know, dear brother, how else to advise you. Ah—but wait just a moment! I do have a little book that will explain it." He brought me *The Spiritual Education of the Interior Man,* by Saint Dimitri. "Here you are—read this page."

I began to read the following: "Those words of the apostle—'pray without ceasing'—should be understood in reference to the prayer of the mind: for the mind can always aspire to God and pray to Him without ceasing."

"Would you explain to me the means by which the mind can always aspire to God and pray unceasingly, without being distracted?"

"That requires a great deal of wisdom, except for the one to whom God Himself has granted such a gift," said the abbot. He offered no further explanation.

I spent the night at the monastery. The next morning I thanked him for his kind hospitality and continued on my journey, without really knowing where I was headed. I grieved over my lack of understanding and comforted myself by reading the Holy Bible. Thus I journeyed for five days, keeping to the main road. Finally, one day toward evening, an old man who appeared to be some kind of cleric caught up with me. In answer to my question, he replied that he was a schima monk* and lived in a monastery, located some six miles off the main road. He invited me to come with him, to visit their monastery. "We take in pilgrims," said he, "and we offer them rest and food in the guesthouse, along with other devout people."

I was reluctant to go with him, so I replied, "My peace of mind does not depend on finding shelter, but rather on obtaining spiritual guidance. I do not need food, for my knapsack is filled with dried crusts of bread."

The monk asked, "What sort of guidance do you seek, and what is it that you do not understand? Come, dear brother, come and visit with us. We have experienced *startsi** who can nourish you spiritually and set you on the path of truth, in the light of God's Word and the teachings of the Fathers."

"Well, you see, Batyushka,* about a year ago, while at Liturgy, I heard the words of the apostle, exhorting men to 'pray unceasingly.' Unable to understand this, I began to read the Bible. There, in several different places, I also encountered this same divine instruction: that we must pray unceasingly, always and in all places, not only while occupied with all manner of activity, not only when we are awake, but even while we sleep. 'I sleep but my heart is awake' [Song of Sol. 5:2]. This surprised me, and I found myself unable to understand how this could be done and by what means it could be achieved. A burning desire and curiosity were aroused in me, and my thoughts dwelt on it day and night. So I began to visit many different churches and to listen to sermons that spoke about prayer. Yet no matter how many sermons I heard, not one of them provided me with an explanation of how to

*Words marked with an asterisk in their first occurrence are found in the glossary.

pray unceasingly. They spoke only of how to prepare oneself for praying, of the fruits of prayer, and so on; but they did not teach how one is to pray unceasingly and what is the nature of this sort of prayer. I frequently read the Bible to verify what I had heard, but I have not yet found the knowledge I seek. I am not at peace with myself and am still quite puzzled by all this."

The starets made the sign of the cross over himself and began to speak: "Thank God, beloved brother, for having awakened in you this irresistible longing to acquire unceasing interior prayer. You must recognize in this the calling of God. Be at peace and rest assured that until now you have been tested in the cooperation of your will with God's calling and have been granted to understand that neither the wisdom of this world nor mere superficial curiosity can attain to the divine illumination of unceasing interior prayer. On the contrary, it is the humble, simple heart that attains to such prayer, through poverty of the spirit and a living experience of it. So it is not at all surprising that you heard nothing about the very essence of prayer nor acquired any knowledge on how to achieve its unceasing activity.

"To tell the truth, although much has been preached on prayer and much is written about it in the teaching of various writers, they are better equipped to preach about the elements that constitute prayer than about the very essence of it, because their thoughts are based mostly on speculation and the deliberations of natural reason, rather than on a living experience of prayer. One will offer an exceptional discourse on the necessity of prayer, another on its power and benefits; yet a third will discuss the means to attaining to perfect prayer—the necessity of applied effort, attentiveness, warmth of heart, purity of thought, reconciliation with one's enemies, humility, contrition, and so on. But what about prayer itself, and how to learn to pray? To these, the most essential and necessary questions of all, very rarely does one obtain any substantial answers from present-day preachers. Such questions are far more difficult for their understanding to grasp than are all those arguments of theirs that I just mentioned, for they require a mystical insight that goes above and beyond mere academic knowledge. And what is even more pathetic is that the vain, natural wisdom of this world compels one to judge the Divine according to human standards. Many people treat prayer in an inverted way, thinking that it is one's efforts and the preparatory steps that give rise to prayer, rather than the prayer itself giving birth to good works and all the virtues. In this case, they mistakenly see the fruits and resulting benefits of prayer as the means to its end, thereby denigrating the very power of prayer.

"All this stands in direct contradiction to Holy Scripture, for the apostle Paul teaches us the following about prayer: 'I urge therefore that first of all supplications . . . be made . . .' [1 Tim. 2:1]. Here we see that the apostle's first emphasis is on the preeminence of the activity of prayer: 'I urge therefore that first of all supplications . . . be made. . . .' Many good works are required of a Christian, but it is prayer that must come first and foremost, for without prayer no other good work can be performed and one cannot find the way to the Lord. Truth cannot be acquired, the flesh with its passions and lusts cannot be crucified, the heart cannot be filled with the light of Christ and united with Him, through salvation, unless these are preceded by frequent prayer. I say *frequent,* because the proper way to pray and to attain to perfect prayer lies beyond our abilities. The apostle Paul says: 'For we do not know how to pray as we ought' [Rom. 8:26]. Consequently, it is only the frequency and regularity of prayer that lie within our abilities, as the means of attaining to pure prayer, which is the mother of all spiritual blessings. 'Acquire the mother and she will bear you children,' says Saint Isaac the Syrian. First learn to pray, and then you will easily perform all the good works. This is not obvious to those who lack a living experience of prayer and the knowledge of the mystical teachings of the Fathers, so they say very little about it."

So engrossed were we in this conversation that without realizing it, we had almost reached the monastery. Not wanting to lose touch with this wise starets and eager to obtain what I desired from him, I quickly said, "Would you be so kind, honorable Father, to explain to me the meaning of unceasing interior prayer and how one can learn it? I can see that you have experience of it and know it well."

The starets lovingly acknowledged my request and invited me to come with him. "Come inside with me now, and I will give you a book of the writings of the Fathers from which, with God's help, you will be able to learn and understand about prayer, clearly and in detail." We entered his cell, and the starets said the following to me: "The unceasing interior Jesus Prayer is the uninterrupted, continual calling upon the divine name of Jesus Christ, with the lips, the mind, and the heart, while calling to mind His constant presence and beseeching His mercy, during any activity one may be occupied with, in all places, at all times, and even while sleeping. The words of this prayer are as follows: 'Lord Jesus Christ, have mercy on me!' If one makes a habit of this supplication, one will experience great comfort and a need to repeat this prayer unceasingly, so that eventually one will not be able to live without it and the prayer will flow of its own accord.

"Now is it clear to you what unceasing prayer is?"

"Very clear, my Father! For God's sake, teach me how to acquire it," I cried out with joy.

"We can read about how to learn the prayer in this book, whose title is the *Philokalia.** It contains the complete and detailed teaching on unceasing interior prayer, as set forth by twenty-five holy Fathers. It is so lofty in wisdom and so beneficial that it is considered to be the foremost and primary manual of the contemplative spiritual life. The blessed Nikifor said that 'without struggle and sweat does it bring one to salvation.' "

"Is it possible that it is more exalted and holier than the Bible?" I asked.

"No, it is not more exalted or holier than the Bible, but it contains enlightened explanations of what is mystically contained in the Bible and is so lofty that it is not easily comprehended by our shortsighted intellects. Let me give you an example of this: the sun is the greatest, the most resplendent and magnificent source of light; but you cannot contemplate or examine it with the simple naked eye. You would need to use a special viewing lens, which, albeit a million times smaller and dimmer than the sun, would enable you to study this magnificent lord of all light and to endure and delight in its fiery rays. Thus the Holy Scriptures are like a brilliant sun, for which the *Philokalia* is the necessary viewing lens.

"Now listen, I will read to you about how to learn unceasing interior prayer." The starets opened the *Philokalia,* selected a passage from Saint Simeon the New Theologian, and began to read: " 'Find a quiet place to sit alone and in silence; bow your head and shut your eyes. Breathe softly, look with your mind into your heart; recollect your mind—that is, all its thoughts—and bring them down from your mind into your heart. As you breathe, repeat: "Lord Jesus Christ, have mercy on me"—either quietly with your lips, or only in your mind. Strive to banish all thoughts; be calm and patient, and repeat this exercise frequently.' "

Then the starets explained all this to me, illustrated it with examples, and we read some more from the *Philokalia*: passages from Saint Gregory of Sinai, the blessed Callistus and Ignatius. After reading all this in the *Philokalia,* the starets further explained it to me in his own words. I was fascinated and listened attentively to every word he said, absorbing it with my mind in as much detail as I was capable of remembering. Thus we spent the entire night, without sleeping a wink, and then went off to matins.

When we were parting, the starets blessed me and said that while learning the prayer, I should come to see him and reveal and confess all to him honestly and openly, for it is difficult and futile to live an inner spiritual life properly, without the guidance of a spiritual director.

Standing in church, I experienced a burning zeal within me to learn unceasing interior prayer as diligently as possible, and I asked God to help me in this effort. Then I thought to myself: how will I visit the starets for counsel and confession, when the monastery guesthouse has a three-day limit for visitors and there are no other residences near the monastery? Finally I happened to hear that there was a village a little over three miles away. I went there in search of a place to stay and was overjoyed that God had led me to find lodging. A peasant hired me to guard his kitchen garden for the entire summer, in exchange for which I could live alone in a hut near the garden. Thank God! I had found peaceful lodging. So I settled into my dwelling and began to learn interior prayer according to the way I'd been taught, and I visited the starets from time to time.

For a week, in the seclusion of the garden, I worked diligently on learning unceasing prayer and I did what the starets had taught me. At first it seemed as if things were moving along. Then a great inner heaviness, laziness, boredom, and drowsiness began to overcome me, while a mass of thoughts clouded my mind. Filled with grief, I went to see the starets and explained my problems to him. He greeted me kindly and said, "That, beloved brother, is the kingdom of darkness waging war against you. There is nothing more dreadful for this darkness than the prayer of the heart, so it will try anything to thwart you and prevent you from learning to pray. Come to think of it, even the enemy can act only by God's will and permission, and only for as long as it may be necessary for us. It appears that your humility still needs to be tested. Consequently, it is too soon for you to be attempting to enter into your deepest heart with such unrestrained zeal, lest you succumb to spiritual avarice. I will read to you what the *Philokalia* says about this."

The starets found a passage from the teaching of Blessed Nicephorus the Solitary and began to read: " 'If, after a few attempts, you are unable to enter into the place of the heart, as you were taught to do, then do what I tell you and, with God's help, you will find what you seek. You know that each person has a larynx through which he exercises his faculty of speech. Banishing all thoughts (you can do this, if you want to), exercise this faculty and continually repeat the following: "Lord Jesus Christ, have mercy on me!" Compel yourself always to repeat this. Should you do this for some period of time, then assuredly this exercise will open the doors of your heart. Experience has proven this.'

"So this is what the holy Fathers prescribe in such cases," said the starets. "Therefore, you must accept this teaching now with complete trust and repeat the Jesus Prayer as often as possible. Take this *chotki** and use it while you repeat the prayer, at least three thousand times a day to begin with. Whether you are standing, sitting, walking, or lying down, continue to repeat: 'Lord Jesus Christ, have mercy on me!' Do not be loud or rush the prayer, but without fail repeat it three thousand times each day, neither increasing nor decreasing this number on your own. Through this exercise God will help you to attain to the unceasing prayer of the heart."

I joyfully accepted his instructions, went home, and began to carry out the bidding of the starets faithfully and accurately. For two days I experienced some difficulty, but then the exercise became so easy and so desirable that if I stopped, I experienced a kind of compelling need to start reciting the Jesus Prayer again. Soon I was praying it with comfort and ease, without any of the force that I initially had to exert.

I related this to the starets, who instructed me to increase the number of repetitions to six thousand times a day. "Be calm and just try to repeat the prayer as faithfully as you can, for the number of times I have assigned to you. God will bestow His mercy on you."

For an entire week, in the solitude of my hut, I repeated the Jesus Prayer six thousand times a day. I was not anxious about anything and paid no heed to any thoughts, no matter how strongly they assailed me. I concentrated only on precisely carrying out the starets's instructions. And do you know what happened? I became so accustomed to the prayer that when I stopped praying, even for a brief time, I felt as though something were missing, as if I had lost something. When I began to pray again, I was immediately filled with an inner lightness and joy. If I happened to meet people, I no longer felt any desire to speak with them; I longed only for solitude, to be alone with my prayer. Thus it was that within a week I had become so accustomed to this prayer.

After ten days of not seeing me, the starets himself came to visit me, and I described my inner state to him. He listened and said, "Now that you have become accustomed to the prayer, take care to preserve and strengthen this habit. Do not pass your time in vain and, with God's help, resolve to repeat the prayer, without fail, twelve thousand times a day. Remain in solitude, rise earlier in the morning, retire later at night, and come to me for counsel every two weeks."

I began to carry out the starets's instructions. By late evening of the first day, I had barely managed to complete the rule of twelve thousand repetitions of the prayer. On the second day, I fulfilled the rule with ease and delight. At first I was weary from continuously repeating the prayer. My tongue became numb and my jaws felt stiff, although the sensations were not unpleasant. I then felt a subtle, delicate pain in the roof of my mouth, followed by a slight pain in the thumb of my left hand, with which I was counting the knots of the chotki. My left wrist felt inflamed, and this feeling spread up to my elbow, creating a most pleasant sensation. Moreover, all this was somehow urging and compelling me to pray more and more. Thus for the first five days I faithfully repeated the prayer twelve thousand times a day. As this habit became stronger, it also became more pleasant and I found myself more willing to practice it.

Early one morning somehow the prayer awakened me. I began to recite my morning prayers, but my tongue was reluctant to say them, while all my desire seemed to be striving, as if with a mind of its own, toward reciting the Jesus Prayer. As soon as I began to repeat it, I was filled with such lightness and joy that it felt as if my tongue and mouth spoke the words of their own accord, without any effort on my part! I spent the entire day enveloped in such joy and somehow detached from everything else—almost as if I were on another planet. By early evening I had easily completed the twelve thousand repetitions of the prayer. I had a strong desire to continue praying, but I dared not exceed the rule given to me by the starets. In the days that followed, I continued to call on the name of Jesus Christ with such ease and feeling so drawn to it.

Then I visited the starets and honestly recounted all this to him in detail. He listened and said, "Thank God that the ease and desire for prayer have been manifested in you. This is a natural consequence that comes from frequent practice and great effort. It is similar to a piece of equipment that can operate for a long time on its own, once its main drive has been activated; but in order for it to continue operating, the drive must be oiled and regularly reactivated. Now do you see with what superior abilities God, in His love for man, has endowed even the most sensual human nature—and what feelings can be experienced even outside a state of grace, even by a sinful soul with unclean passions, as you yourself have already experienced? Yet how magnificent, how delightful and enjoyable it is when the Lord bestows the gift of unceasing self-acting prayer and purifies the soul of its passions! This state is indescribable, and the revelation of the mystery of such prayer is a foretaste of heavenly bliss on earth. This is granted to those who seek the Lord in the simplicity of a heart filled with love! I now give you leave to repeat the prayer as much as you desire and as frequently as possible. Strive to devote every waking moment to prayer. Do not count the number of repetitions anymore, but call on the name of Jesus Christ, submitting yourself humbly to the will of God and awaiting His help. I believe that He will not abandon you and will set you on the right path."

Accepting this guidance, I spent the entire summer continuously repeating the Jesus Prayer with my lips. I was very much at peace and often even dreamed that I was uttering this prayer. If I happened to meet people during the day, without exception they all appeared very dear to me, as if they were family, though otherwise I did not concern myself too much with them. All thoughts seemed to vanish on their own, and I thought of nothing else but the prayer. My mind was recollected and attentive to it, while at times and of its own accord, my heart would feel a warmth and a kind of pleasure. When I happened to go to church, the long monastic service would seem so short and was no longer as tiring as it once had been for me. My solitary hut seemed like a magnificent palace, and I knew not how to thank God for sending such a starets and guide for the salvation of a wretched sinner such as I.

It was not for long that I enjoyed the counsel of my kind, divinely inspired starets, however, for at the end of that summer he died. As I tearfully parted with him, I thanked him for the fatherly counsel he had given to wretched me and begged him to give me, for a blessing and keepsake, the chotki he always used to pray with. And so I was left all alone. The summer finally drew to an end, and the kitchen garden was cleared. I was left with nowhere to live. The peasant released me from my job, paying me a wage of two rubles, and filled my knapsack with dried bread for my journey. Once again I set off wandering through different places, but now my travels were free of worry. Calling on the name of Jesus Christ now filled my days with joy. Each person I encountered seemed dearer to me, as if all were filled with love for me.

At one point I began to wonder what to do with the wages I'd earned for guarding the kitchen garden. What did I need money for? "Aha!" I thought, "I've got it! The starets is no longer around and there is no one to teach me. So I'll buy myself a copy of the *Philokalia* and continue learning about interior prayer." I made the sign of the cross over myself and went on walking and praying. When I came to a provincial town, I searched through the shops for a copy of the *Philokalia*. I found one, but they were asking three rubles for it, while I had only two! After I had bargained for a long time, the shopkeeper still refused to lower the price. Finally he said, "Go to that church over there and ask the parish elder. He has an old copy of this book; maybe he'll sell it to you for two rubles." I went there and actually managed to buy the *Philokalia* for two rubles! It was an old, worn copy, but I was thrilled. I managed to mend it somewhat by covering it with a piece of fabric, and I placed it in my knapsack, together with my Bible.

I set out again, continuously praying the Jesus Prayer, which had become more precious and sweeter to me than anything else in the world. There were days when I covered forty-seven miles or more, and I didn't even feel the effort of walking. The prayer alone filled my consciousness. When it was bitterly cold, I would pray more fervently, and soon I'd feel warm all over. If hunger threatened to overcome me, I would call upon the name of Jesus Christ with renewed vigor, and soon my hunger was forgotten. If I felt ill and pain racked my back and legs, I would give myself over to the prayer and soon was deaf to the pain. If someone offended me, I needed only to remember the sweetness of the Jesus Prayer, and all hurt and anger vanished, all was forgotten. It was as if I'd become a half-wit, for I had no cares about anything, nothing interested me. I cared not for the vain concerns of this world and longed only for solitude. I was now used to desiring only one thing: to pray unceasingly, for that filled me with joy. God alone knows what was happening to me! Yet of course, all these feelings were sensual, or, as my late starets would say, a natural consequence of habit. However, in my unworthiness and foolishness, I dared not venture yet to learn and aspire to the prayer of the inner heart. I awaited the fulfillment of God's will, setting my hopes on the prayers of my departed starets. And so, though I had not yet achieved the unceasing self-acting prayer of the heart, still I thanked God! For now I understood clearly the meaning of the apostle's words that I had heard: "Pray without ceasing!"

Second Narrative

For a long time I wandered through different places accompanied by the Jesus Prayer, which encouraged and comforted me wherever I went, no matter what or whom I encountered. Finally, I began to think it might be better for me to settle down somewhere, so as to find enough time and solitude to study the *Philokalia*. Although I had managed to read bits of it whenever I stopped for the night or to rest during the day, I dearly longed to immerse myself in it without interruption and, with faith, to learn from it the true way to salvation through the prayer of the heart.

However, despite my wishes and because of the disability I'd had in my left arm from early childhood, I could not find any suitable work. Since I was unable to manage the upkeep of a permanent residence, I headed for Siberia to visit the grave of Saint Innocent of Irkutsk. It seemed to me that the Siberian forests and steppes would allow for quieter and more peaceful traveling and make it easier to pray and read. And so I set out, repeating the prayer continuously with my lips.

Finally, after a short time, I felt that the prayer began to move of its own accord from my lips into my heart. That is to say, it seemed as if my heart, while beating naturally, somehow began to repeat within itself the words of the prayer in rhythm with its natural beating: (1) Lord . . . (2) Jesus . . . (3) Christ . . . and so on. I stopped reciting the words of the prayer with my lips and began to listen attentively to the words of my heart, remembering what my starets said about how pleasant this would be. Then I began to experience a delicate soreness in my heart, and my thoughts were filled with such a love for Jesus Christ that it seemed to me that if I were to see Him, I would throw myself down, embrace His feet, and never let them go, kissing them tenderly and tearfully. And I would thank Him for His love and mercy in granting such consolation through His name to His unworthy and sinful creature!

Then a wholesome warmth began to fill my heart, and it seemed to spread throughout my chest. This warmth especially moved me to an attentive reading of the *Philokalia*, both to verify the feelings I had experienced and to further my studies of the interior prayer of the heart. I was afraid that without this verification I might fall into delusion or mistake natural activity for the action of grace and succumb to the pride, which the starets had spoken of, in having attained so quickly to this prayer.

So I took to walking mostly at night and spent my days sitting in the forest, under the trees, and reading the *Philokalia*. Ah, how much new knowledge, how much wisdom that I had never yet possessed, was revealed to me in this book! As I began to put it into practice, I tasted a sweetness I could not have even imagined until now. Although it is true that several passages I read were incomprehensible to my foolish mind, the effects of this prayer of the heart clarified what I'd failed to understand. At times my starets came to me in my dreams and explained so much to me. Above all else he inclined my ignorant soul toward humility. For more than two months of that summer I basked in this blissful state while I walked, keeping to the forests and the byroads. When I came to a village I would ask for dry bread to fill my knapsack with, and for a handful of salt. Then I would fill my bark jar with water, and on I would go for almost another seventy miles.

Perhaps it was due to the sins of my wretched soul, or for lack of something in my spiritual life, or the need for better guidance and more experience, but by the end of the summer I was assailed by temptations. On one such occasion I had come out onto a main road and was overtaken at dusk by two men, whose haircuts made me think they were soldiers. They began to demand money from me. When I replied that I didn't have a penny, they did not believe me and shouted insolently, "You're lying! Pilgrims always pick up a lot of money!" One of them said, "Don't waste your time arguing with him," and he clobbered me so hard over the head with a club that I fell down unconscious.

I don't know how long I lay unconscious, but when I came to I realized that I was lying near the forest, just off the road. I was disheveled and my knapsack was gone. All that was left were the severed ropes that had once held it on my back. Thank God they hadn't stolen my passport, which I carried inside my old hat, in case I needed to produce it quickly on demand. I stood up and burst into bitter tears, not so much from my aching head as over the fact that my books were gone—the Bible and the *Philokalia*, which were in the knapsack they had stolen.

So I grieved and wept day and night. Where was my Bible now, the one I had been reading from my early childhood and had always carried with me? Where was my *Philokalia*, which had given me such guidance and comfort? Woe is me, I had been deprived of the first and last treasures of my life—and I hadn't even had my fill of them yet! The robbers should have murdered me instead of leaving me to go on living without this spiritual nourishment. I would never replace it now!

For two days I barely dragged my feet, overwhelmed by my grief. By the third day I was so exhausted that I collapsed under a bush and fell asleep. I dreamed that I saw myself back at the monastery, in the cell of my starets, pouring out my grief to him. The starets comforted me and said, "Let this be a lesson to you in detachment from earthly material possessions; it will ease your journey toward heaven. This was permitted to happen to you so as to protect you from falling into spiritual gluttony. God wants from the Christian a complete denial of his own will, of his desires and of all attachment to them, so that he can totally submit himself to His Divine Will. He orders all things for the good and salvation of man: 'who desires all men to be saved . . .' [1 Tim. 2:4]. So take courage and believe that 'with the temptation God will also provide the way of escape' [1 Cor. 10:13]. And you will soon be comforted in far greater measure than you now grieve."

Upon hearing these words I awakened, feeling a new inner strength, and my soul was filled with light and peace. "God's will be done," I said, and making the sign of the cross over myself, I got up and went on my way. Once again the prayer came alive in my heart, just as it had done previously, and for three days I journeyed in peace.

Suddenly I caught up with a convoy of convicts, accompanied by a military escort. As I approached them I saw the two men who had robbed me. Since they were walking on the fringes of the convoy, I threw myself at their feet and earnestly begged them to tell me what they had done with my books. At first they ignored me, but then one of them said, "For a fee we'll tell you where your books are. Give us a ruble." I swore that I would pay them, even if I had to go begging for it, for Christ's sake. "Here—take my passport as a pledge, if you want," said I. They told me that my books were in the wagon in the rear, along with other stolen items that had been confiscated from them.

"How can I get them back?"

"Ask the captain in charge."

I hurried to the captain and told him my whole story. Among other questions, he asked me, "Can you really read the Bible?"

"Not only can I read," I replied, "but I can even write. You will see by the inscription in the Bible that it belongs to me. And here, my name and surname are in my passport too!"

Then the captain said, "These swindlers are military deserters. They were living in a mud hut and robbing everyone in sight. A clever coachman nabbed them yesterday as they tried to steal his three-horse team. I suppose I'll return your books to you, if they are here, but you'll have to accompany us to our next layover for the night. It's not far ahead, a little over two miles; we can't stop the wagon and the convoy just to get your books."

I walked gladly alongside the horse on which the captain rode and struck up a conversation with him. I noticed that he was an honest and kind man who was on in years. He asked me who I was, where I was headed, and where I hailed from. I answered all his questions honestly, and before long we had reached the hut where the convoy was to spend the night. He found my books, returned them to me, and said, "Where will you go now, in the dark? Spend the night here, in the foyer." So I stayed.

Now that the books were in my possession again, I was so happy that I knew not how to thank God. I clasped the books to my bosom and held them there until my arms went numb. Tears of joy streamed down my face and my heart beat tenderly with delight!

The captain had been watching me and said, "It's obvious that you love to read the Bible." I was so overjoyed that my tears spilled over and I could not answer him. "My brother, I also read the Bible faithfully each day," he said, and, unbuttoning his uniform jacket, he produced a small Bible that had been printed in Kiev and was bound in silver. "Sit down and I'll tell you what brought me to all this.

"How about some supper!" he shouted.

We sat down to eat and the captain began his story. "From the time I was a young man I have served in the army, not in a garrison unit. I knew my job and was a second lieutenant, well liked by my commanding officers. But I was young and so were my buddies, and unfortunately I started drinking heavily and eventually became an alcoholic. When I was sober, I was a model officer; but as soon as I hit the bottle again, I could not function for up to six weeks at a time. They put up with me for a long time until finally, in a drunken stupor, I insulted a commanding officer. I was demoted to the rank of soldier for three years, transferred to a garrison unit, and threatened with severe punishment if I did not straighten myself out and stop drinking. No matter how hard I tried to abstain in this miserable condition and no matter what cures I tried, I simply could not give up my addiction. Finally they decided to place me under military arrest, and when I heard this, I was at my wit's end.

"One day, as I sat in the barracks thinking, a monk came by unexpectedly, collecting alms for the church, and each of us gave whatever he could. As he approached me, he said, 'Why are you so sad?' We struck up a conversation, and I poured out all my woes to him. The monk expressed compassion for my plight and said, 'The very same thing happened to my brother. Here is what helped him: his spiritual father gave him a Bible and firmly instructed him that when he felt the urge to drink wine, he must pick up the Bible immediately and read a chapter from it. Each time the urge to drink returned, he was to read yet another chapter. My brother took his advice and, in a short time, his passion for alcohol disappeared. So for fifteen years now he has not had a drop of alcohol. Why don't you do the same? It'll work—you'll see. I have a Bible that I think I'll bring to you.'

"I listened to him and said, 'How can your Bible help me when neither my own efforts nor any medical cures succeeded in keeping me sober?' I said this because I had never read the Bible. The monk replied, 'Don't say that. I assure you that it will help.'

"The next day the monk indeed brought me his Bible. I opened it, looked inside, read some of it, and said, 'I won't accept it. I can't understand a single word of it. I'm not used to reading Church Slavonic.'* The monk continued to assure me that the very words of the Bible were imbued with the power of grace, for they were the words of God Himself. 'It does not matter if you don't understand it at first; just keep on reading diligently. A saint once said, "If you don't understand the words of God, at least the evil spirits understand what you read and they tremble before it." Your addiction to alcohol is certainly the work of the devil. Let me tell you something else: Saint John Chrysostom writes that even the very room where a Bible is kept frightens the spirits of darkness and makes it impossible for them to lay their evil snares.'

"I forget how much money I gave the monk, but I did accept his Bible. I then stored it away in a small trunk along with my other belongings and forgot about it. Sometime later I was overcome again by an irresistible urge to drink. I was dying for some wine, so I quickly opened my small trunk, to get some money and run over to the tavern. The first thing that my eyes fell upon was the Bible, and I clearly remembered all that the monk had told me. I opened it and began to read the first chapter of Matthew. I read the entire chapter without understanding a word of it. Then I remembered the monk's advice, 'If you don't understand it right away, keep on reading diligently.'

" 'All right,' I thought to myself, 'I'll read another chapter.' I read it and I began to understand. 'Why not try a third chapter?' I thought. But as soon as I started reading, the barracks bell sounded, announcing it was time to retire. It was obviously too late to go out, so I stayed put.

"When I arose in the morning, I was all ready to go for a drink when a thought struck me: 'I wonder what would happen if I read a chapter from the Bible?' I did just that and did not go out. Then again I felt the urge to drink wine. I again took to reading and felt much better. This encouraged me so much that each time I felt an urge to drink, I would read a chapter from the Bible. The more I did this, the easier it became to resist. Finally, when I had read through all four Gospels, the urge to drink had vanished to such a degree that I now felt an aversion to alcohol. It is now exactly twenty years that I have not touched a drop of any alcoholic beverage.

"Everyone was astonished by this transformation in me. Three years later my officer's rank was restored to me. In due time I was promoted again, until finally I attained the rank of commanding officer. I married a kind woman and we settled down. Now, thank God, we have a good life together; we give to the poor when we can, and we take in pilgrims. Why, my own son is already an officer—and a fine man he is!

"Listen: from the time I was healed of alcoholism, I made a vow to myself that for the rest of my life I would read the Bible, one Gospel every day, no matter how busy I was. So this is what I have been doing. On days when work runs me ragged, I come home, lie down, and make my wife or son read one of the Gospels to me, in its entirety, so as not to break my daily rule. In gratitude to God, and to His glory, I had this Bible bound in pure silver, and I always carry it with me, in my breast pocket."

I listened with delight to the captain's story and said, "I once knew someone who had the same experience. In our village there was a very gifted craftsman, who worked at the local factory. He was a kind man who did expensive work. Unfortunately, he also took to drinking frequently. A God-fearing man suggested to him that whenever he felt the urge to drink wine, he should repeat the Jesus Prayer thirty-three times, in remembrance of the Holy Trinity and the thirty-three years of Jesus Christ's earthly life. The craftsman heeded this advice, started saying the prayer, and in no time he stopped drinking completely. And that was not all—three years later he entered a monastery!"

"Which is more exalted," asked the captain, "the Jesus Prayer or the Bible?"

"It's all the same," I replied, "for the Divine Name of Jesus Christ contains within itself all the biblical truths. The holy Fathers say that the Jesus Prayer is the abbreviated version of the entire Bible."

The two of us finally said our prayers, and the captain started reading from the Gospel of Saint Mark, chapter one. I listened, while in my heart I prayed the Jesus Prayer. At two o'clock in the morning the captain finished reading the Gospel of Saint Mark, and we went to bed.

I rose early, as was my custom, and found that everyone was still asleep. At the first crack of dawn I threw myself into reading my precious *Philokalia.* What joy filled me as I opened that book! It was as if I'd been reunited, after a long separation, with my own father, or with a friend who had been resurrected from the dead. I covered the book with kisses and thanked God for restoring it to me, and immediately began to read Theophilus of Philadelphia, in the second part of the *Philokalia.* I was surprised to read that a man could simultaneously perform three different activities: "While sitting in the refectory," he writes, "give food to your body, give your attention to the reading of the day, and give your mind over to prayer." Yet when I remembered the joyful evening we had spent last night, my own living experience verified what I had just read. Thus, a mystery was revealed to me: namely, that the mind and the heart are separate entities.

When the captain arose, I went to thank him for his kindness and to take my leave of him. He offered me tea and gave me a ruble, and we parted. And I set off on my journey again, full of joy.

I had walked about three quarters of a mile when I remembered my promise to give those soldiers a ruble, which I now happened to have in my pocket. "Should I give it to them or not?" I wondered. One of my thoughts said, "They beat you up and robbed you. Besides, they're under arrest, so they couldn't even spend it." Another thought said, "Remember what the Bible says: 'If your enemy is hungry, feed him' [Rom. 12:20]. Even Jesus Christ Himself said, 'Love your enemies' [Matt. 5:44], and then: 'And if anyone would sue you and take your coat, let him have your cloak as well' " [Matt. 5:40]. This convinced me, and I decided to go back. As I approached the camp, all the criminals were being lined up outside for the next part of the journey. I hurried over to the two men, put the ruble piece in their hands, and said, "Repent and pray; Jesus Christ loves man; He will not abandon you!" Then I walked away and headed in the opposite direction.

I had walked a little over thirty-three miles along the main road when I thought of turning off onto a bypath so I could be alone to read.

For a long time I walked through forests and only rarely ran across small villages. Often I spent an entire day sitting in the forest, carefully reading the *Philokalia* and learning so many wondrous things from it. My heart burned with a desire for union with God through interior prayer, which I strove to attain to under the guidance and verification of the *Philokalia*. Yet I also grieved that I had not yet found a permanent dwelling where I could spend all my time reading in peace.

During this time I also read my Bible and felt that I was beginning to understand it better than I had before, when so much was still unclear and puzzling to me. How right the Fathers are when they say the *Philokalia* is the key to unlocking the mysteries of Holy Scripture. With its guidance, I began to understand parts of the hidden meaning of the Word of God. The meanings of such statements as "the hidden inner man of the heart," "true prayer," "worshiping in the spirit," "the Kingdom of Heaven is within us," "the intercession of the Holy Spirit with unutterable groanings," "abide in me," "give me your heart," "to put on Christ," the "betrothal of the Spirit to our hearts," calling from one's heart: "Abba, Father!" and so on, were now being revealed to me. As I began to pray now with my heart, everything around me was so delightfully transformed: the trees, the grass, the birds, the ground, the air, the light—all seemed to proclaim that they exist for the sake of man and bear witness to the love of God for man. All creation prays to God and sings His praises. From this I understood what the *Philokalia* calls a "knowledge of the language of all creation," and I saw how it is possible for man to communicate with all of God's creatures.

I journeyed thus for a long time until, finally, I found myself in a place so uninhabited that for three days I did not see a single village. I had eaten all my dried bread, and I despaired at the thought that I would die of hunger. Yet as soon as I started praying, the despair would vanish. I gave myself over entirely to the will of God and was filled with joy and peace. When I had walked along part of the road that ran next to the forest, ahead of me I saw a mongrel dog come running out of the forest. It approached when I called to it and began to play affectionately with me. I was overjoyed and thought to myself, "Now there's God's mercy for you! Surely there must be a flock grazing in this forest, and of course this trained dog belongs to the shepherd; or perhaps there is a hunter nearby. Whatever the case, at least I'll be able to beg for some bread—I haven't eaten in twenty-four hours. Or else I can ask where the nearest village is."

The dog had been jumping around me, and when it realized I had nothing to offer, it ran off into the forest down the same narrow path by which it had come out. I followed it, and about five hundred yards later I saw that the dog had run into a hole between some trees, from which it kept looking out and barking.

At that very moment a skinny, pale, middle-aged peasant emerged from behind a large tree. He asked me how I had come to be there and I, in turn, asked him what he was doing here. We struck up a friendly conversation, and the peasant invited me into his mud hut. He told me that he was a forester and was guarding this part of the woods, which had been sold for felling. He offered me bread and salt, and we began to talk. "I envy you," said I, "because you live in such comfortable solitude, so far removed from everyone, while I wander from place to place, mixing with all sorts of people."

"If you'd like to," he said, "maybe you can live here too. There's an old mud hut not far from here that belonged to the previous watchman. It's run down, of course, but it's livable in the summer. You have a passport, and we'll have enough bread to eat; they supply me with it weekly from the village. There's a stream here, which never dries up. For ten years now, brother, I myself have eaten only bread. I drink water and never anything else. There is one thing, however: in the fall, when the peasants finish working on the land, about two hundred of them will gather here to fell the trees in this forest. Then my job here will be over, and you won't be allowed to remain either."

When I heard all this, I was so overjoyed that I could have thrown myself at his feet. I knew not how to thank God for showing me such mercy. That which I'd desired and longed for was now being given to me so unexpectedly. There were still more than four months left until late fall. Here I could find the peace and solitude that I needed to immerse myself in reading the *Philokalia* and learning how to attain to the unceasing prayer of the heart. So I settled down joyfully in the hut he pointed out to me, for whatever time had been given me to live there. I talked some more with this simple brother who had offered me shelter, and he told me about his life and his thoughts on it.

"In my village," he said, "I had a good position; my trade was dyeing fustian and linen. I led a prosperous life, though not a sinless one. Often I cheated in business and took false oaths; I cursed, drank too much, and got into fights. There was an old deacon in our village who had an extremely old book about the Last Judgment. He would visit the Orthodox faithful and read to them from it, for which they gave him money. And he also visited me. Give him about ten kopecks and he could read into the night, till the cock crowed. So I'd sit and work, listening to him read about the torments that await us in hell, how the living would be transformed and the dead would be resurrected, how God would come down to judge us, how the angels would sound their trumpets, of the fire and brimstone, and how the worm would devour the sinners. One time, as I listened to all this, I got scared and thought to myself, 'There's no way I'll avoid that torment! Maybe it's time I started saving my soul—maybe I could even pray my sins away.' I thought about this for a long time and decided to give up my business. Since I had no family ties, I sold my hut and became a forester in exchange for being provided with bread, clothing, and candles for my prayers, by the village *mir*.*

"So I've lived here for more than ten years. I eat once a day, only bread with some water. I get up each day at the cock's crow and say my prayers and do my prostrations until dawn, burning seven candles in front of the icons. During the day, when I make my rounds of the forest, I wear iron chains weighing seventy-two pounds next to my skin. I don't curse anymore, or drink any wine or beer, or get into any fights, and I've never been with women or girls in my life.

"At first I preferred this kind of life, but lately I find myself constantly attacked by thoughts. God knows if sins can really be prayed away—and it is a hard life, you know. And then, is it really true what that book says—that dead men will be resurrected? Someone who died a hundred years ago or more—why, there's not even a speck of dust left of him. For that matter, who really knows if there will even be a hell, right? Why, no one has ever come back from the dead! It seems to me that once a man dies, he rots and vanishes without a trace. Maybe that book was written by the clergy, by some officials, just to scare us fools, to make us more humble. Life is full of hardships as it is, without any consolation—and there won't be anything in the next life. So what's the point? Isn't it better to take it easy, at least in this life, and to enjoy yourself? Such thoughts hound me," he continued, "and I wonder if I shouldn't just go back to my old job!"

Listening to him speak, I sympathized and thought to myself: they say that it is only the educated and the intelligent who are freethinkers and believe in nothing. But here is one of our own brethren—a simple peasant—and what doubts he is capable of entertaining! It appears that the powers of darkness are allowed access to everyone, and perhaps it is easier for them to attack the unsophisticated. A person must acquire wisdom and strengthen himself as much as possible with the Word of God against the spiritual enemy.

So as to help and strengthen this brother's faith as much as I could, I took the *Philokalia* out of my knapsack, opened it to chapter 109, the work of the venerable Hesychios, and read it to him. I then explained that abstaining from sin only because one fears punishment is a useless and fruitless task. "The soul cannot free itself from sins of thought other than by guarding the mind and the purity of the heart, all of which is achieved by interior prayer. Moreover," I added, "the holy Fathers say that the efforts of those who strive for salvation only from a fear of hell's torments, or even solely from a desire to enter the Kingdom of God, are mercenary. They say that to fear suffering is the way of the servant, while to desire a reward in the Kingdom is the way of the mercenary. Yet God desires that we come to Him as sons, that we be honest and delight in the redemptive union with Him in our hearts and souls—but only out of love and devotion to Him. No matter how you wear yourself out with physical labors and struggles, if you do not keep the remembrance of God in your mind and the Jesus Prayer in your heart, you will never find peace from these thoughts and you will always be easily swayed by sin, even by the smallest temptations. Why don't you start saying the Jesus Prayer, brother? It would be possible and so easy to do with the solitude you live in, and you will see its benefits in no time. No godless thoughts will besiege you, and you will acquire faith and love for Jesus Christ. Then you will know how it is that the dead will be resurrected, and you will be given to understand the Last Judgment as it really will take place. Your heart will be so free of burdens and so full of joy from this prayer that you will be amazed, and you'll no longer feel lonely or doubt the efforts you make toward your salvation."

Then I explained to him how to begin saying the Jesus Prayer and how to repeat it continuously, as the Word of God instructs us and the holy Fathers teach us to do. It seemed to me that he was willing to do this and was much calmer now. I took leave of him then and shut myself up in the ancient mud hut that he had told me about.

My God! What joy, peace, and delight I knew the moment I set foot in that "cave," or better yet "tomb." It seemed to me to be the most magnificent palace, filled with every joy and consolation! I thanked God with tears of joy and thought, "Well, now, with all this peace and quiet I must seriously get back to my own task and ask the Lord to guide me." So I began by reading the *Philokalia* very carefully, starting with the first chapter and going all the way to the end. It did not take too long to read it through, and I realized what wisdom, holiness, and depth it contained. Yet it covered so many different subjects and contained so many different teachings of the holy Fathers that I was unable to understand everything or to piece together all that I wanted to learn, especially about interior prayer, so I could draw from it the knowledge of how to attain to the unceasing self-acting prayer of the heart. I longed for this, in keeping with God's commandment and as it was spoken through His apostle: "But earnestly desire the higher gifts" [1 Cor. 12:31] and again: "Do not quench the Spirit" [1 Thess. 5:19].

I thought about this for a long time. What could I do? I would start badgering the Lord with prayers; perhaps the Lord would somehow enlighten me. So I did nothing but pray continuously for the next twenty-four hours, not stopping for even a moment. My thoughts were calmed and I fell asleep. In my dream I saw myself sitting in the cell of my departed starets. He was explaining the *Philokalia* to me, saying, "This holy book is full of great wisdom. It is a mystical treasury of the meanings of the hidden judgments of God. It is not made accessible everywhere and to everyone, but it does offer instruction according to the measure of each reader's understanding. Thus, to the wise it offers wise guidance, while to the simpleminded it yields simple guidance. That is why you simpleminded ones should not read it section by section, in the order that the teachings of the different holy Fathers are printed in the book.

"First read the book of Nicephorus the Solitary (in part 2); then read the entire book of Saint Gregory of Sinai, excluding the short chapters; then read Simeon the New Theologian on the three kinds of prayer, and his Discourse on Faith; and afterward read the book of Callistus and Ignatius. The work of these Fathers contains the complete instruction and teaching on the interior prayer of the heart and can be understood by all.

"Then, if you should want an even clearer teaching on prayer, turn to section 4 for the summary on methods of prayer, by Callistus, the most holy Patriarch of Constantinople." In my dream I held the *Philokalia* in my hands and began to look for this passage, but I could not find it right away. The starets flipped through a few pages and said, "Here it is! I will mark the place for you." He picked up a piece of coal from the ground and made a mark with it in the margin, next to the passage he had found. I had listened carefully to everything the starets had said and tried to remember it in as much detail as possible. Since it was not yet dawn when I woke up, I lay in bed and went over every detail of my dream and everything the starets had told me. Finally I began to wonder, "God alone knows if this is really the soul of the late starets who is appearing to me in my dream, or if it is all in my mind, since I think so often about him and the *Philokalia*."

Still puzzled by all this, I got out of bed, for the light of day was dawning. And what do you think happened? I looked at the rock that served as a table in my mud hut and saw the *Philokalia* lying there, open to the very passage that the starets had pointed out to me, with the very markings he had made in charcoal! It was exactly as I had dreamed it—even the piece of coal lay next to the book! This astonished me, for I clearly remembered that the book had not been there the evening before; I had wrapped it up and placed it at the head of my bed. I was also quite sure that there had been no markings next to this specific passage. This incident finally convinced me of the reality of my dreams and that my starets of blessed memory had found favor in the eyes of God.

So I started reading the *Philokalia*, in the very order the starets had outlined for me. I read it through once and then a second time, and my soul burned with a desire and an eagerness to experience personally all that I had read about. The meaning of interior prayer was revealed clearly to my understanding: by what means one could attain to it, what were its fruits, how it delights the soul and the heart, and how to discern whether this sweet delight is from God, from natural causes, or the result of delusion.

So I began first to seek the place of the heart, according to the teaching of Simeon the New Theologian. I closed my eyes and gazed mentally into my heart; I tried to visualize it in the left part of my chest cavity and carefully listened to its beating. I began doing this exercise for half an hour, several times a day. At first I saw only total darkness, but soon a picture of my heart, along with the sound of its natural beating, formed in my mind. Then I began to repeat the Jesus Prayer in my heart, in steady rhythm with my breathing, as taught by Saint Gregory of Sinai, Callistus, and Ignatius: namely, by concentrating my mind in the heart while visualizing it in my mind, I inhaled saying, "Lord Jesus Christ," and then exhaled saying, "Have mercy on me." At first I did this exercise for an hour or two. As I progressed, I increased the time, until finally I was able to repeat the exercise for almost the entire day. If weariness, laziness, or doubts assailed me, I immediately turned to reading the *Philokalia,* specifically those passages that deal with the work of the heart, and all desire and eagerness were restored.

After about three weeks I began to experience a soreness in my heart, followed by the most delightful kind of warmth, joy, and peace. This increasingly stirred me and kindled my desire to practice this prayer more diligently, so that I thought about nothing else and was filled with an immense joy. From then on, at times I would experience different sensations in my heart and in my mind. Sometimes my heart would bubble over with such sweet delight and was filled with such lightness, freedom, and consolation that I was totally transformed and enraptured. At other times I would be consumed with a burning love for Jesus Christ and for all of God's creation. Sometimes sweet tears of gratitude to the Lord, for His mercy to me a cursed sinner, would pour out of me of their own accord. And again, at times, my former foolish understanding was so illumined that suddenly I was able to ponder and comprehend so easily what previously I could not have even imagined. Sometimes the sweet warmth in my heart would overflow and spread through my entire being, so that I tenderly experienced the presence of God all about me. At other times I would experience the greatest inner joy from calling upon the name of Jesus Christ, and I realized the meaning of what He had said: "The Kingdom of God is within you" [Luke 17:21].

As I was experiencing these and other delightful consolations, I noticed that the effects of the prayer of the heart are manifested in three ways: in the spirit, in the feelings, and through revelations. In the spirit there is the sweetness of God's love, inner peace, the rapture of the mind, purity of thought, and the delightful remembrance of God. In the feelings there is a pleasant warming of the heart, a sweet delight that fills all the limbs, the heart bubbling over with joy, an inner lightness and vitality, the delight of being alive, and an inner detachment from illness and offenses. Revelations bring enlightenment of the intellect, an understanding of Holy Scripture, a knowledge of the language of all creatures, a detachment from all anxious cares, a taste of the sweet delights of the interior spiritual life, and a conviction in the close presence of God and in His love for us.

I spent about five months in the solitude of this prayerful exercise, enjoying the experiences I described. I became so accustomed to the prayer of the heart that I practiced it continuously, until I finally felt that my mind and heart began to act and recite the prayer without any effort on my part. This continued not only when I was awake, but even as I slept, and nothing could interrupt it. It did not cease for even a moment, no matter what I happened to be occupied with. My soul was filled with gratitude to the Lord, while my heart languished in unceasing joy.

The time came for felling the trees in the forest, and the workers began to arrive. It was also time for me to leave my solitary abode. I thanked the forester, said a prayer, and knelt to kiss that plot of ground, which God had given to one as undeserving of His mercy as I am, to live on. I put my knapsack, containing the books, on my back and set out on my journey.

For a very long time I wandered through different places, until I arrived in Irkutsk. The self-acting prayer of the heart was my consolation and joy throughout the journey and in all my encounters. It never ceased to delight me, albeit in varying degrees. Wherever I happened to be, whatever I was doing, it never got in the way and was never diminished in any way at all. If I was working, the prayer flowed from my heart on its own and the work would go faster. If I was listening attentively to something or reading while the prayer continued unceasingly, I would simultaneously be aware of both, as if I'd been divided in two or as if there were two souls in my one body. My God! What a mystery man is! "O, Lord, how wondrous are thy works! In wisdom hast thou made them all" [Ps. 104:24].

My travels were also filled with many wonderful experiences and incidents. Were I to recount them all, twenty-four hours would not suffice! But here is one example: it was dusk one winter evening as I walked alone in the forest. I was heading toward a village about a mile and a half ahead, where I planned to spend the night, when suddenly I was attacked by a wolf. In my hands I held the starets's old knotted wool chotki (I always carried them with me). I swung the knots to chase the wolf away—and what do you think happened? The chotki was whisked out of my hand and somehow became tangled right around the wolf's neck, and he took off. As he went crashing through a thorny bush, his back legs became tangled up in it, while the chotki caught on the branch of a dead tree. The wolf began to thrash about, but he could not free himself because the chotki had tightened around his throat. With faith I made the sign of the cross over myself and approached the wolf, intending to set him free, mainly because I feared that if he tore the chotki and ran off with it, then I would lose my precious chotki. Just as I came near and grabbed the chotki, it snapped, as the wolf broke loose and took off without a trace.

Thanking God, I prayed for my blessed starets and managed to get to the village safe and sound. I stopped at the inn, to ask for lodging for the night. As I entered the hut I saw two men sitting at a table in the corner and drinking tea. One was an old man, the other was fat and middle-aged, and neither appeared to be of the lower class. I asked the peasant tending their horses who they were. He said that the old man was a teacher in a public school and the other was a clerk of the county court; both were upper-crust people. "I'm taking them to a fair about thirteen miles from here," he said.

After sitting for a while, I asked a peasant woman for a needle and some thread and, moving closer to the candle, I began to mend my chotki. The clerk looked at me and said, "Looks like you did your prostrations with such zeal that your chotki broke!"

"It was not I who tore it," I replied, "it was a wolf."

The clerk chuckled and said, "My, my! Do wolves pray too?" I explained exactly what had happened in the forest and how precious the chotki was to me. The clerk laughed again and said, "Miracles always happen to you holy frauds! But where's the holiness in all this? You probably just threw something at the wolf and frightened him away. Dogs and wolves are afraid of objects being hurled at them, and it doesn't take much to get caught in forest thickets. There's so much happening in this world—how can one believe that everything is a miracle?"

The teacher had been listening to the clerk and said to him, "Do not jump to such conclusions, sir! You are not familiar with the scholarly facts of the matter. I do see both the sensible and spiritual mystery of nature in this peasant's story."

"And how is that?" asked the clerk.

"Well, you see, although you lack a higher education, you must have studied a condensed version of the sacred history of the Old and New Testaments, the one that is published in catechism form for use in schools. Do you remember when the first created man, Adam, was in a state of innocent grace and all animals were obedient to him? They approached him with fear and he named each one. The starets to whom this chotki belonged was a holy man—and what is holiness? It is simply the return of sinful man, through efforts and struggles, to that innocent state of grace that the first man enjoyed. When the soul is sanctified, so is the body. Holy people always held chotki in their hands. This very contact of their hands and the holiness that emanated through them infused the knots with the power of the innocent state of the first man. That is the mystery of the spiritual nature of life! Down through the ages, and even to the present time, all animals naturally inherited the ability to sense this power. They experience it in their sense of smell, for the nose is the main organ of sensation in all beasts and animals. That is the mystery of the sensible nature of life!"

The clerk replied, "You educated people carry on about powers and wisdom! For us it's all much simpler: pour a shot of vodka, toss it down, and there's your power," and he got up and walked over to the cabinet.

"That is your business," said the teacher, "but leave scholarly matters to us."

I was pleased with the way the teacher had spoken, so I approached him and said: "If I may, Batyushka, I'd like to tell you more about my starets."

I told him of the dreams in which he had appeared to me, how he had instructed me and marked the passages in the *Philokalia* in charcoal. The teacher carefully listened to all this while the clerk, who was stretched out on a bench, grumbled: "It's like they say—you can lose your mind reading the Bible too much. How true that is! What ghost goes around at night, marking up books? You just knocked the book down on the floor in your sleep and it was smudged by some soot. There's your miracle! Oh, you scoundrels! I've seen enough of your kind!" Having mumbled this, the clerk turned to the wall and fell asleep.

I said to the teacher, "If you like, I'll show you that very book and you'll see that it has precise markings in it and not just sooty smudges." I took the *Philokalia* out of my knapsack and showed it to him, saying, "I marvel at such wisdom; how could a bodiless soul pick up a piece of charcoal and write with it?"

The teacher looked at the markings and replied, "That belongs also to the realm of spiritual mysteries. Let me explain this: you see, when spirits appear in bodily form to someone on earth, they fashion a material body for themselves from the air and elements around them. Once their task is done they return the elements to the material world, from which they were borrowed to create the bodies. Just as the air is resilient, has elasticity, and can be compressed, so the soul clothed in it can pick up material objects and perform actions such as writing. By the way, what is that book you have there? Let me see it!"

He opened the book at random to the writing of Saint Simeon the New Theologian. "Ah, this must be a theological work; I've never seen it before."

"Batyushka, this book consists almost solely of teachings on the interior prayer of the heart in the name of Jesus Christ," I replied. "It is explained in complete detail here by twenty-five holy Fathers."

"I do know about interior prayer," said the teacher. I bowed to the ground before him and asked him to tell me something about interior prayer.

"This is what the New Testament says: man and all creation are subject to 'vanity, not of [their] own will,' and 'groan inwardly, struggling and desiring to enter into the liberty of the sons of God' [Rom. 8:20ff]. Interior prayer is this mystical inward groaning of creation and the innate aspiration of souls toward God. It is not something that needs to be learned, for it is innate in everyone and everything!"

"How can one attain to it, discover it, and experience it in the heart?" I asked. "How can one recognize and accept it with one's will, and acquire it so that it becomes active, to delight, to enlighten, and to save a person?"

"I do not remember if this is written about in any theological treatises," replied the teacher.

"But here—it is all written here," I said.

The teacher picked up a pencil, jotted down the title of the *Philokalia,* and said, "I simply must order this book from Tobolsk, so I can study it." Then we took leave of each other.

As I started again on my journey, I thanked God for that conversation with the teacher, but I prayed for the clerk, that the Lord would somehow arrange that he read the *Philokalia* at least once and grant him wisdom for his salvation.

Another time, it was in the spring that I came to a village where I found lodging for the night at a priest's house. He was a kind man and lived alone, so I spent three days with him. After observing me during this time, he said, "Stay here with me. I need a conscientious man here, and I'll pay you a wage. You see that we are building a new stone church, near the old wooden chapel. I have not been able to find a reliable man to keep an eye on the workers and to sit in the chapel, accepting donations for the new building. You could handle this, and it would suit your way of life. You could sit alone in the chapel and pray to God. There is also a separate booth for the watchman to sit in. Please stay, at least until the new church is built." I tried to get out of doing this, but the priest was so insistent that finally I had to agree.

Through the summer I lived in that chapel, until the fall came. At first it was peaceful and very conducive to reciting my prayer, even though many people visited the chapel, especially on feast days. Some came to pray, some to dawdle, while others came to steal from the collection plate. I regularly read the Bible and the *Philokalia,* and when visitors saw this, some would strike up a conversation with me. Others would merely ask me to read to them.

After a while I noticed that a young peasant girl came frequently to the chapel and spent a long time praying to God. I listened to her muttering and discovered that some of the prayers she was repeating were very odd-sounding, while others seemed to be completely distorted. "Who taught you all this?" I asked. She replied that her mother, who was a churchgoing woman, had taught her. Her father was a schismatic who belonged to a sect that rejected the priesthood. I sympathized with all this and then advised her to pray according to the proper tradition of the holy church: namely, the Lord's Prayer and "Rejoice O Virgin Theotokos."* Finally, I said, "Why don't you make a habit of saying the Jesus Prayer? It reaches out to God more directly than any other prayer, and through it you will attain salvation for your soul."

The young girl took my advice seriously and very simply began doing what I had taught her. And do you know what happened? After a short time she informed me that she had become so accustomed to the Jesus Prayer that she felt drawn to reciting it continuously, if such a thing were possible, and that while she prayed she was filled with gladness, whereas when she stopped, she was filled with joy and a desire to pray again. I was overjoyed by this and advised her to continue praying in the name of Jesus Christ.

The end of the summer was drawing near. Many of the visitors to the chapel were now coming to see me. They came not only to hear me read to them and for advice, but they also brought all their problems to me, even seeking help in locating misplaced or lost items. Obviously, some of them took me for some sort of fortuneteller. Finally, the same young girl came back, filled with grief and seeking advice. What should she do? Her father had decided to marry her off, against her will, to one of the schismatics in his sect, and the wedding was to be performed by one of the peasants. "How could that be a legal marriage?" she cried. "It will be nothing but debauchery! I want to run away—it doesn't matter where I go!"

"Where would you run?" I asked. "They'll only find you again. Nowadays, there is nowhere you could hide yourself well enough. No matter where you go, they will find you. Why don't you pray to God more earnestly about this and rely on His judgment about changing your father's mind and saving your soul from sin and heresy? That would be far more sensible than running away."

As time went on, life became unbearably noisy for me and full of distracting temptations. Finally the summer was over and I decided to leave the chapel to continue on my own journey. I went to the priest and said, "Batyushka, you know what I am seeking. I need quiet surroundings to pray, and there are too many harmful distractions here. I have fulfilled by obedience to you and stayed through the summer. Release me now and give me your blessing for my solitary journey."

The priest did not want to let me go, and he tried to convince me to stay. "What's stopping you from praying right here? There's nothing for you to do here except to sit in the chapel. Your daily bread is provided for you. Say your prayers there day and night, if you like, and live with God, brother! You are very gifted, and your presence here is good for us. You don't gossip idly with visitors, and you are doing something profitable for God's church by faithfully taking in the collections. This is more pleasing to God than your prayers in solitude. What do you need solitude for? It's merrier to pray in community with others. God did not create man so that he could get to know only himself, but so that people would help each other, lead each other to salvation according to each one's abilities. Take a look at the saints and the ecumenical Fathers! They were concerned and cared for the Church day and night and traveled all over to preach. They did not go off in solitude and hide from people."

"God gives to each man his own gift, Batyushka. There have been many preachers, but there have also been many hermits. Each found his own unique calling and followed it, believing that through this God Himself was guiding him on the path to salvation. How then would you explain the fact that so many saints gave up their ecclesiastical offices, administrative positions, and priestly duties and fled into the solitude of the desert, to avoid the confusion and distractions of living among people? Saint Isaac the Syrian fled, leaving behind his episcopal diocese. The venerable Athanasius of Athos fled from his large monastery. They did this precisely because those places were too distracting, too full of temptations for them, and because they genuinely believed the words of Jesus Christ: 'For what will it profit a man, if he gains the whole world and forfeits his life?' " [Matt. 16:26].

"But they were saints!" said the priest.

"If the saints needed to protect themselves from the dangers of mingling with people," I replied, "then what must a poor sinner resort to!"

In the end I finally parted with this kind priest, and he lovingly saw me on my way.

After walking almost seven miles I stopped for the night in a village. At the inn I found a peasant who was extremely ill, and I advised his friends that he should receive his last communion. They agreed, and by morning they had sent for the priest from the village parish. I remained so that I could venerate the holy gifts and pray while this great sacrament was administered. In the meanwhile I went out into the street and sat down on a mound of earth to wait for the priest. Suddenly I saw a young girl running toward me from the backyard—the one who had spent so much time praying at the chapel.

"How did you end up here?" I asked.

"The date was set for my betrothal to that schismatic," she replied, "so I left." Then she bowed to the ground before me and said, "Be merciful—let me go with you and take me to some women's monastery! I don't want to be married. I'll live in a monastery and pray the Jesus Prayer. They'll take me in on your word."

"Mercy!" I said. "And just where am I going to take you? I don't know a single women's monastery in this part of the country. Besides, how could I take you with me when you don't even have a passport? For one thing, no one will take you in anywhere, and for another, you won't be able to hide anywhere nowadays. You would be caught at once and sent back home, and they may even punish you for vagrancy. Why don't you just go home and pray to God, and if you don't want to get married, then make up some illness as an excuse. That's called pretending for the sake of salvation. The holy Mother Clementa did this, and so did the blessed Marina when she took refuge in a men's monastery. And there were also many others."

While we were sitting and talking, we saw four peasants come tearing down the road toward us in a wagon. They grabbed the girl, put her in their wagon, and sent her off with one of the peasants. The other three tied my hands together and forcibly led me back to the village where I had just spent the summer. I tried to explain the situation to them, but they kept shouting, "We'll teach you to seduce our girls, little holy man!" We arrived toward evening, and they took me to the village courthouse, chained my legs, and locked me up in a jail cell to await trial in the morning. The priest found out that I was in jail and came to visit me. He brought me some dinner, and in an attempt to comfort me he said that, as my spiritual father, he would testify on my behalf and tell them that I was not the kind of man to do what they were accusing me of. He stayed with me for a while and then departed.

Later that evening, the magistrate happened to be riding through the village on his way somewhere. He stopped to see the village deputy and was informed of what had happened. He gathered everyone together and ordered me brought to the courthouse. We went and stood there, waiting for him. The magistrate arrived in high spirits; he sat down at the table, still wearing his hat, and shouted, "Hey, Epiphan! The girl—your daughter—she didn't steal anything from your house, did she?"

"No, Batyushka, nothing!"

"Has she been caught in any funny business with that fool over there?"

"No, Batyushka!"

"Fine! Then this is my decision on how we're going to settle this:

you handle your own daughter. As for this young know-it-all, we'll teach him a lesson tomorrow and chase him out of the village. He'll be told in no uncertain terms never to come back here again. That's all!"

Having passed this judgment, the magistrate stood up and went home to sleep, while I was returned to the jail. Two village policemen came in the morning, gave me a thrashing, and let me go. I left, thanking God that He had deemed me worthy to suffer for His name. This comforted me greatly and further kindled the unceasing prayer of my heart.

I was not offended by anything that had happened to me. It was as if it had happened to someone else and I had been merely an observer. Even the beating I received was within my power to endure. The prayer that delighted my heart made me unaware of everything else.

After walking almost three miles, I met the young girl's mother, who was on her way home with purchases from the market. She saw me and said, "Our bridegroom has backed off from the marriage. You see, he was angry with Akulka for running away from him." Then she gave me some bread and a patty, and I went on my way.

The weather was dry, and I had no desire to spend the night in another village. So that evening, when I saw two fenced-in haystacks in the forest, I settled down under them for the night. When I fell asleep, I dreamed that I was walking along the road and reading chapters from the work of Saint Anthony the Great in the *Philokalia*. Suddenly the starets caught up with me and said, "You're reading the wrong passage. This is what you should read," and he pointed to the thirty-fifth chapter of Saint John of Karpathos, where I read the following: "Sometimes the teacher submits to ignominy and suffers temptations for the sake of those who will benefit spiritually from this." The starets also pointed out the forty-first chapter, by the same Saint John, which said: "Those who pray most earnestly are the ones who are assailed by the most terrible and fierce temptations."

Then the starets said, "Be strong in spirit and do not despair! Remember what the apostle said: '. . . He who is in you is greater than he who is in the world' [1 John 4:4]. Now you have experienced for yourself that a man is tempted only as much as he can endure it; 'but with the temptation God will also provide the way of escape' [1 Cor. 10:13]. Hoping in God's help is what strengthened holy men of prayer and led them on to zeal and fervor. Such men not only gave their lives over to unceasing prayer, but out of their love they also revealed and taught it to others, whenever the opportunity presented itself. Saint Gregory of Thessalonika says the following about this: 'It is not only we who should heed God's command to pray unceasingly in the name of Christ. We must also reveal and teach this prayer to others, to everyone, in fact: monastics, lay people, the wise, the simple, husbands, wives, and children. We must awaken in them a desire to pray unceasingly.' The venerable Callistus Telicudis says something very similar: 'Neither mental prayer to the Lord [i.e., interior prayer] nor contemplative illumination nor any means of elevating one's soul should be hoarded in one's own mind. They must be recorded, written down, and made available to others for the sake of love and the common good of all.' The Scriptures themselves speak of this: 'Brother helped by brother is like a strong fortress' [Prov. 18:19]. However, in this case one should flee vanity in every possible way and guard oneself, so that the seed of God's Word is not sown into the wind."

When I awakened, my heart was filled with great joy and my soul was strengthened, and I went on my way.

After this, a long time passed before another incident occurred. Perhaps I will tell you about it. It was on March 24 when I experienced an irresistible desire to receive Holy Communion on the following day, which was the Feast of the Annunciation of the Most Pure Theotokos. I asked for the whereabouts of the local church and was told that it was twenty miles away. So for the rest of that day and night I walked, in order to get to matins on time. The weather could not have been worse. First it snowed, then it rained; the wind was strong and it was very cold. Along the way I had to cross a small creek, and when I reached the middle of it, the ice broke under my feet and I fell into the water up to my waist. When I arrived for matins I was soaked, but I stood through matins and then the Divine Liturgy, at which God had granted me to receive Communion.

In order to spend that day peacefully, without disturbing the spiritual joy that filled me, I asked the church watchman if I could spend the night in his room. That entire day my heart was filled with indescribable joy and delight. I lay on the plank bed in this unheated room as if I were resting in the bosom of Abraham, while the prayer flowed intensely. A love for Jesus Christ and the Mother of God washed over my heart in waves of delight and steeped my soul in a soothing rapture. Toward evening I suddenly felt a strong pain in my legs and remembered that they were still wet. I ignored this and listened more attentively to the prayer in my heart, and soon I no longer noticed the pain. The next morning I tried to get out of bed and realized that I could not move my legs. They were completely paralyzed, as weak as if they were limp pieces of string. The watchman was barely able to drag me off the bed. For two days I sat, unable to walk, and on the third day the watchman began to chase me out from his room, saying, "If you die here, who's going to bury you?" Somehow I barely managed to crawl out of there, dragging myself on the ground with my hands, and collapsed on the church steps, where I lay for about two days. People walked right past me, completely ignoring me and my pleas for help.

Finally some peasant came up to me, sat down, and struck up a conversation. "What will you pay me if I cure you?" he asked. "The exact same thing once happened to me, so I know the cure."

"I have nothing to give you," I said.

"What have you got there in your knapsack?"

"Only some dried bread and books."

"Well, how about working for me, for at least one summer, if I cure you?"

"I can't do any work. You see that I have the use of only one arm, and the other one is almost completely withered."

"So what can you do?"

"Nothing, really—but I do read and write."

"Aha, you can write! Well, then, teach my son. He reads a little, and I want him to learn to write. But tutors are expensive—they want twenty rubles to teach him." I agreed to this, and with the watchman's help the peasant dragged me off and put me in an old abandoned bathhouse in his backyard.

Then he set about curing me. He scoured the fields, yards, and garbage dumps and gathered almost a bushel of rotting bones: bird and cattle bones, among others. He washed them, ground them down with a rock, and placed them in a large earthen pot. He covered this with a lid with a small opening in it and lowered it upside down into an empty jar sunk in the ground. He smeared the lid of the earthen pot with a thick layer of clay. Then he made a pile of wood around it and lit a fire, which he kept burning for more than twenty-four hours. As he added wood to the fire, he said, "Now we'll get some tar from these bones."

The next day he dug the jar out of the ground. It contained a little over a pint of viscous liquid that had dripped into it through the hole in the lid of the earthen pot. It was a reddish, oily liquid that smelled abominably, like raw meat. The bones, which had initially been black with putrefaction, were now clean and white—as transparent as mother-of-pearl, or actual pearls. I rubbed this liquid into my legs five times a day. And what do you think? On the second day I was able to wiggle my toes. On the third day I could bend and unbend my knees. On the fifth day I walked around the yard with the help of a cane. In a word, by the end of a week my legs had recovered their former strength! I thanked God for all this and thought to myself: what wisdom has gone into God's creation! That those dry, rotting, almost completely decomposed bones could contain such vital power, color, and odor and have such an effect on living organisms, as if bringing life to deadened limbs! This is indeed a pledge of the coming resurrection. If only that forester, with whom I spent the summer and who doubted the final resurrection of all life, could see this now!

Once I was cured, I began teaching the little boy. Instead of using a grammar book, I wrote out the Jesus Prayer, showed him how to form the letters, and had him copy it. Teaching the boy was very restful for me, because during the day he was apprenticed to a local estate steward and could study with me only while the steward slept, from daybreak until the late-morning Liturgy. He was a bright boy and was soon able to write a few things fairly well. When the steward found out that the boy could write, he asked him, "Who is teaching you?" The boy replied, "A pilgrim with a disabled arm who is staying with us in the abandoned bathhouse."

The curious steward, who was Polish, came to see me and found me reading the *Philokalia*. He started talking with me and asked, "What are you reading?" I showed him the book. "Ah," he said, "that's the *Philokalia!* I saw this book at our *ksenda's** when I lived in Vilna. I once heard that it contains some very strange magic and methods for praying that were written down by Greek monks and that are similar to what those fanatics in India and Bukhara do. They sit and breathe up a storm so they can experience some stirring in their hearts, and in their stupidity, they mistake these natural feelings for prayer, thinking that they are given to them by God Himself. We should pray simply because this is our obligation before God. Get up in the morning, say the Our Father as Christ taught us, and you're set for the whole day—but not this endless repetition, beating the same thing to death, over and over again! Why, you could go out of your mind—and hurt your heart in the process!"

"Do not think that way about this holy book, Batyushka," I replied.

"It was not written by ordinary Greek monks, but by the greatest and holiest men of long ago, who are revered by your Church as well: Saint Anthony the Great, Saint Macarius the Great, Mark the Anchorite, Saint John Chrysostom, and others. It was from them that the monks of India and Bukhara adopted the method for interior prayer of the heart, but my starets told me that they distorted and ruined it. But in the *Philokalia,* all the teachings on the prayer of the heart are rooted in the Word of God, the Holy Bible, where the same Jesus Christ Who taught us the Our Father, also commanded us to pray unceasingly, saying, 'Love the Lord your God with all your heart and all your mind' [Matt. 22:37]; 'Take heed, watch . . . and pray' [Mark 13:33]; 'Abide in me and I in you.' [John 15:4] And the holy Fathers cite the witness King David bears in the Psalter: 'O taste and see that the Lord is good!' [Ps. 34:8]. They explain this by saying that the Christian must do everything possible to acquire and experience the delights of prayer, continually seeking the consolation it brings—and not just say the Our Father once a day. Here, let me read to you how these saints condemn those who do not strive to learn and practice the delightful prayer of the heart. They write that such people make the following mistakes: they contradict the divinely inspired Scriptures; they do not set their sights upon a higher and more perfect spiritual state for their souls and, instead, are satisfied only with external good works; they do not hunger and thirst for the truth, thus depriving themselves of bliss and joy in the Lord; because they judge themselves on the basis of their external works, they frequently fall into delusion or pride and alienate themselves."

"What you are reading is quite lofty," said the steward, "but it hardly applies to us ordinary people who live in the world!"

"Here, let me read you something simpler, about how even good people, living in the world, managed to learn unceasing prayer." I found a passage from Saint Simeon the New Theologian in the *Philokalia,* about George the Younger, and read it to him.

The steward was impressed by this and said, "Let me borrow this book and I'll look through it when I have some free time."

"I suppose I could give it to you for twenty-four hours, but no longer, because I read it daily and cannot manage without it."

"Well, at least copy out what you just read. I'll pay you for it."

"I don't need your money. I'll copy it for the sake of love, and I only hope that God will grant you the desire to practice this prayer."

With great pleasure I immediately copied the passage I had read, and he took it home and read it to his wife. They were both impressed by it and began inviting me over. I would go, bringing the *Philokalia* with me, and read to them while they drank tea and listened. One time they asked me to stay for dinner. The steward's wife, a kind elderly woman, sat with us as we ate fried fish. Suddenly she choked on a fish bone and, after trying everything possible, we could not get it out. She had a great deal of pain in her throat, and after about two hours took to her bed. We sent for the doctor, who lived thirty miles away, but since it was already evening, unfortunately I had to go home.

I slept lightly that night and dreamed that I heard my starets's voice. I could not see him, but I heard him say, "Your landlord cured you—and you can't even help the steward's wife? God commanded us to have compassion for our neighbor's suffering."

"I'd be more than glad to help—but how? I don't know what to do!"

"Here is what you do: the old lady has a lifelong aversion to lamp oil. Not only is she unable to swallow it, but she cannot abide even the smell of it without getting nauseated. So you must get her to swallow a spoonful of the lamp oil, and this will induce vomiting and dislodge the bone. The oil will also coat the wound that the bone made in her throat, and it will heal."

"But how will I get her to take lamp oil if she has such an aversion to it? She won't swallow it!"

"You tell the steward to hold her head while you quickly pour it down her throat. Use force if you have to."

When I woke up I went at once to the steward's home and told him all this in detail. "What good will your oil do now?" he said. "Her throat is already hoarse, she's hallucinating, and her neck is all swollen! But then again, maybe we should give it a try. Oil is a harmless medicine, even though it won't do any good either."

He poured some lamp oil into a shot glass, and somehow we managed to get her to swallow it. The vomiting started immediately, and soon the fish bone came out, along with some blood. She felt better and fell into a deep sleep.

I came back in the morning to check on her and saw that she was calmly drinking tea. Both she and her husband were astonished by this cure, but especially by the fact that the wife's aversion to lamp oil had been revealed to me in a dream, for they alone knew about this. At that point the doctor arrived and the steward's wife told him what had happened to her, while I described how the peasant had cured me. After listening to us, the doctor said, "Neither case is all that unusual. The same natural powers were active in both instances. However, let me write it down so I don't forget it." He produced a pencil and made some notes in his notebook.

After this incident, word spread quickly around the neighborhood that I was a visionary, a healer, and a witch doctor. People started coming to me from all over with their affairs and problems. They brought me gifts, began to treat me with great respect, and looked after all my comforts. I put up with this for a week, but then I became afraid of falling into vainglory and being harmed by all these distractions. So I left during the night without saying a word to anyone.

Thus I embarked once again on my solitary journey. I experienced such a lightness within me, as if an immense burden had been removed from my shoulders. The prayer increasingly comforted me, so that often my heart would bubble over with boundless love for Jesus Christ. Gentle streams of consolation would flow from this delight through all the joints in my body. The remembrance of Jesus Christ was so engraved in my mind that when I meditated on biblical events it was as if I could see them right before my very eyes. I was filled with a warm tenderness and shed tears of joy. Such joy filled my heart that I have no words to describe it!

At times I would go for three whole days without encountering any human habitation, which, to my immense delight, made me feel as if I were the only man alive on earth—one wretched sinner in the presence of the merciful and man-loving God. This solitude consoled me and enabled me to experience the delights of the prayer with far greater sensitivity than I do when I am surrounded by people.

Finally I arrived in Irkutsk. There I venerated the relics of Saint Innocent and began to think to myself, "So, where do I go from here?" I had no desire to stay there for any length of time, for the city was heavily populated. I walked down the street, lost in my thoughts, when I met one of the local merchants. He stopped me and asked, "Are you a pilgrim? Why don't you come over to my house?" I went, and soon we arrived at his lavish house. He asked me about myself and I told him about my travels. When I had finished, he said, "It is to old Jerusalem that you should make a pilgrimage. The shrines and relics there cannot compare to anything else in the world!"

"I would gladly go," I replied, "but there is no way to get there by land. I could get as far as the sea, but I cannot pay for a sea voyage. I would need some money for that."

"If you like," said the merchant, "I could make it possible for you to go. Just last year I sent one of our old-timers there."

I fell at his feet and he said, "Listen here, I'll give you a letter of introduction to my son. He lives in Odessa and does business with Constantinople, so his ships sail there. He will gladly arrange passage for you on one of his vessels. Then in Constantinople he will instruct his agents to book passage for you on another ship that sails to Jerusalem and to pay for it. It's not all that expensive."

When I heard this I was overcome with joy. I showered my benefactor with gratitude for his kindness. Then I thanked God for the fatherly love and care that He had bestowed on such a wretched sinner as I, who was no good to himself or to others, and who ate the bread of others in idleness.

I enjoyed the hospitality of the generous merchant for three days, and he provided me with the promised letter of introduction to his son. So there I was, on my way to Odessa, in hope of reaching the holy city of Jerusalem. Yet I did not even know for sure if the Lord would grant me to venerate his life-giving tomb.

Third Narrative

Just before leaving Irkutsk I visited my spiritual father, with whom I had spoken frequently, and said to him, "Well, here I am, off to Jerusalem. I just came to say good-bye and to thank you for the Christian love you have shown to me, an unworthy pilgrim."

"May God bless your journey," he replied. "But you know, you have not told me all that much about yourself—who you are, where you are from. You told me so much about your travels, I would be curious to know where you are from and about your life before you became a pilgrim."

"Of course," I said, "I'll be glad to tell you about that too. My story is not all that long. I was born in a village in the Orlovsk province. After my parents died, there were just the two of us left—I and my older brother. He was ten years old and I was two, going on three. Our grandfather took us in to raise us. He was a prosperous and honest old man who kept an inn on the main thoroughfare, and thanks to his kindness many a traveler stayed at the inn. So we went to live with him. My brother was very high-spirited and often took off on his own, running around the village, while I spent more time with Grandfather. On feast days we attended church with him, and he often read from the Bible at home—in fact, from this very same one that I now carry with me. When my brother got older, something went wrong in his life, and he took to drinking heavily. I was seven years old at the time. I remember that once, when we were lying down together on the stove, he pushed me off and I hurt my left arm when I fell. After that I lost the use of this arm, and now it has all withered up.

"Grandfather realized that I would not be able to work on the land, so he began to teach me to read and write. Since we had no grammar books, he somehow managed to use this very Bible instead. He started from the very beginning and had me writing words so I could learn the letters of the alphabet. I do not know how I did it, but by repeating everything he said, I eventually learned how to read. Finally, when Grandfather's vision grew weak, he frequently made me read to him from the Bible, correcting me as I went along.

"There was a county clerk who often stayed at the inn, and he had such a beautiful handwriting. I enjoyed watching him write and tried to copy his writing. He began to teach me, giving me paper and ink and sharpening my quills. That was how I learned to write. Grandfather was very pleased by this and would say to me, 'Now that God has revealed reading and writing to you, it will make a man out of you. You must thank the Lord for this and pray more often.' So we would attend all the church services, but we also prayed a great deal at home. I would chant 'Have mercy on me, O God,' while Grandfather and Grandmother did their prostrations or simply knelt.

"Finally, when I turned seventeen, Grandmother died. Grandfather would say to me, 'We don't have a mistress of the house any longer—how are we going to manage without a woman? Your older brother has made a mess of his life, so I want you to get married.' I protested because of my disabled arm, but Grandfather insisted. They found a mature, kind twenty-year-old girl for me and we were married.

"One year later, Grandfather became ill and was on his deathbed when he called for me. As he spoke words of parting, he said, 'I am leaving you this house and everything I own. Live by your conscience, do not cheat anyone, but above all else pray to God, for everything comes from Him. Do not place your hope in anything or anyone, but only in God. Go to church, read the Bible, and remember me and the old lady in your prayers. I am giving you a thousand rubles. Be careful with the money and do not spend it foolishly, but neither be stingy with it. Give to God's Church and to His poor.'

"So he died and I buried him. My brother grew very jealous because I alone had inherited the inn and the rest of the estate. He became enraged with me and was so enmeshed in evil that he actually plotted to kill me. Finally, this is what he did one night, while we were sleeping. There were no guests at the inn, and he broke into the closet where I kept the money, stole it from the chest, and set fire to the closet. By the time we awakened, the fire had spread through the whole hut and inn. We barely managed to jump out the window, wearing nothing but our nightclothes.

"Since we kept the Bible under our pillows, we were able to take it with us. As we stood and watched our house burning, we said to each other, 'Thank God, at least we rescued the Bible! At least we have something to console us in our distress.' Thus our entire estate burned down and my brother disappeared without a trace. Much later we found out that he had begun to drink heavily and was heard to boast about how he had stolen the money and had set fire to the inn.

"We were left completely destitute, without any clothing or even a pair of *lapti** to wear. Somehow we managed to borrow some money to build a small cabin, and we started living in it as landless peasants. My wife did beautiful handiwork—weaving, spinning, sewing. She took in work, laboring day and night to support me. With my withered arm I could not even make shoes, so I would sit while she wove or spun and read to her from the Bible. She would listen and sometimes burst into tears. 'Why are you crying?' I'd ask. 'Thank God that at least we are alive.' And she would reply, 'The Bible contains such beautiful words that it touches me so deeply.'

"Remembering Grandfather's admonitions, we fasted frequently, chanted the akathist to the Theotokos every morning, and did one thousand prostrations before going to bed at night, so as not to fall into temptation. Thus we lived peacefully for two years. It is interesting that although we had never heard of the prayer of the heart, did not understand it, and simply prayed with our lips, doing mindless prostrations like blockheads performing somersaults, we still had the desire to pray. Not only was it easy for us to recite long prayers without really understanding them, but we did so with great delight. It seems that teacher was right when he told me that one could pray secretly within himself, without being consciously aware of the prayer or of how it acts on its own in the soul and awakens the desire to pray, according to each person's knowledge and ability.

"After living this way for two years, my wife suddenly became ill with a very high fever. She received her last Communion and died on the ninth day of her illness. I was left completely alone, without any means of supporting myself. So I started wandering about and begging, of which I was quite ashamed. In addition, I was overwhelmed with such grief over losing my wife that I didn't know what to do with myself. When I walked into my cabin and saw her clothing or a kerchief she wore, I would let out such a howl and even faint. Finally it became impossible for me to bear my grief living at home. So I sold my hut for twenty rubles and gave to the poor whatever was left of my wife's and my clothing. Because of my arm, I was given a permanent disability passport, and I took my Bible and set off without any specific destination in mind.

" 'Where will I go now?' I thought. 'I'll go to Kiev first, to venerate the relics of God's worthy saints and ask for their help and intercession.' This decision instantly made me feel much better, and my journey to Kiev turned out to be a joyous one. This was thirteen years ago, and ever since then I have been wandering through different places. I have visited many churches and monasteries, but nowadays I keep mainly to the steppes and fields. I am not sure if the Lord has ordained it for me to reach the holy city of Jerusalem. If it is God's will, perhaps it is time for my sinful bones to be buried there."

"How old are you now?"

"I'm thirty-three."

"The age of Jesus Christ at His death!"

Fourth Narrative

But for me it is good to be near God; I have made the Lord God my refuge. . . .

—Ps. 73:28

When I came to my spiritual father I said, "How true it is what that Russian proverb says: 'Man proposes, but God disposes.' I had planned to set out today and start on my journey to the city of Jerusalem. However, something quite different happened. A totally unforeseen incident has kept me here for three more days. I could not resist coming to see you, to tell you about this, for I needed your advice on how to handle it. I will tell you about this unexpected incident.

"After I had taken my leave of everyone, with God's help I set out on my journey. Just as I was about to pass through the gates of the city, I saw a familiar man standing at the doorway of the last house. He was once a pilgrim, just as I am, and I had not seen him for three years. We greeted each other, and he asked me where I was headed.

"I replied, 'I'd like to get to the old Jerusalem, God willing.'

" 'Thank God!' he exclaimed. 'I know a good traveling companion for you.'

" 'God be with you and with him,' I said, 'but surely you know that I never travel with any companions, since I'm used to walking alone.'

" 'Hear me out—I know that this traveling companion will be just right for you. You will both suit each other quite nicely. You see, the father of the master of this house where I work has also made a vow to visit old Jerusalem. You will get used to each other. He's a local man, of the lower middle class—an elderly man who is kind and actually quite deaf. So it doesn't matter how much you shout at him, he won't hear a thing. If you need to speak with him, you must write it down on paper and then he'll answer. So he will not bother you on the journey, because he won't be talking to you. He hardly speaks even in his own home, but you would be indispensable to him on the journey. His son is providing him with a horse and wagon to get to Odessa, where he will sell both. The old man would like to go on foot, but he needs the horse for his luggage and some packages he is taking to the Lord's tomb, and you could load your knapsack on his wagon. Think about it! How can you let an old, deaf man go off on his own, in a horse-drawn wagon, on such a long journey? We have been looking for some time for a traveling companion for him, but they're all asking too much money. And then it is dangerous to send him off with a stranger, especially since he's carrying money and parcels with him. Do say yes, brother; I assure you it will work out just fine. Agree to do this to the glory of God and for love of your fellowman. I will vouch for you to his family, and they will be overjoyed to hear it. They are kind people and care a great deal for me. I've been working for them for two years already.'

"We had been standing and talking at the entrance to the house. Then he took me inside and introduced me to the master. I realized that this was an honest, decent family, so I agreed to their proposal. We decided to leave, God willing, on the third day after Christmas, right after the Liturgy.

"You see what kinds of coincidences happen in one's life! Yet God and His Divine Providence always guide all our plans and deeds, just as it is written: 'For God is at work in you, both to will and to work for his good pleasure' " [Phil. 2:13].

My spiritual father listened to my story and said, "I rejoice with all my heart, dearest brother, that the Lord has ordained for me to see you again, so soon and so unexpectedly. Since you have some free time on your hands, I will lovingly ask you to stay a bit longer and tell me more about the educational experiences you have encountered on your lengthy pilgrimages. I have listened with such pleasure and delight to all your other stories."

"I will be more than happy to do so," I replied, and I began to talk.

So many things, both good and bad, have happened to me, that it would be impossible to recount them all. Why, I've even forgotten some, for my attention was always more focused on what was guiding and prodding my lazy soul to pray. So I did not spend much time thinking about all the rest—or, rather, I tried to forget the past, as the apostle Paul teaches us, saying: ". . . forgetting what lies behind and striving forward to what lies ahead" [Phil. 3:13]. Even my late starets of blessed memory would tell me that obstacles to the prayer of the heart come from two sources: from the left and from the right. This means that if the enemy fails to prevent us from praying, through vain thoughts and sinful imaginings, then he stirs within us memories of all sorts of edifying things, or he entices us with pleasant thoughts—anything at all—just to lure us away from prayer, which is something unbearable to him.

This is what is called "right-hand theft," and it causes the soul to scorn converse with God and to turn to the pleasure of conversing with its own self or with other creatures. He taught me, therefore, that during prayer I must reject even the most pleasant spiritual thoughts. Moreover, if I should happen to notice during the course of a day that I am spending more time on edifying speculation or conversation than on the essential hidden prayer of the heart, I should consider even this as being immoderate, or as self-seeking spiritual gluttony. This applies especially to beginners, for whom it is vital that the time they spend on prayer must significantly exceed even the time they spend on any other pious activities.

Still, neither can one forget all the rest. It can happen that an experience becomes so ingrained in one's mind that even if one does not think about it often, it remains clearly etched in the memory. A case in point would be the pious family with whom God granted me to spend a few days; I will tell you now about them.

While I was journeying through the Tobolsk province, I happened to be passing through one of the cities of that district. I was down to the last of my dried bread, so I stopped in one of the houses to ask for some. The master of the house said to me, "Thank God that you have come at the right moment! My wife has just taken some fresh bread out of the oven. Here is a warm loaf for you; pray to God for us." I thanked him and started to put the bread in my knapsack when the mistress of the house saw me and said, "Look at your knapsack—it's all worn out! Let me give you another one." And she gave me a good, sturdy one instead. I thanked them with all my heart and went on my way. As I was leaving the city, I stopped in a small shop and asked for some salt. The shopkeeper gave me a small bagful and I rejoiced in my spirit, thanking God for bringing unworthy me to such good people. Now I would not have to worry about food for a whole week. I could sleep peacefully and be satisfied. Bless the Lord, O my soul!

I had walked about three and a half miles beyond the city when I came across a poor village along that road. There stood a wooden church, simple but nicely decorated with frescoes on the outside. As I walked past it I felt a desire to go inside and worship in this temple of God, so I went on the porch and prayed for a while. Two children, aged five or six, were playing on the grass along the side of the church. I thought they were the priest's children, even though they were extremely well dressed. Still I said my prayers and went on my way. I had walked only ten steps away from the church when I heard shouting behind me: "Dear beggarman! Dear beggarman, wait!" The children, a boy and a girl, had seen me and were running toward me and shouting. I stopped and they ran up to me and each grabbed one of my hands. "Come with us to Mommy—she loves the poor," they said.

"I am not a beggar," I replied. "I'm just a man passing through."

"Then why do you have a knapsack?"

"I keep bread for the road in there. But tell me, where is your mommy?" I asked.

"She's over there, behind the church, just behind that little grove."

They led me into a beautiful garden, in the middle of which stood a large manor house. We went inside, and how neat and clean everything was! The mistress of the house ran out to meet us. "Welcome! Welcome! From where has God sent you to us? Sit down, kind sir, sit down!" She removed the knapsack from my back, put it on the table, and sat me down in one of the softest chairs. "Wouldn't you like something to eat, or some tea? Is there anything at all that you need?"

"I thank you most humbly," I replied, "I have a sack full of food. Although I do drink tea, we peasants are not all that used to it. Your eagerness to help and your affectionate welcome are more precious to me than any refreshments. I will pray to God that He bless you for the biblical spirit of your love of pilgrims." When I had said this I experienced an intense desire to enter into my inner self again. The prayer was kindled in my heart and I needed peace and silence, so I could give reign to this self-kindling flame of prayer and keep others from seeing all the external manifestations that accompany it, such as tears, sighs and the unusual facial gestures and movement of my lips. So I got up and said, "Please excuse me, *Matushka*,* it's time for me to leave. May the Lord Jesus Christ be with you and with your kind little children."

"Oh, no! God forbid that you should leave—I won't let you go! My husband will be coming home from the city this evening. He works there as an appointed judge, and he'll be so happy to meet you! He considers every pilgrim to be a messenger of God. If you leave now he will be very upset not to have met you. Besides, tomorrow is Sunday and you can pray at the Liturgy with us and then we'll eat together whatever God has provided. We always have guests on each feast day—as many as thirty of Christ's needy brethren. But you have not even told me anything about yourself—where you come from and where you are headed! Stay and talk with me, I love to hear about spiritual matters from devout people. Children, children! Take the pilgrim's knapsack and put it in the chapel—that's where he will spend the night."

I was surprised to hear what she was saying and thought to myself: am I dealing here with a human being, or is she some sort of an apparition?

So I did stay to meet the master of the house. I briefly told him about my journey and that I was headed for Irkutsk.

"Well, then," said the mistress, "you will have to pass through Tobolsk. My mother is a schima nun* now and lives in a women's monastery there. We will give you a letter of introduction and she will receive you. Many people go to her for spiritual counsel. By the way, you can also bring her a book by Saint John of the Ladder, which she asked us to order from Moscow. How nicely all this fits together!"

Finally it was time for dinner, and we all sat down at the table, where four more ladies joined us. After the first course, one of them got up from the table, bowed to the icon, then to us. She served the second course and sat down again. Then another of the ladies repeated this and served the third course. Observing all this, I asked the mistress of the house, "If I may ask, little mother, are these ladies related to you?"

"Yes, they are sisters to me: this one is the cook, this one is the coachman's wife, that one is the housekeeper, and the last is my maid. They are all married—I don't have a single unmarried girl in my house."

Having observed and listened to everything, I was even more astonished. I thanked God for bringing me to such devout people and experienced the intense activity of the prayer in my heart. Since I was eager to be alone so as not to hinder this prayer, I got up from the table and said to the mistress, "No doubt you will need to rest after dinner. I am used to taking a walk, so I will stroll around the garden."

"No," she replied, "I do not need to rest. I will walk with you in the garden, and you will tell me something edifying. If you go alone, the children will pester you. As soon as they see you, they won't leave your side for a moment, because they truly love the needy brethren of Christ and pilgrims."

There was nothing for me to do but go with her. In order to avoid talking about myself when we entered the garden, I bowed to the ground before the mistress and said, "Matushka, in the name of God, please tell me how long you have been living such a devout life and how you achieved such piety."

"Perhaps I should tell you the whole story of my life. You see, my mother is the great-granddaughter of Saint Joasaph, whose relics rest in Belogorod and are open for veneration. We owned a large town house and rented one wing of it to a nobleman, who was not too well off financially. When he died, his widow was pregnant, and then she died after giving birth. My mother had compassion on the poor orphaned child and took him in to raise him. I was born one year later. We grew up together, studied under the same tutors, and became as close as brother and sister. Sometime later my father died, and my mama moved from the city to live right here in the country, on her estate. When we grew up, my mother gave me in marriage to this orphaned young man who had grown up in our house. She settled her entire estate on us and entered a monastery, where she had a cell built for herself. In giving us a mother's blessing, she admonished us to live as Christians, to pray earnestly to God, and above all else to strive to fulfill the most important of God's commandments: to love our neighbors and to feed and help Christ's needy brethren, with simplicity and humility to raise our children in the fear of God, and to treat our servants as brothers. So we have lived here by ourselves these last ten years, trying our best to heed our mother's instructions. We have a guesthouse for the poor, where there are more than ten crippled and needy people in residence at the moment. Perhaps tomorrow we will visit them."

When she had finished her story I asked, "Where is that book by Saint John of the Ladder that you wanted delivered to your mother?"

"Let's go inside and I will find it for you."

No sooner had we sat down to read than the master of the house arrived. Upon seeing me he embraced me warmly, and we exchanged the Christian kiss of peace. Then he took me into his own room and said, "Come, dear brother, to my study and bless my cell. I think that you have had enough of her"—he pointed to his wife. "As soon as she sees a man or woman who is a pilgrim, or someone who is ill, she is more than glad to spend day and night with them. Her entire family has been this way for generations." We went into his study. There were so many books and magnificent icons there, as well as a life-giving crucifix with a life-sized figure of Christ on it and a Bible next to it. I prayed and then said to him: "Sir, what you have here is God's paradise. Here is the Lord Jesus Christ Himself, His Most Pure Mother, and His holy saints; and these"—I pointed to the books—"are their divinely inspired, living words and teachings, which can never be silenced. I would expect that you enjoy frequent spiritual converse with them."

"Yes, I admit it," said the master. "I do love to read."

"What sort of books do you have here?" I asked.

"I have many spiritual books," he replied. "Here is the *Chet'-Minei** for the entire year, the works of Saint John Chrysostom and Saint Basil the Great. There are many theological and philosophical works, as well as collections of many sermons of the most recent and celebrated preachers. My library is worth five thousand rubles."

"By any chance, would you have a book about prayer?" I asked.

"I love to read about prayer. Here is the most recent work on that subject, written by a priest in Saint Petersburg." He reached for a volume on the Lord's Prayer, the Our Father, and we began to read it with pleasure.

A short time later, the mistress of the house brought us some tea, while the children brought in a large silver basket filled with some sort of biscuits or pastries that I had never before eaten. The husband took the book from me, gave it to his wife, and said, "Since she reads so beautifully, we will make her read to us while we take some refreshment." She started reading and we listened. As I listened to her, I was able simultaneously to attend to the prayer in my heart. The more she read, the stronger the prayer became and filled me with delight. Suddenly, it seemed to me as if someone passed before my eyes in a flash, through the air—as if it were my late starets. I shuddered, but not wanting them to notice this, I quickly said, "Forgive me, I must have dozed off." At that moment I felt as if the starets's spirit had penetrated my own spirit, as if he had illumined it. I experienced a certain enlightenment in my understanding, and a multitude of thoughts about prayer came to me. I had just made the sign of the cross over myself in an attempt to banish these thoughts when the mistress finished reading the book and her husband asked me if I had enjoyed it. So we started a discussion on it.

"I liked it very much," I replied. "The Lord's Prayer, the Our Father, is more exalted and more precious than all the recorded prayers we Christians have, for it was given to us by the Lord Jesus Christ Himself. The commentary on it was very good, except that it focuses primarily on Christian works. In my reading of the holy Fathers, I have read also the contemplative, mystical commentaries on this prayer."

"In which of the Fathers did you read this?"

"Well, for example, in Saint Maximus the Confessor and, in the *Philokalia*, in Saint Peter of Damascus."

"Do you remember anything you read? Please, tell us about it!"

"Why, of course! Let's take the first words of the prayer: *Our Father, Who art in heaven.* In the book we read today the interpretation of these words is to be understood as a call to brotherly love for one's neighbors, as being all children of the one Father. This is true, but the Fathers explain this further, on a deeper spiritual level. They say that the words of this maxim are a call to raise the mind to heaven, to the heavenly Father, and to remember our obligation to place ourselves and live our lives in the presence of God at each and every moment. The words *hallowed be Thy Name* are explained in your book as being a sign of reverence, so that the Name of God would never be uttered disrespectfully or taken in false oaths. In a word, the holy Name of God must be spoken reverently and not taken in vain. The mystical commentators see these words as a direct request for the gift of interior prayer of the heart—a request that the most holy Name of God be engraved upon the heart and hallowed by the self-acting prayer, so that it might sanctify all our feelings and spiritual powers.

"The words *Thy Kingdom come* are explained by mystical commentators in the following way: may inner peace, tranquillity, and spiritual joy come into our hearts. Your book explains the words *give us this day our daily bread* as a request for the material needs of our bodies—not in excess, but enough to fill our own needs and to help the needy. However, Saint Maximus the Confessor interprets *daily bread* to mean the feeding of the soul with heavenly bread—the Word of God—and the union of the soul with God, through constant remembrance of Him and through the unceasing interior prayer of the heart."

"Ah! That is a great deed, but it is almost impossible for those who live in the world to attain to interior prayer!" exclaimed the master of the house. "We're lucky when the Lord helps us simply to say our prayers without laziness!"

"Don't look at it that way, Batyushka. If it were so impossible and overwhelmingly difficult, then God would not have admonished us all to do it. His strength is made perfect also in weakness. From their own experience the Fathers offer us ways and methods that make it easier for us to attain to the prayer of the heart. Of course, for hermits they teach special and more advanced methods, but they also prescribe convenient methods that faithfully guide lay people to attain to the prayer of the heart."

"I have never come across anything as detailed as this in my reading," said the master.

"Please, if you would like me to, I will read to you from the *Philokalia*."

I went to get my *Philokalia*, found the article by Saint Peter of Damascus in section 3, and read the following: " 'More important than attending to breathing, one must learn to call upon the Name of God at all times, in all places, and during all manner of activity. The Apostle says: *pray without ceasing;* that is, he teaches constant remembrance of God at all times, in all places, and under any circumstances. If you are busy doing something, you must remember the Creator of all things; if you see light, remember Him who gave it to you. If you look at the sky, the earth, the waters and all that is in them, marvel and glorify the Creator of all. If you are putting your clothes on, remember Him Whose gift they are and thank Him Who provides everything in your life. In short, let every action be an occasion for you always to remember and praise God. And before you know it, you are praying unceasingly and your soul will always rejoice in this.' Do you see now how this method for achieving unceasing prayer is convenient, easy, and accessible to any person who has at least some measure of human feelings?"

They were very impressed by all this. The master embraced me with delight and thanked me. Then he looked through my *Philokalia* and said, "I will order this from Petersburg as soon as I can. For now I will copy this passage so I don't forget it. Read it to me again." He wrote it down quickly and neatly. Then he exclaimed, "My God! Why, I even have an icon of the holy Damascene!" (It was probably one of Saint John of Damascus.) He picked up a picture frame, inserted the handwritten sheet behind the glass, and hung it beneath the icon.

"There," he said, "the living word of God's saint, hanging right under his image. It will serve to remind me always to put his redemptive advice into practice."

After this we sat down to dinner, and the same people as before sat with us, men and women. What reverent silence and peace there were at the dinner table! After the meal we all, adults and children, spent a long time in prayer. I was asked to chant the Akathist to the Most Sweet Jesus.

After prayers the servants went to bed, while the three of us remained in the room. The mistress brought me a white shirt and socks. I bowed to the ground before her and said, "Matushka, I will not take the socks, for I have never worn them in my life. We peasants are used to always wearing *onoochi**. She hurried out of the room and brought back her old robe, made of thin yellow fabric, and ripped it in half to make two onoochi. "Look," said the master, "the poor man's footwear is falling apart." He brought a pair of his own *bashmaki** that were new and in a large size, the kind that were worn over boots. "Go in that empty room and change your clothes," he said. I did so, and when I returned they made me sit down and began to change my shoes. The husband started to wrap the onoochi around my feet, while his wife pulled the bashmaki on top of them. At first I protested, but they insisted, saying, "Sit and be quiet—Christ washed the feet of His apostles." There was nothing else I could do, so I burst into tears and they wept with me. Afterward, the mistress retired for the night with the children, while the master and I went to the summerhouse in the garden.

For a long time we did not feel sleepy, so we lay awake and talked. Then he began to ply me with questions: "Now tell me the truth, in God's name and on your conscience. Who are you? You must come from a good family and have chosen willingly to become a fool for Christ.* You write and read very well; you speak correctly and are able to think and discuss things properly. These things could not have been learned from a peasant upbringing."

"I spoke the honest truth, from the sincerity of my heart, when I told you and your wife about my background. I never thought to lie or deceive you. Why would I do that? Everything I have shared with you is not my own, but what I learned from my late starets, who was filled with divine wisdom, and what I carefully read in the holy Fathers. My ignorance has been enlightened most of all by interior prayer, which I did not acquire on my on. It came to life in my heart through God's mercy and the guidance of my starets. But this is something that is possible for each man. All it takes is to descend silently into one's heart and call more frequently on the enlightening name of Jesus Chirst, and immediately one will experience inner illumination. Then all things will be revealed to the understanding and one will comprehend even certain mysteries of the Kingdom of God through such enlightenment. Even to know that one can plumb the depths of one's own being, see one's inner self, be delighted by this self-knowledge, experience warm tenderness and shed tears over one's fallen state and distorted will, is already a deep and enlightened mystery. It is possible, and not all that difficult, to discuss and converse wisely with people, for the mind and heart existed before any human learning or human wisdom was acquired. If one has a mind, it can be educated, either by science or by experience; but where there is no understanding, then no amount of discipline will help. The fact is that we are far removed from our own real self, and we have little desire to confront that self. Instead, we run from any encounter with our real self, choosing aimless trifles over the truth. Then we try to convince ourselves that we'd be more than glad to live the spiritual life and take up praying, but there's never enough time for it, because all the cares and worries of our lives take up all our time. And yet, what is more important: the redemptive eternal life of the soul, or the short-lived life of the body, which we spend so much time attending to? It is this, which I spoke of, that leads people either to good judgment or to stupidity."

"Forgive me, dear brother, I did not question you merely from curiosity, but from a kindhearted sense of Christian empathy, and also because two years ago I had an experience that now prompted my question. You see, a beggar with a military discharge passport came to us. He was old, decrepit, and so poor that he barely had any clothes or shoes on him. He spoke little and so simply that one took him for a peasant from the steppes. We took him into the guesthouse for the poor, and some five days later he became so ill that we moved him into this summerhouse, and my wife and I began to nurse and care for him. Finally it became clear that he was close to dying, so we prepared him by calling our priest to come and hear his confession, to give him Communion, and to administer the sacrament of Holy Unction. The day before he died he got out of bed, asked for a pen and a sheet of paper, and requested that his door be locked and no one allowed inside while he wrote his last will and testament to his son. He asked also that after his death we mail it to the address he would provide in Saint Petersburg. I was astounded to see that not only did he write a beautiful and exceedingly cultured hand, but the composition was excellent; it was grammatically correct and very gentle in style. Tomorrow I will read his will to you—I kept a copy of it. All this surprised me and made me curious enough to ask him about his background and life. He made me vow that I would not reveal anything while he was still alive, and then, to the glory of God, he told me the story of his life.

" 'I was a very wealthy prince, living an opulent and dissipated life of great luxury. My wife died and I lived alone with my son, who was fortunate to be serving as a captain in the Guards. One day we were preparing to go to a ball at an important person's house when I became furious with my valet. Unable to control my temper, I hit him very hard on the head and ordered him sent back to his village. This happened in the evening, and the next day the valet died from an inflammation on his brain. Yet I was not bothered too much by this. I regretted my rash behavior but soon forgot about the incident. Six weeks later the dead valet began to appear to me, at first in my dreams. He hounded me every night, reproaching me and continually repeating, "Unscrupulous man! You are my murderer!" Then I also began to see him when I was fully awake. The longer this went on, the more frequently he would appear to me, until he was hounding me almost continuously. Finally I began to see not only him but also other dead men whom I had sorely offended, and even women whom I had seduced. They all continuously reproached me, robbing me of all my peace until I could no longer sleep or eat or do anything at all. I became so utterly exhausted that my skin stuck to my very bones. No matter what cures they attempted, not even the most experienced doctors could help me. I went abroad to try new cures, but after six months my condition had not improved in the least. The tormenting apparitions mercilessly grew worse and worse, and I was brought home barely alive. Indeed, my soul experienced the fullest measure of the torments of hell, before it had even left my body. It was then that I was convinced of the existence of hell and what it is really like.

" 'In this tormented state I acknowledged my sins, repented, confessed, and set free all my servants. I vowed that for the rest of my life I would inflict all manner of toil and hardship upon myself and humble myself in poverty, so that because of my sins I would become the lowest servant to people of the lowest class. As soon as I had firmly resolved to do this, all the tormenting apparitions vanished. I cannot fully describe the joy and delight that I experienced from having made my peace with God, and it was this experience that taught me what paradise is and how the Kingdom of God is revealed in our hearts. Soon I was completely cured and set out to fulfill my vow. I obtained a military discharge passport and, without telling anyone, I left my native land. It is now fifteen years since I have been wandering through Siberia. Sometimes I would hire myself out to peasants, to do whatever work I was capable of, and other times I would beg for food in the name of Christ. Ah, but in spite of all my poverty I knew such bliss, happiness, and peace of conscience! This can be fully experienced only by someone who has been brought from the torments of hell into God's Kingdom, by the mercy of the holy Intercessor.'

"When he finished telling me all this, he gave me his will to mail to his son, and the next day he died. I have kept a copy of it in my briefcase, tucked inside my Bible. If you would like to read it, I'll get it for you. Here it is!"

I unfolded it and read the following:

> In the name of God, glorified in the Trinity, the Father and the Son and the Holy Spirit.
>
> My dearest son!
>
> It has been fifteen years since you last saw your father. Although you have not had any news of him, from time to time he has managed to hear about you and has cherished a father's love for you. That love compels me to send to you these last words from my deathbed, with the hope that they will serve as a lesson in your life.
>
> You know how I suffered for my carelessness and my thoughtless life; but you do not know of the bliss I experienced during the years of my anonymous pilgrimage and how I delighted in the fruits of repentance.
>
> I die in peace in the home of one who has been a kind benefactor to me and also to you, for the blessings poured out upon the father must also touch the sensitive son. Express to him my gratitude in whatever way you can.
>
> I leave you with my paternal blessing and adjure you always to remember God, to guard your conscience, and to be prudent, kind, and discerning. Treat your subordinates as favorably and kindly as you can, and do not scorn the poor and homeless, remembering that your dying father found peace and tranquillity for his tormented soul only in poverty and pilgrimage.

Beseeching God's blessings on you, I peacefully close my eyes in the hope of eternal life, through the mercy of mankind's Intercessor, Jesus Christ.

Your father . . .

Thus the kind master and I lay in the summerhouse and chatted. Then I asked him, "I would think, Batyushka, that keeping a guesthouse for the poor brings you its own worries and problems. There are quite a few of our fellow pilgrims who wander because they have nothing better to do or because they are too lazy to work. Sometimes they even cause trouble on the road, as I have had occasion to see for myself."

"We have not had too many such cases," he replied. "Mostly they have been genuine pilgrims. Yet we tend to welcome the troublemakers even more and urge them to stay longer with us. By living among our kind beggars, among the brethren of Christ, they are often reformed and leave the guesthouse as meek and humble people. We had a case like this just recently. One of our local middle-class townsmen became so depraved that everyone began to chase him from their doorsteps with sticks. No one would give him so much as a piece of bread. He was a violent, pugnacious drunk and he even stole. He came to us in this condition, quite starved, and asked for some bread and wine, the latter being what he was extremely eager for. We welcomed him kindly and said, 'Live with us and we will give you as much wine as you want, but only under the condition that when you get drunk, you will go immediately to bed and sleep it off. Should you create the slightest disturbance or trouble, we will not only throw you out and never let you come back here, but I will even report you to the magistrate or the town governor and have you sent to a penal colony for suspicious vagrancy.' He agreed to all this and came to live with us. For a week or more he really did drink a great deal, as much as he wanted. Yet he always kept his promise and went to bed, because he was too addicted to wine (and could not risk being deprived of it). Or else he would go into the garden and quietly lie down there. When he was sober, his fellow beggars tried to urge him to stop drinking, or at least to start by cutting down. Gradually he began to drink less and less, until finally, some three months later, he was completely dry. He has a job somewhere now and no longer needs to beg for his bread. Why, just the day before yesterday he came over to thank me."

What wisdom, I thought, has been wrought under the guidance of love, and I exclaimed, "Blessed be God, Who has revealed His mercy in the household that is under your care!"

After this conversation the master and I slept for about an hour, or an hour and a half, until we heard the bell for matins. We got up and went to church. Just as we walked inside we saw the mistress, who had been there for some time already with the children. We stood through matins and then the Divine Liturgy, which followed soon after. The master and I stood with the little boy in the altar, while his wife and daughter stood near the altar window so they could observe the elevation of the Gifts. My God! How they prayed as they knelt, with tears of joy streaming down their faces! Their faces were so radiant that just watching them brought forth the fullness of my own tears.

After the Liturgy the gentlefolk, the priest, the servants, and all the beggars went to the dining room to eat. There were some forty beggars, and everyone—the crippled, the infirm, the children—all sat down at one table. What silence and tranquillity there was! Drawing on my boldness, I quietly said to the master, "In monasteries they read from the lives of the saints during meals. You could do the same, since you have the complete text." He turned to his wife and said, "Actually, Masha, why don't we start doing that regularly? It would be most edifying. I will read first, at this meal, then you will read at the next one, and then Batyushka can read. After that, whoever else knows how to read may take turns."

The priest, who was eating, said, "I love to listen, but as for reading, well, with all due respect, I do not have the time for it. The minute I get home I have so much to do, so many duties and concerns to attend to, I hardly know where to begin. First one thing needs to be done, then another; then there are all the children and the cows need to be let out. My days are so completely taken up with all this that I'm not up to reading or studying. I've long since forgotten even what I learned at seminary." When I heard this I shuddered, but the mistress, who was sitting next to me, grasped my hand and said, "Father speaks this way from humility. He always humbles himself, but he is righteous and the kindest of men. He has been a widower for twenty years now and has been raising a whole family of grandchildren, as well as serving frequent services in church." Her words reminded me of the following saying of Nikitas Stethatos in the *Philokalia:* "The nature of things is measured by the interior disposition of the soul; that is, the kind of person one is will determine what he thinks of others." He goes on to say: "He who has attained to genuine prayer and love no longer puts things into categories. He does not separate the righteous from the sinners, but loves all equally and does not judge them, just as God gives the sun to shine and the rain to fall both on the just and the unjust."

This was followed again by silence. A completely blind beggar from the guesthouse sat across from me. The master fed him, cutting up the fish and handing him a spoon filled with broth.

Observing him closely, I noticed that the beggar's mouth was constantly open and his tongue kept moving about inside, as if it were trembling. This made me think that perhaps he was a man of prayer, so I continued to watch him. At the end of the meal one of the old women suddenly became so ill that she began to moan. The master and his wife took her into their bedroom and lay her down on the bed. The wife stayed to watch over her, while the priest went to get the Presanctified Gifts,* just to be on the safe side. The master ordered his carriage and went to fetch the doctor, while the rest of us departed.

I felt a kind of prayerful inner quiet, a strong need to pour my soul out in prayer, and it had already been forty-eight hours since I had experienced any silence or solitude. It felt as if a flood were building up in my heart that strained to burst forth and spill out into all my limbs. Since I was struggling to contain it, I felt a soreness in my heart, albeit a pleasurable one, that insistently demanded the peace of silence and could be satisfied only by prayer. Through this it was revealed to me why people who had attained to genuine self-acting interior prayer fled the company of others and took refuge in anonymous solitude. I understood also why the venerable Hesychios said that even the most beneficial conversation was idle chatter when taken to excess, just as Saint Ephraim the Syrian said, "Good speech is silver, but silence is pure gold."

As I considered all this, I walked to the guesthouse, where everyone was resting after the meal. I climbed up into the attic, calmed down, rested, and prayed a bit. When the beggars had arisen from their rest, I found the blind man and walked with him just beyond the kitchen garden, where we sat down alone and began to talk.

"For God's sake, would you tell me if you are praying the Jesus Prayer for spiritual benefit?"

"I have been praying it unceasingly for a long time now."

"And what is it that you experience from it?"

"Only that I cannot be without the prayer day or night."

"How did God reveal this practice to you? Tell me everything, dear brother."

"Well, you see, I once belonged to a local guild and earned my living as a tailor. I traveled to other provinces and villages, making clothing for the peasants.

"One time I happened to spend a longer time in one of the villages, living with a peasant for whose family I was making clothing. On one of the feast days I noticed three books lying near the icon case, and I asked, 'Who in the household knows how to read?' 'No one,' they replied. 'These books were left to us by our uncle, who knew how to read and write.' I picked up one of the books and opened it at random. On one of the pages I happened to read the following, which I still remember to this day: 'Unceasing prayer is calling always upon the Name of God, whether one is conversing or sitting down, walking, working, or eating, or occupied with any other activity—in all places and at all times one should call upon the Name of God.' After reading this I began to realize that it would be quite convenient for me to do this. So I began to repeat the prayer in a quiet whisper while I sewed and found it much to my liking. The others living with me in the hut noticed this and began to make fun of me. 'What are you, some sort of wizard?' they asked. 'What are you whispering all the time? Are you weaving some sort of spell?' So to cover up what I was doing, I stopped moving my lips and began to pray only with my tongue. Eventually, I grew so accustomed to the prayer that day and night my tongue would form the words on its own, and this became quite pleasant for me.

"So I lived this way for quite a while, going from village to village to sew, until all of a sudden I became completely blind. Almost everyone in our family suffers from 'dark water.'* When I became poverty-stricken, our guild placed me in an almshouse in Tobolsk, the capital of our province. I was on my way there when the master and mistress urged me to stop over here so they could provide me with a cart that would take me to Tobolsk."

"What was the name of the book you read? Was it by any chance the *Philokalia*?"

"Honestly, I do not know; I didn't even look at the title."

I brought my *Philokalia* to him and in part 4 I found the passage by Patriarch Callistus, which the blind man had just quoted from memory. I read it back to him and he cried out, "That's it, that's exactly it! Keep on reading, brother—this is just wonderful!"

When I got to the line "One should pray with the heart," he began to ply me with questions: "What does this mean?" and "How do you do this?" I told him that all the teachings on the prayer of the heart were provided in detail in this book, the *Philokalia.* He earnestly beseeched me to read the whole thing to him.

"I'll tell you what we'll do," I said. "When are you leaving for Tobolsk?"

"I could leave this very moment," he replied.

"Then let's do this: since I am thinking also of heading out tomorrow, we can travel together and I can read to you everything concerning the prayer of the heart. I'll also explain how to locate the place of the heart and how to enter into it."

"But what about the cart?" he asked.

"Eh, who needs a cart? As if we don't know how far Tobolsk is! It's only about a hundred miles, and we'll walk slowly. Think how good it will be for the two of us alone to travel together. It will be much easier for us to talk and read about prayer as we walk." So we agreed on this.

That evening the master himself came to call us to dinner. After the meal we informed him that the blind man and I would be traveling together and that we did not need the cart, since it would be easier this way for us to read the *Philokalia.* When he heard this, the master said, "I too enjoyed the *Philokalia.* In fact, I've already written a letter, enclosing some money, which I'll mail to Saint Petersburg on my way to the courthouse tomorrow. I've asked them to send it to me at the very first return of post."

The next day we set off, after warmly thanking our hosts for their most exemplary love and hospitality. They both accompanied us for over half a mile from their house. Thus it was that we took our leave of them.

The blind man and I walked short distances at a time, some six to ten miles a day. The rest of the time we sat in secluded spots and read from the *Philokalia.* I read to him all that there was on the prayer of the heart, following the order that my late starets had indicated to me, beginning with the book of Nicephorus the Solitary, Saint Gregory of

Sinai, and so on. How greedily and attentively he took in everything and how it pleased and delighted him! Then he began to ask me such questions about prayer that my mind was not equal to answering them. When we had read all the necessary passages from the *Philokalia*, he earnestly beseeched me actually to show him how the mind can find the heart, how to bring the Name of Jesus Christ into it, and how to experience the delightful interior prayer of the heart. I explained the following to him: "You are blind and can see nothing, but are you not able to visualize in your mind that which you once could see with your eyes—a person or some object or one of your limbs, such as a hand or a foot? Are you not able to visualize it as vividly as if you were actually looking at it and to concentrate and focus even your blind eyes on it?"

"I can do that," said the blind man.

"Well, then, do the same thing and try to visualize your heart with your mind. Focus your eyes as if you were looking at it, right through the wall of your chest cavity. Try to visualize it as vividly as possible in your mind, and with your ears listen to the steady rhythm of its beating. When you have succeeded with this, then begin to repeat the words of the prayer, in accompaniment to each beat of your heart, keeping your eyes focused on it all the while. Thus with the first beat you will say, verbally or mentally, the word *Lord;* with the second, *Jesus;* with the third, *Christ;* with the fourth, *have mercy;* with the fifth, *on me.* Repeat this over and over again. It should be easy for you, since you have already learned the basics of the prayer of the heart. Eventually, when you get used to it, then you can begin to repeat the full Jesus Prayer in your heart, in time with a steady rhythm of inhaling and exhaling, as the Fathers taught. As you inhale, you visualize your heart and say, 'Lord Jesus Christ.' As you exhale, you say, 'have mercy on me!' Do this as much and as often as you can, and soon you will experience a delicate but pleasant soreness in your heart, which will be followed by warmth and a warming tenderness in your heart. If you do this, with God's help you will attain to the delightful self-acting interior prayer of the heart. However, as you do all this, guard against mental imaginings and any sort of visions. Reject everything your imagination produces, for the holy Fathers strictly teach that interior prayer must be a visionless exercise, lest one fall into delusion."

The blind man listened attentively to everything and then earnestly began to practice the specified method of prayer. He would spend an especially long time on it at night when we stopped to rest. After about five days he began to feel an intense warmth and an indescribably pleasant sensation in his heart, along with a great desire to devote himself continually to this prayer, which was stirring in him a love for Jesus Christ. From time to time he would begin to see a light, though he discerned no visible things or objects in it. At times, when he entered into his heart, it seemed to him that a strong flame, like that of a burning candle, would flare up delightfully within his heart and would illuminate him as it rushed up and outward through his throat. This light made it possible for him to see things even at a great distance, which did occur on one occasion.

We happened to be walking through a forest, and he was fully and silently absorbed in his prayer. Suddenly he said to me, "What a pity! The church is already burning, and there—the belfry has collapsed."

"Stop imagining things," I said. "That's nothing but a temptation. You must quickly banish all thoughts. How can you possibly see what's happening in the city when we're still almost eight miles away from it?"

He took my advice, continued praying, and was silent. Toward evening we arrived in the city, and I actually saw several burned-down buildings and a collapsed belfry, which had stood on wooden piles. Many people were milling about, amazed that the belfry had not crushed anyone when it collapsed. I estimated that this tragedy had occurred exactly at the time the blind man had told me about it. So he began saying to me, "You said I was imagining things, and yet it happened just as I described it. How can one not love and be grateful to the Lord Jesus Christ, Who manifests His grace to sinners, to the blind and the unwise! I thank you too for teaching me the work of the heart."

"You can love Jesus Christ and be as grateful to Him as you will," I said, "but beware of accepting visions as direct revelations of grace, because such things can often occur as natural manifestations, according to the natural order of things. Man's soul is not absolutely bound by space and matter. It can also see events through darkness and at very great distances, as if they were happening nearby. It is we who do not give power and momentum to this capability in our souls, and we squelch it beneath the bonds of either the carnal fleshiness of our bodies or our confused thoughts and scattered ideas. Yet, when we focus our attention on the inner self, divert our concentration from everything external, and refine our mind, then the soul finds its truest fulfillment and exercises its highest powers, which is quite natural. I heard from my late starets that nonpraying people or people who have a certain ability or suffer from sick disorders are able to see, in the darkest room, the aura of light that radiates from all things, to distinguish between various objects, to sense the presence of their double, and to know the thoughts of others. But what occurs during the prayer of the heart is the direct result of God's grace, and it is so delightful that no tongue can describe it, attribute it to anything material, or compare it to anything at all. All physical sensations are base in comparison to the delightful experience of grace acting within the heart."

My blind man listened seriously to all this and was even more humbled by it. The prayer continued to increase within his heart, delighting him beyond description. I rejoiced in this with all my heart and earnestly thanked God for granting me to have met such a blessed servant of His.

At last we arrived in Tobolsk, where I took him to the almshouse. After kindly parting with him, I left him there and continued on my own journey.

For a month I walked slowly, reflecting in depth on how edifying and encouraging the good experiences in life can be. I read the *Philokalia* frequently to verify all that I had told the blind man of prayer. The edifying example of his experience kindled in me a zeal, gratitude, and love for the Lord. The prayer of the heart delighted me so much that I thought there could be no one happier than I in the whole world and could not imagine how there could be any greater or deeper contentment in the Kingdom of Heaven. Not only did I experience all this within my soul, but everything around me appeared to be enchanting and inspired me with love for and gratitude to God. People, trees, plants, and animals—I felt kinship with them all and discovered how each bore the seal of the Name of Jesus Christ. At times I felt so lightweight, as if I had no body and were not walking but rather joyously floating through the air. At other times I entered so fully into myself that I saw clearly all my inner organs, and this caused me to marvel at the wisdom that went into creating the human body. Sometimes I knew such joy that I felt as if I had been crowned a king. It was at such moments of consolation that I wished that God would grant me to die as soon as possible, so that I could pour myself out in gratitude at His feet in the spiritual world.

Yet it became apparent to me that my enjoyment of these experiences was tempered or had been regulated by God's will, because I soon began to experience some sort of anxiety and fear in my heart. "I hope this is not another sign of some upcoming disaster or misfortune," I thought, "such as that incident with the village girl to whom I taught the Jesus Prayer in the chapel!" Clouds of thoughts descended upon my mind, and I remembered the words of the blessed John of Karpathos, who said that often the teacher submits to humiliation and suffers misfortune and temptations for those who will benefit from him spiritually. After struggling for a while with such thoughts, I began to pray more earnestly, and this banished them completely. I was encouraged by this and said to myself, "God's will be done! Anything that Jesus Christ may send my way I am ready to endure for my wretchedness and arrogant disposition—for even those to whom I had recently disclosed the secret of entering the heart and of interior prayer had been prepared directly by God's hidden guidance, before I met them." This thought calmed me, and once again I set off with consolation and with the prayer, feeling more joyous than I had been before.

It rained for about two days and the road had completely turned to mud, so that my legs sank into it and I was barely able to walk. So I walked through the steppe and thus did not come across any human habitation for almost ten miles. At last, one day toward evening, I came upon a farmstead right near the road. I was overjoyed and thought to myself, "I can ask to spend the night and rest up here, and I'll accept whatever God sends my way tomorrow morning. Perhaps even the weather will be better."

As I approached I saw a drunk old man wearing a military overcoat and sitting on a mound of earth by the farmhouse. I bowed to him and said, "Would it be possible to ask someone if I could spend the night here?"

"Who else could let you do that but me?" the old man bellowed. "I'm in charge here! This is a post office and I'm the postmaster."

"Well, then, Batyushka, will you permit me to spend the night here?"

"Do you have a passport? Let's see some legal proof of who you are!"

I gave him my passport, and he had it in his hands when he asked, "Well, where's the passport?"

"You're holding it in your hands," I replied.

"Oh, well, then—let's go inside the hut."

The postmaster put on his glasses, studied the passport, and said, "It's a legal document, all right. You can stay the night. I'm a good man, you know. Here—I'll even offer you a welcome drink."

"I've never had a drink in my entire life," I replied.

"Well, who cares! At least have dinner with us."

"I sat down to table with him and his cook, a young peasant woman who had already had one too many herself. They sat me down to eat with them, and during the entire meal they quarreled, scolding each other. By the end of the meal they were well into a fight. Then the postmaster went off to sleep in the pantry, while the cook began clearing the table, washing the cups and spoons and cursing her old man.

I sat for a while and decided it would be some time before she calmed down, so I said, "Matushka, where could I sleep for the night? I'm exhausted from my journey."

"Here, Batyushka, I'll make you up a bed." She pulled another bench up to the one near the front window, covered it with a felt blanket, and put a pillow at the head of it. I lay down and shut my eyes to make it look as if I were sleeping. The cook continued to putter around for a long time until at last she had cleaned up. She doused the fire and had started coming over to me when suddenly the entire window in the front corner of the house—the frame, the glass, and splinters from the lintel—came showering down with a frightful crash. The entire hut shook, and from just outside the window there came a sickening groan, shouting, and loud scuffling noises. The peasant woman sprang back in terror and jumped into the middle of the room, where she went crashing down on the floor. I jumped up half conscious, thinking that the very ground under me had split wide open. Then I saw two coach drivers entering the hut. They carried between them a man so covered with blood that you couldn't even see his face, which horrified me even more. He was a royal courier who had been on his way here for a change of horses. His coach driver had miscalculated the turn into the gates, the carriage pole had knocked out the window, and, as there was a ditch in front of the house, the wagon had overturned. The courier was thrown clear, and he deeply gouged his head against a sharp stake in the ground that was propping up the earthern mound that served as a bench. He demanded some water and wine to wash his wound with, and after bathing it with some of the wine, he drank a glass of it himself. Then he shouted, "Get the horses!" I went over to him and said: "Batyushka, how can you travel when you're in such pain?"

"A royal courier has no time to be sick," he replied and galloped away. The coach drivers dragged the unconscious peasant woman to the stove in the corner of the room and covered her with a bast hearth rug.

"She's only in shock from being so frightened. She'll come out of it." The postmaster had another drink to ease his hangover and went back to bed, leaving me all alone.

Soon the peasant woman got up and began to pace back and forth, from one corner of the room to the other, until finally she walked out of the hut. I said my prayers and realized how exhausted I was; but I did manage to catch some sleep just before dawn.

In the morning I took my leave of the postmaster and set off. As I walked I offered up my prayer with faith, hope, and gratitude to the Father of all blessings and consolations, Who had delivered me from an impending disaster.

Six years after this incident I was passing a women's monastery and stopped in their church to pray. The abbess was most hospitable to pilgrims and invited me inside after the Liturgy, asking that some tea be brought to me. Then some unexpected guests arrived for the abbess, and she went to greet them, leaving me alone with her nuns. The one who started to pour my tea struck me as a truly humble woman, so I could not resist asking her, "Matyushka, have you been in this monastery a long time?"

"Five years," she replied. "I was out of my mind when they brought me here. God was merciful to me and the mother abbess let me stay and take the veil."

"What caused you to go out of your mind?" I asked.

"I was in shock from a terrifying experience that happened while I was working at a post office. It was at night and I was sleeping when some horses knocked out one of the windows, and I went mad from fear. For an entire year my family took me from one shrine to another, and it was only here that I was healed." Upon hearing this my soul rejoiced and glorified God, Who so wisely orders all things for the good.

"There were also many other incidents," I said, turning to my spiritual father. "Were I to relate them all, in the order they occurred, three days and nights would not suffice to tell it all. However, I will tell you about one more incident."

One clear summer day, near the road I saw a cemetery, or what one would call a churchyard, a church, with nothing but houses for the clergy. The call to Liturgy sounded, and I started walking to the church. Some local people were also headed in that direction, while others sat on the grass not far from the church. When they saw me hurrying along, they said, "Don't hurry, there's time enough to stand around before the service starts. The services here are very long, because the priest is in poor health and he drags them out." Indeed, the service was very long. The priest was a young man, but frightfully thin and pale. He celebrated and moved about very slowly, yet with great devotion. At the end of the service, with great depth of feeling he gave an excellent and intelligible sermon on the various ways one can acquire a love for God.

The priest invited me to his home and asked me to stay for lunch. Sitting at table, I said to him, "How devoutly and slowly you serve, Batyushka!"

"Yes," he replied, "even though the parishioners don't like it and grumble. But what can one do? I love to reflect on every word of a prayer and to relish it, for each word that is pronounced without an inner experience and appreciation of it brings no benefit either to one's own self or to others. It all boils down to the interior life and recollected prayer! And yet," he continued, "how few concern themselves with the interior life! This is because people do not want to do it, because they do not care about inner spiritual enlightenment," said the priest.

"But how is one to acquire it?" I asked again. "It would seem to require such depths of wisdom."

"Quite a bit. In order to be spiritually enlightened and to live a recollected interior life, one must take any single passage from the Holy Scriptures, focus all one's attention and meditate on it, for as long as possible, and the light of understanding will be revealed. The same must happen with prayer: if you want it to be pure, correct, and delightful, then you must choose any brief prayer, consisting of a few but powerful words. Repeat it frequently, for long periods of time, and then you will acquire a taste for praying."

The priest's advice pleased me. How practical and simple it was, and yet how deep and wise! In my mind I thanked God for having led me to such a true shepherd of His church.

When the meal was over, the priest said to me, "Why don't you take a nap after dinner while I read the Bible and prepare tomorrow's sermon." So I went to the kitchen, which was empty except for an extremely old woman who sat alone in the corner, hunched over and coughing. I sat down near the window, took the *Philokalia* out of my bag, and began to read quietly to myself. After a while I happened to hear that the old woman in the corner was whispering the unceasing Jesus Prayer. I rejoiced to hear this continuous repetition of the Lord's most holy Name, so I said to her, "How good it is, Matushka, that you pray unceasingly! It is the best thing a Christian can do for his salvation."

"Yes, Batyushka," she replied, "at my old age the only joy for me is to ask the Lord's forgiveness."

"How long has it been since you have made such a habit of this prayer?"

"Since I was a little girl, Batyushka. I couldn't live without it, for the Jesus Prayer saved me from ruin and death."

"How is that? Please tell me about it, to the glory of God and in praise of the blessed power of the Jesus Prayer." I put the *Philokalia* back in my bag and moved closer to the old woman, and she began to speak.

"I was a young, good-looking girl. My parents arranged to give me in marriage, and the very day before the wedding my bridegroom was coming to see us. On his way over, about ten steps from the house, he suddenly collapsed and died without even a gasp! I was so frightened by this that I refused ever to marry and decided to lead a celibate life, visiting shrines and praying to God. However, because I was so young I was afraid to travel alone, lest I be molested by evil people. Then an old woman I knew, who was a pilgrim, advised me that whatever road I happened to be walking on I should unceasingly repeat the Jesus Prayer. She solemnly promised me that no harm could come to me on my journey while I repeated this prayer. I believed this and, indeed, everything went well, even when I traveled to distant shrines. My parents gave me money for these trips.

"As I grew old, I became infirm and this priest was kind enough to feed me and let me stay here."

I listened to her with such delight, not knowing how to thank God for a day so full of such edifying lessons. Then I asked the kind and devout priest for his blessing and, rejoicing, I set off again on my own journey.

Then again, not too long ago, as I was on my way here I passed through the Kazansk district and had another experience that taught me how clearly and vitally the power of praying in the name of Jesus Christ is revealed, even in those who practice it without a conscious awareness of doing so, and how the frequency and duration of repeating it is the surest and quickest way to acquiring the fruits of this prayer. It happened once that I spent the night in a Tatar village. On entering it I saw a carriage and a Russian coachman standing next to the window of one of the huts. The horses were feeding next to the wagon. I was happy to see this and resolved to ask for lodging there, thinking that at least I would be spending the night with Christians. I went up to him and asked, "Who is your passenger?"

"The master is traveling from Kazan to the Crimea," he replied.

While the coachman and I were talking, his master drew apart the curtains inside the carriage. He looked out and, seeing me, said, "I am also spending the night here, but I did not go inside the hut, because Tatar houses are so wretched that I decided to sleep in the carriage." Then, since it was a pleasant evening, he got out to take a walk and we struck up a conversation.

Among my many questions that he responded to, he told me the following about himself.

"Up to the age of sixty-five I served as a high-ranking captain in the navy. As I grew old I developed gout, an incurable infirmity. I retired and went to live in the Crimea on my wife's farm, and I was almost constantly sick. My wife was an extravagant and impulsive woman who loved to play cards. She was bored living with a sick man, so she left me and went to Kazan to live with our daughter, who happened to be married to a civil servant there. She cleaned me out and even took all the servants with her, leaving me only with one eight-year-old boy, my godson.

"I lived alone for about three years. The boy who served me was very capable and took care of all my household chores. He cleaned the room, fired the stove, cooked porridge for me, and heated the samovar. Yet despite all this he was extremely lively and energetic and an impossible mischief-maker. He was incessantly running around, banging, shouting, and carrying on, all of which greatly disturbed me. Because of my illness, and probably from boredom as well, I always loved to read spiritual literature. I had a great book of Saint Gregory Palamas's teaching on the Jesus Prayer, which I read from almost continually. At times I would also practice the prayer itself. My boy was a nuisance, and no threats or punishments could keep him from his pranks. So I came up with an idea: I began to make him sit on a footstool next to me and ordered him to repeat continually the Jesus Prayer. At first he was not very happy about this and tried everything he could to get out of doing it, or else he would just say nothing at all.

In order to get him to obey, I took to keeping a rod beside me. When he was repeating the prayer, I would quietly read a book or listen to his pronunciation. But as soon as he stopped, I would show him the rod and it would frighten him enough to start the prayer again. This had a very calming effect on me, for it brought quiet to my house. After a short time I noticed that there was no more need of the rod, for the boy was now obeying me more eagerly and willingly. Then I noticed a complete change in his wild character; he became quieter and more reserved and performed his household chores better than before. This made me happy and I started giving him more freedom. Do you know what happened finally? He became so used to the prayer that he repeated it continually, almost all the time, whatever he happened to be doing, and without any urging from me. When I questioned him about it, he replied that he had an irresistible desire to pray unceasingly.

" 'And what do you feel when you pray?' I asked the boy.

" 'Nothing, really—except that it's very nice when I'm praying.'

" 'So—is that good?'

" 'I don't know—what can I say?'

" 'Are you happy?'

" 'Yes, I'm happy.'

"He was already twelve years old when the Crimean War broke out and, taking him with me, I went to stay with my daughter in Kazan. There he lived in the kitchen with the other servants, and he was very bored. He complained to me that the others would play and fool around among themselves, bothering him and making fun of him and preventing him from praying. Finally, after about three months he came to me and said, 'I'm going home. It's unbearably boring and noisy for me here.'

" 'How can you travel so far alone in the winter?' I asked. 'Wait until I'm ready to go, and I'll take you with me.'

"The next day my boy disappeared. We searched everywhere for him, but he was nowhere to be found. At last I received a letter from the Crimea, from some people who had stayed behind on our farm, informing me that on April 4, the day after Easter, the boy had been found dead in my empty house. He was lying on the floor in my room, with his hands devoutly folded on his chest, a cap under his head, and he was wearing the same thin frock coat that he had worn when he lived with me, and was wearing when he left. And so he was buried in my garden. After I received this news I was completely astonished at how the boy had managed to get to the farm so quickly. He left on February 26 and was found on April 4. To cover about two thousand miles in one month—why, even with God's help, you'd still need horses! You would have to travel about sixty-five miles a day—and then, without any warm clothing or a passport or a penny in your pocket. Let's say that maybe somebody gave him a ride along the way, but even that could not have happened without God's specific providence and care for him. Well, now, my boy tasted the fruits of prayer," the master concluded, "while I, at my ripe old age, have not yet attained to the measure of it that he had acquired."

I said to him, "Batyushka, there is a splendid book by the blessed Gregory Palamas, which you used to read. I know that book, but it primarily discusses the oral form of the Jesus Prayer. What you should read is a book called the *Philokalia.* There you will find the complete and perfected teaching on how to attain to the spiritual level of the Jesus Prayer, in the mind and in the heart, and taste of its sweetest fruits." Then I showed him the *Philokalia* and noticed that he was quite pleased to accept my advice. He promised to obtain a copy of the book for himself.

"My God," I thought to myself, "what wondrous manifestations of God's power are revealed through this prayer and how wise and edifying are such occurrences! A rod had taught the boy to pray and it even served as a means of acquiring consolation! Could it not be that the very grief and sufferings that we encounter on the path of prayer are, in fact, God's own 'rod'? If so, why is it that we are so afraid and distraught when these are sent our way, by the very hand of our Heavenly Father, Who is filled with such boundless love, and when these 'rods' teach us to be more attentive to our prayer and lead us to that inexpressible consolation?"

When I finished relating my stories, I said to my spiritual father, "For God's sake, forgive me—I have talked for too long! The holy Fathers say that even spiritual conversation is vainglory if it is unrestrained. It is now time for me to go and join my fellow traveler to Jersualem. Pray for me, a wretched sinner, that in His infinite mercy the Lord will grant me a good journey."

"My beloved brother in Christ, with all my heart I wish that the grace of God, abounding with love, will bless your journey and go with you, as the angel Raphael went with Tobias!"

The Pilgrim Continues His Way

from the narratives of the pilgrim about the grace-filled activity of the Jesus Prayer

The Pilgrim's Account of the Fifth Meeting

Already a year had passed since the last meeting with the pilgrim. Then, finally, a soft knock on the door and a courteous voice announced the arrival of this dear brother, much to the heart-felt delight of the one who awaited him. . . .

STARETS: "Enter, beloved brother! Let us both thank the Lord, Who blessed your journey and your return!"

PILGRIM: "Glory and thanks be to the Most High Father of all bounties for all that He provides according to His wisdom—all that is best for us, pilgrims and strangers in a 'foreign land!' Here I am, a sinner who parted with you last year, and who by God's mercy was deemed worthy again to see you and to hear your warm welcome. And, of course, you expect to hear from me a detailed report about God's holy city—Jerusalem—which my soul longed to visit and on which I cast my unwavering intentions. Yet what we wish for does not always come to pass. That is what happened to me, and it is no wonder. For how could I, a wretched sinner, be deemed worthy to walk on that hallowed land, which bears the imprints of the Lord Jesus Christ's divine footsteps?

You remember, Father, that I left here last year with a companion, a deaf old man, and with a letter from an Irkutsk merchant to his son in Odessa asking him to arrange passage for me to Jerusalem. Well, we arrived safely in Odessa with no delays. My companion immediately booked passage on a ship sailing to Constantinople and departed, while I stayed on and began to search for the son of the Irkutsk merchant, to whom the letter was addressed. I quickly found his residence, but much to my surprise and regret, I discovered that my benefactor was no longer among the living: three weeks earlier, following a brief illness, he had died and had been buried. Although this saddened me deeply, I gave myself over to the Will of God. The entire household was in mourning. The widow of the dead man, who was left with three small children, mourned so much that she cried all the time, and several times a day, she would collapse, convulsed in grief. It appeared that she would not live long either in the throes of such grief. Still, despite all this, she welcomed me kindly. As her circumstances did not permit her to send me to Jerusalem, she took me in as a guest for two weeks, until the dead man's father returned to Odessa, as he had promised, to attend to the bereaved family's business affairs and to settle the accounts. So I stayed.

I lived there for a week, then a month, and yet another. But instead of arriving, the merchant sent a letter announcing that his own circumstances were preventing him from coming. He advised them to settle all their outstanding accounts and asked that the whole family come to him in Irkutsk without delay. There began a flurry of preparations. Realizing that they had no time for me, I thanked them for the hospitality that they had shown to a stranger, bid them farewell, and set off to continue my travels through Russia.

For some time I wondered: where should I go now? Finally, I decided that I would go first to Kiev, where I had not been for many years. So I set off. . . .

At first I certainly grieved, because my desire to visit Jerusalem had not been fulfilled; but, I reflected, even this is part of God's providence—and I found comfort in the hope that the Lord, Who loves mankind, would accept my intention as if it were the deed and would not deprive my wretched journey of guidance and spiritual benefit. . . .

That is exactly what happened, for I met people along the way who revealed so many things to me that I had not known, and who enlightened my dark soul unto its salvation. . . . Had circumstances not steered me to travel in this direction, I would not have met these spiritual benefactors of mine.

And so, during the day I walked in the company of the prayer, and at night, I found lodging and read my *Philokalia* to strengthen and to rouse my soul in its battle with the invisible enemies of salvation.

Finally, when I had traveled about seventy *versts** from Odessa, I had a strange experience: I encountered a long string of wagons that was transporting goods—about thirty carts—and I caught up with them. One of the lead carriers, at the head of the train, was walking next to his horse; the others remained in a group and followed at some distance. We had to pass a pond fed by springs, in which chunks of ice, broken by the spring thaw, swirled around the perimeter of the pond, making a dreadful noise. Suddenly, the young lead carrier stopped his horse, bringing the rest of the string of carts to a stop. All the other carriers ran up to him and saw that he was undressing. They asked him why he was undressing, and he replied that he had a strong desire to swim in the pond. The carriers were astonished—some began to laugh at him; some scolded him, calling him crazy; and the eldest, the brother of the carrier who was undressing, tried to stop him and convince him to get back on the road.

The lead carrier defended himself and refused to listen. Some of the younger carriers amused themselves by dipping buckets for watering the horses into the pond and splashing water on the carrier who wanted to swim—one splashed water on his head, one on his neck, saying: "There you go, we'll give you a bath!" The moment that the water touched his body, the carrier cried out, "Oh! How wonderful!" and he sat on the ground while the splashing continued. Shortly after, he lay down and instantly, peacefully died. Everyone was frightened and was unable to understand what had caused this. The older carriers were worried, saying that the incident must be reported to the authorities; others decided that it was his fate to meet with such a death.

I stayed with them for about an hour and then went on my way. After walking about three and a half miles, I saw a village next to the main road. As I entered the village, I met an elderly priest walking down the street. I considered telling him about the incident I had witnessed, to hear what he thought about it. The priest took me to his home and after telling him about what I had seen, I asked him to explain to me why this had happened. . . .

"There is nothing I can tell you about this, kind brother, except that there is much in life that is extraordinary and incomprehensible to our minds. I think that God ordains such things in order to show man more clearly His order and providence at work in nature by using specific occurrences that are accompanied by unnatural and spontaneous changes in the laws of nature. I, myself, once witnessed a similar incident. Not far from our village, there is a very deep, precipitous ravine; although not too wide, it is ten or more *sazhen** deep. It's scary even to look down into its dark depths. Somehow they managed to build a bridge for pedestrians over this ravine.

"Once, a peasant from my parish, a family man of good standing, experienced an irresistible urge to throw himself off the bridge into that deep ravine. He struggled for an entire week with that thought and that urge. Finally, no longer able to resist this powerful impulse, he arose one morning, rushed off and jumped into the ravine. Soon after his moans were heard, he was dragged out of the ravine with great difficulty and with both his legs broken. When people asked him why he had fallen, he replied that although he was now in great pain, his soul was at peace after giving in to an irresistible urge which had so tormented him all week, that he was ready to sacrifice his life just to fulfill that desire.

"He was treated for over a year in the city hospital, where I visited him. Seeing the doctors around him, I often wished, as you did, to hear them explain why something like that had happened. The doctors all told me that this was the result of an 'obsession'. . . . When I asked them to give me a scientific explanation of this and why it afflicts people, I learned nothing more from them other than that this is one of nature's mysteries that has not yet been explained by science. . . . I remarked to them that if man were to turn to God in prayer while experiencing such mysteries of nature, and if he were to disclose this to good people around him, then even a so-called overwhelming 'obsession' would not achieve its purpose. Truly, there are many occurrences in life that cannot be clearly explained."

Evening had approached while we were talking, and I stayed on to spend the night. In the morning, the district police officer sent his clerk to ask for permission to bury the dead man in the cemetery, stating that the autopsy had revealed no signs of insanity and that the doctor had determined the cause of death to be a sudden stroke.

"You see," the priest said to me, "even medicine could not determine the cause for his irresistible attraction to the water."

After bidding farewell to the priest, I went on my way.

After traveling for several days, I was quite tired when I came upon a large commercial town called Byelaya Tserkov. Since evening was approaching, I sought lodging for the night. In the marketplace, I met a man who looked as if he also might be a traveler, and who was asking around the shops for the location of some local resident's house. When he saw me, he walked up to me and said, "It's obvious that you're a pilgrim too, so let's go together, and we'll find a local burgher who goes by the name of Yevreinov. He is a good Christian who owns a prosperous coaching inn and loves to take in pilgrims. Here, I have something I wrote down about him."

I gladly agreed, and we soon found his apartment. Although we did not find the host himself at home, his wife, a kind elderly woman, warmly welcomed us and put us up in a private room in the attic where we could rest. We made ourselves comfortable and rested a bit, then the host arrived and invited us to dine with him. At dinner, we struck up a conversation about who we were and where we came from—and somehow or other the question came up about why he went by the name of Yevreinov.

"I will tell you something remarkable about this," he replied, and began to tell us his story.

"You see, my father was a Jew, born in the city of Shklov, and he hated Christians. From his earliest years, he prepared to become a rabbi and diligently studied all the Jewish tales that were spread to refute Christianity. One day, he happened to pass through a Christian cemetery and saw a human skull with both its jaws intact (filled with disfigured teeth), which seemed to have been taken from a recently dug grave. Filled with bitterness, he began to snicker at the skull; he spit on it, cursed it, and kicked it. Not satisfied with this, he picked up the skull and impaled it on a picket stake, as they do with the bones of animals to ward off birds of prey. After satisfying himself in this manner, he went home.

"The very next night, just as he fell asleep, a stranger suddenly appeared to him in a vision and strongly reproached him, saying, 'How dare you commit such an outrage on the mortal remains of my bones? I am a Christian, and you are an enemy of Christ!' This apparition returned several times that night, robbing him of all peace and sleep. Then that apparition began to come to him even during the day, and he would hear the echoing of its reproaching voice. As more time passed, the apparitions increased in frequency. Finally, after becoming despondent, frightened, and exhausted, he ran to his rabbis, who prayed over him and performed exorcism. However, not only did the apparition not leave him, but it became even more frequent and aggressive.

"Word of his condition spread, and a Christian, who knew him through business dealings, heard about it. He advised him to convert to Christianity and attempted to convince him that this was the only way he could rid himself of this disturbing apparition. Although this was highly undesirable for the Jew, he nonetheless replied, 'I'll be glad to do whatever you want, only to be rid of this torturous and unbearable apparition.'

"The Christian was overjoyed by these words and urged him to submit a request to the local bishop to be baptized and to join the Christian Church. They formulated a request, and the Jew, however reluctantly, signed it. And from that moment of signing the request, the apparition ceased and never bothered him again. This made him extremely happy and he calmed down. He then experienced such an ardent faith in Jesus Christ that he immediately went to the bishop, told him about this, and expressed a sincere desire to be baptized. He quickly and diligently learned the dogmas of the Christian faith and was baptized. Afterward, he came here, married my mother, a good Christian woman, and led a devout life in prosperity. He was generous to the needy, which he also taught me to be; and before he died, he charged me to continue in this manner and gave me his blessing. And this is why I am named Yevreinov!"

I listened to this story with deep respect and feeling, and I thought to myself, "My God! How merciful is our Lord Jesus Christ and how great is His love! By what different paths He draws sinners to Himself, and how wisely He transforms insignificant events into stepping stones toward greater things! Who could have foreseen that the Jew's pranks over the dead bones would lead him to a genuine knowledge of Jesus Christ and would serve to guide him toward a devout life?"

After dinner, we gave thanks to God and to the host and went to rest in our attic room. We were not sleepy yet, and my companion and I struck up a conversation. He told me that he was a merchant from Mogilets, and that he had lived for two years in Bessarabia as a novice in one of the local monasteries, but only with a temporary passport. He was now on his way home to obtain a permanent discharge from the merchants' association in order to enter a monastery. He praised the local monasteries in Bessarabia, their monastic rules and customs, as well as the strict life led by many of the pious startsi who lived there. He assured me that comparing the monasteries in Bessarabia to those in Russia was akin to comparing heaven and earth, and he urged me to go there as well.

While we were conversing, a third lodger arrived. He was a non-commissioned officer on temporary discharge from the army, and he was heading home on leave. We noticed that he was very tired from his travels, so we said our prayers together and lay down to sleep. Rising early in the morning, we began preparing to leave; but just as were ready to go to thank the host, we suddenly heard the church bells ring for matins. The merchant and I began to discuss what we should do. How could we possibly leave after hearing the church bells without attending the church of God? We decided that it was better for us to attend matins and to pray in the holy temple, after which our departure would be more pleasant. That is exactly what we decided to do. We even invited the officer to come with us, but he replied: "Praying on the road? What good is it to God if we attend church? When we get home, that's where we'll pray! You go if you want to, but I won't. While you're at matins, I'll get ahead of you by about three miles, and I really want to get home as soon as possible." The merchant replied to him, "Be careful, my friend, about anticipating the future—God may have other plans for you!"

And so, we went to church, while the officer set off. After matins (served very early here), we returned to our room and began to pack our bags. We noticed that the hostess was approaching with a samovar, and she said, "And where are you off to? Here, drink some tea, and, while you're at it, have dinner with us too. As if we'd let you go off hungry!" So we stayed. We had been drinking tea for barely half an hour, when suddenly the non-commissioned officer came running toward us, all out of breath.

"I've come to you, full of grief and joy."

"What's the matter?" we asked him.

"Well, listen! As soon as I parted with you and set off, I thought about stopping at the inn to change some *assignaty** for smaller bills, and while I was at it, to have a vodka to ease the journey. At the inn, I got my change and took off with wings on my feet. About two miles down the road, I decided to count my money, to see if the innkeeper had given me the right amount. I sat at the side of the road, took out my wallet, counted the money, and it was all there. Suddenly, I reached for my passport, which I kept in the same place, and it was gone—only my papers and money were there. I was so frightened, I almost lost my head. And then it dawned on me: of course! I must have lost it when I was changing money at the inn—I must hurry back! I ran and ran, assailed by awful thoughts: What if it's not there? It's got to be! I'll be in a mess of trouble!

"When I got there, I questioned the innkeeper, but he replied, 'I haven't seen it.' Again I was overcome with sorrow and frantically began to search for it in those places where I'd stood or walked around. And what do you think? Just my luck! I found my passport, folded as usual—it was lying there in the hay and the garbage on the floor, trampled into the dirt. Thank God! I was overjoyed. I felt as if a ton had been lifted off my chest! Of course, it was covered with grime and dirty stains, and I could get a sound beating for that—but that's alright! At least I'd get home and back again in one piece! I came back to tell you about all this—but also, on top of everything else, as I was running in fear, I skinned my foot raw, and now I can barely walk—so I'm asking for some lard to apply to the wound."

"There you have it, my friend! This happened because you didn't listen and didn't come with us to pray," began the merchant. "You wanted to get so far ahead of us, yet you ended up right back here with us, and with a limp at that! I told you not to try to predict what lies ahead, and I was right! And, as if it weren't enough that you didn't go to church, you even said things like, 'What good would it be to God if we pray?' That, my friend, is not good at all. . . . God certainly does not need our sinful prayers; but in His love for us, He does love it when we pray.

"It is not only pure prayer, which the Holy Spirit Himself rouses within us and enables us to offer, that is pleasing to Him—for He requires this of us, charging us in this manner, 'Abide in me and I in you.' He even treasures each seemingly minor deed that is done for Him—every intention, every motive, and even every thought that is to His glory and toward our salvation. God's infinite mercy rewards all this most generously. The love of God returns a thousandfold more than man's deeds are worthy of. If you but give a worthless mite and it is for God, He will reward you with a gold piece. If you but consider turning to the Father, He has already met you halfway. If you but feebly utter these few words, 'Accept me! Have mercy on me!', He has already embraced you by the neck and is showering you with kisses.

"This is the kind of love that our heavenly Father has for such as unworthy as we! And only with this kind of love does He rejoice over each step, even the smallest, that we take toward our salvation. You may think: Where is the glory for the Lord, and what good is there in it for you, if you pray for a bit and then become distracted again; or if you only perform some insignificant good deed—for example, you recite some prayer or other, do five or ten prostrations, sigh from the depths of your heart, and call on the Name of Jesus Christ; or you acknowledge some good thought or other, or feel inclined to read something edifying, or restrain from eating, or bear some minor offense in silence. . . .

"To you, all this appears to be insufficient for your complete salvation, as if it were useless activity. Not so! Not a single one of these minor acts is lost, and each will be honored by the All-Seeing Eye of God and will be rewarded a hundredfold, not only in eternity, but even in this life. Saint John Chrysostom[1] also confirms this: 'No good deed,' says he, 'no matter how insignificant it may be, will be scorned by the

Righteous Judge. If sins are assessed in such detail, that we will end up answering for words, for desires and for thoughts—then how much more will the good deeds, however small, be assessed with special attention and will justify us before our All-Loving Judge?'

"Let me give you an example that I myself witnessed last year. In a monastery in Bessarabia, where I was living, there was a starets-monk who lived a good life. He was once assailed by a temptation—a strong desire for dried fish. And since it was impossible at that time to get it in the monastery, he was contemplating going to buy it at the market. . . . He struggled with this thought for a long time, considering that a monk should be satisfied with the regular food served to all the monks, that he should do his utmost to avoid sensual pleasures, and that even to walk among the crowds in the marketplace is a temptation and unbecoming for a monk. Finally, the enemy's tricks won over his reason and, submitting to his self-will, he decided to go and get the fish.

"He left the cloister and while walking along the city street, he noticed that he did not have his chotki in his hands and thought, 'How can I continue on my way? I am like a warrior without his sword. Not only is this unbecoming, but lay people who see me will judge me and will be led into temptation seeing a monk without his chotki.' Just as he had decided to go back for them, he searched his pocket and found them there. Taking them out, he made the sign of the cross over himself, slipped them over his hand, and calmly continued on his way.

"As he approached the marketplace, he saw a horse standing near the shops with a big cartload of huge vats. Suddenly, the horse was frightened by something and took off like a bolt, with hooves pounding. It collided with him, grazing his shoulder, and knocked him down to the ground, although not injuring him too much. Then, about two steps away from him, the load tipped over, smashing the cart to pieces. He was frightened, of course, but he quickly got up and, at the same time, marveled at how God had saved his life. For had the load tipped over but a split second sooner, he, too, would have been smashed to pieces, just like the cart.

"Without giving this any further thought, he purchased the fish, went home, ate it, and, after praying, he went to bed. . . . When he fell into a light sleep, a dignified but unfamiliar starets appeared to him and said, 'Listen, I am the patron of this monastery, and I want to teach you something, so that you understand and remember the lesson that was given to you today. . . . Look here: Your weak struggles against the temptation of sensual pleasures, and your laziness in striving for self-understanding and renunciation, gave the enemy easy access to you, and he was able to plan for you this fatal incident that you witnessed today. But your guardian angel foresaw this and inspired you to pray and to remember your chotki; and, since you heeded this inspiration, obeyed and actually acted on it, that very act saved you from death. Can you see God's love for man and how generously He rewards even the smallest gesture of turning to Him?' After saying this, the starets hurried from the cell. As the monk bowed before his feet, he awoke to find that he was no longer in bed but on his knees, prostrated at the threshold of the door. He wasted no time in telling many others, including me, about this vision for their spiritual benefit.

"Truly boundless is God's love for us! Is it not amazing that for a small act, such as, removing the chotki from his pocket, slipping them over his hand and calling on the Name of God just once—that for something so small, a man was granted life! And on the scales of man's fate, one brief moment of calling on Jesus Christ outweighed a multitude of hours wasted in laziness. . . . Truly, a small mite was rewarded with a goldpiece. . . . You see, friend, how powerful prayer is, and how mighty the Name of Jesus Christ that we call on! In the *Philokalia,* Saint John of Karpathos[2] says that when we call on the Name of Jesus in the Jesus Prayer and say: 'Have mercy on me, a sinner', the mystical voice of God replies to each such supplication,

'Child, your sins are forgiven.' And he goes on to say that whenever we pray, in no way are we different from the saints, the blessed, and the martyrs. For, as the holy Chrysostom says, 'Prayer cleanses instantly, though it be uttered by us who are filled with sin.' Great is God's mercy toward us. Yet we, sinful and dishonest, do not want to set aside even a small amount of time to offer Him thanks. Instead of praying, which is more important than anything else, we fill that time with life's cares and worries, forgetting God and our indebtedness to Him! As a result, we often fall prey to misfortune and disasters; but the abundant loving Divine Providence uses even this to teach us and to turn us to God."

As soon as the merchant had finished talking with the officer, I said to him, "Well, Sir, you have so delighted my sinful soul, I bow before your feet in gratitude." On hearing this, he turned to talk with me as well. "Apparently you are interested in stories about spiritual matters? Just a moment—I'll read you something similar to what I was just talking about. Here, I have a small pocketbook called the *Agapia* or *Salvation for Sinners*. It contains accounts of many miraculous incidents."

He took the book out of his pocket and began to read a wonderful story about a certain pious Agaphonik, whose devout parents had taught him from childhood to stand daily before the icon of the Mother of God and to recite the prayer Rejoice, O Virgin Theotokos!, and so on. He did this every day. Then, as an adult, he went to live alone and became so overwhelmed by life's cares and worries that he recited this prayer less frequently, until finally he stopped praying it altogether. He once took in a pilgrim for the night, who informed him that he was a hermit from Thebaid and that he had seen a vision that had directed him to go to Agaphonik and to reprimand him for neglecting the prayer to the Mother of God. Agaphonik explained that the reason for his neglect was that after praying it for many years, he had seen no benefit in doing so.

Then the hermit said to him, "Think back, O sinful and blind one, how many times did this prayer help you and save you from misfortune? Remember your adolescence—how you were miraculously saved from drowning? Don't you remember when that contagious epidemic sent many of your neighbors to their graves, while you remained healthy? And don't you remember when you were riding with your friend, and you both fell out of the carriage? He broke his leg, yet nothing happened to you. And don't you know that a man of your acquaintance, who was once young and healthy, is now an invalid, while you remain in good health and suffer nothing?" After reminding Agaphonik of many more such incidents, he finally said: "You should know that you were spared in all those incidents through the patronage of the Most Holy Theotokos for that brief prayer, through which you daily roused your soul toward union with God. . . . Listen, you forge ahead and do not stop glorifying the Queen of Heaven through this prayer, lest she abandon you."

When he finished reading, we were called to dinner. Then, fortified with food, we thanked our host and started off on our journey, each going his separate way, according to his plans.

I proceeded to walk for about five days, comforting myself with memories of the stories that I had heard from the devout merchant from Byelaya Tserkov. As I was approaching Kiev, for no apparent reason, I suddenly experienced a kind of fatigue, a weakness, along with gloomy thoughts. It was difficult to pray, and I felt myself overcome by some kind of sloth. Then I saw a thicket and a wooded area off the road, and I headed there to get some rest and to sit somewhere behind a secluded bush to read the *Philokalia*, in order to strengthen my weakened soul and alleviate my faintheartedness. After finding a quiet spot, I began to read the Venerable Cassian the Roman,[3] in part 4 of the *Philokalia*, on the eight thoughts.[4]

After about half an hour of delightful reading, I suddenly saw a man, deep in the forest, about 116 yards from me, who was kneeling perfectly still. This gladdened me, and I thought that surely he was praying to God. I returned to my reading and, after another hour or more, I looked again at this man, and he was still kneeling motionless. I was very touched by this and thought about what devout servants of God there are.

As I was reflecting on this, the man suddenly collapsed on the ground and lay motionless. I was surprised by this, and since I had not been able to see his face, for he had knelt with his back to me, I was overcome with curiosity to see who he was. As I approached him, I found that he was sleeping lightly. He was a village lad about twenty-five years old, attractive and with a clean but pale face. He was dressed in a peasant caftan, tied about the waist with a bast rope, and he had nothing else—no knapsack, not even a staff. The rustle of my approach woke him, and he stood up. I asked him who he was, and he told me that he was a state peasant from the Smolensk province and was traveling from Kiev.

"So where are you heading now?" I asked.

"I don't know myself," he replied, "wherever God takes me."

"Has it been long since you left home?"

"Yes, it's my fifth year."

"And where did you live during this time?

"I visited various holy places, monasteries, and then some churches. What's the point of living at home? I'm an orphan, have no relatives; and what's more, I have a lame leg. So, I roam the wide world!"

"It seems that someone pleasing to God has taught you not to roam aimlessly, but to visit the holy places," I told him.

"Well, now, you see," he replied, "because I was poor, I was a shepherd in our village since childhood, and all was well for about ten years. Then, one day, when I had brought my herd home, I realized that I'd not noticed that my village elder's best sheep was missing. And our village elder was a mean and inhumane peasant. When he got home and saw that his sheep was missing, he came running to me and began to swear and threaten me, saying that I must go find his sheep, or else, he vowed, 'I'll beat you to death, I'll break your hands and feet.'

"Knowing how cruel he was, I went looking for the sheep in those places where the herd had grazed that day. I looked and looked and looked—till past midnight—but there was no trace of it. It was a very black night, because it was almost autumn. As I went deep into the forest—and you can barely get through the forests in our province—a storm suddenly started. The very trees were moaning and swaying! Wolves began to howl in the distance, and I was so scared that my hair stood on end. But that's not all—it got worse and worse, and I thought I'd faint from fear and horror. And I fell on my knees right then and there and made the sign of the cross over myself, and with all my strength I said, 'Lord Jesus Christ, have mercy on me.' As soon as I said this, I felt at ease, like I'd never had any grief at all. And all my fear vanished, and it felt so good inside my heart, as if I'd gone up to heaven. . . . This made me so happy that I began to repeat this prayer continuously. And I don't even remember any more how long that storm lasted, or how the night passed. The next thing I know, it's light out, and I'm still kneeling on the same spot. So I get up calmly, and I realize that I just can't find that sheep. So I went home, but it still felt so good in my heart, and I still longed to say the prayer.

"As soon as I got back to the village and the village elder saw that I hadn't brought back his sheep, he beat me half to death. That's when he twisted my leg. So, after that beating, I lay barely able to move for six weeks. All I knew was that I was repeating that prayer and that it comforted me. Then I got a bit better and went off to roam the world. Since it bored me to hang around people all the time, and then, with all that sin around—well, I made pilgrimages to holy places and wandered through the forests. So this is now the fifth year that I'm doing this."

As I listened to this, my soul rejoiced that the Lord had deemed me worthy to meet a man so filled with grace, and I asked him, "And now, do you still continue constantly to recite that prayer?"

"Couldn't live without it," he replied. "I just remember how good I felt in that forest, and it's like somebody nudges me to my knees, and I start to pray. . . . I don't know if my sinful prayer is any good, because sometimes, after I pray, I feel so much joy, and I don't know why myself. It's like there's a freedom inside me and a happy peace; but sometimes I feel tired, bored and depressed. But still, I want to pray—always—until I die."

"Do not be confused, kind brother: all is pleasing to God, all is for salvation. The Holy Fathers say that whatever may happen during prayer, be it inner freedom or weariness, it's all good. No prayer, be it good or poor, is lost before God. Inner freedom, warm desire and spiritual sweetness are indications that God is rewarding and comforting you for your valiant efforts. While weariness, inner darkness, and aridity indicate that God is purifying and strengthening the soul and is saving it through the exercise of patience. And through humility, He is preparing it to partake of the sweetness of grace that is to come. Here, I'll prove all this by reading to you from Saint John of the Ladder[5]."

I found the section and read it to him. He listened attentively, with pleasure, and then he thanked me profusely. Then we parted. He headed straight back into the depths of the forest. I returned to the road and continued my journey, thanking God Who had deemed me, a sinner, worthy of such edification.

With God's help, I arrived in Kiev on the next day. My first and foremost desire was to fast, to go to confession and to partake of the Communion of the Holy Mysteries of Christ in this holy place. To this end, I found lodging close to the Saints of God[6], so it would be convenient for me to go to God's place of worship. A kind old Cossack took me in, and since he lived alone in his hut, I found peace and silence there.

During the week that I was preparing for my confession, I thought about making as detailed a confession as possible. I began to reflect on my youth and to remember all my sins in detail, so as not to forget anything. I wrote down everything I remembered, down to the smallest details, and ended up with a long list. I had heard that about four and a half miles from Kiev, in the Kitayev Hermitage, there was a spiritual father who lived an ascetic life and was extremely wise and prudent. Whoever went to see him was always deeply moved, and they returned with spiritual guidance for their salvation and a spiritually enlightened soul.

I was overjoyed by this and immediately went to see him. After speaking and consulting with him, I gave him my list to look at. He read it, and then he said to me, "You, kind brother, have written many empty words. Listen to me: (1) You should not confess again those sins of which you have already repented and have been absolved, and which you have not repeated since. Otherwise, this shows a lack of trust in the power of the sacrament of Confession; (2) You should not mention others who are connected with your sins, but accuse only yourself; (3) The Holy Fathers forbid confessing sins in too much detail and with insinuations—they should be confessed in general, lest too much personal scrutiny lead both you and the confessor into temptation; (4) You have come to repent, but you are not repentant for not knowing *how* to repent—that is, you offer repentance in a cold and careless manner; (5) You did list all the trivial things, but you overlooked that which is most important—you did not admit to the most grievous sins. You did not acknowledge or write down the fact that *you do not love God, that you despise your neighbor, that you do not believe in the words of God in Scripture, and that you are filled with pride and ambition.* The entire abyss of evil and all our spiritual corruption reside in these four sins. They are the main roots from which spring all the shoots of our sinful acts."

I was surprised to hear this, and I ventured to say, "Forgive me,

Venerable Father, but how is it possible not to love God, our Creator and Benefactor? What else is there to believe in except God's words in Scripture—they contain all truth and holiness. As for my neighbor, I wish good for each and every one. For that matter, why should I despise them? As for pride, there is nothing I can be proud of—except for my countless sins. There is nothing in me that is praiseworthy. And what can I possibly lust after and covet, what with my poverty and my disability? Of course, if I were educated or rich, then undoubtedly I would be guilty of what you have just said."

"It is unfortunate, kind one, that you understood so little of what I explained to you. Here, to teach you more quickly, I will give you a list that I also follow whenever I go to confession. Read it and you will find clear and precise proof of all that I just told you."

The confessor gave me the list, and I began to read it.

The Confession of the Interior Man That Leads to Humility

By diligently looking into myself and examining the disposition of my soul, I became convinced that I do not love God, that I have no love for my neighbor, that I have no faith in spiritual realities, and that I am filled with pride and ambition. By thoroughly studying my feelings and actions, I actually found all the following in myself:

1. *I do not love God.* For if I did love Him, then I would ceaselessly think of Him with genuine pleasure, and each thought of God would bring me joyous delight. On the contrary, I far more frequently and far more willingly think about earthly matters, while thoughts of God are difficult for me and give rise to inner aridity. If I loved Him, then conversing with Him through prayer would nourish me; it would delight me and would draw me into unceasing communion with Him. Yet it's quite the reverse—not only do I take no delight in prayer, but I find it difficult to pray. I struggle with reluctance, I am weakened by

laziness, and I am ready to be distracted by any insignificant matter, just to shorten my prayers or even to stop praying altogether. When I am occupied with empty activities, time flies unnoticeably; but when I turn my thoughts to God, when I place myself in His presence, each hour seems like a year.

If someone loves another, his thoughts are always with the other, throughout the day—he pictures the other in his mind and is concerned for the other. No matter what he is occupied with, the beloved friend is ever in his thoughts. While I barely set aside even an hour during the day to immerse myself in deep meditation about God and to surrender myself to His burning love. Yet I eagerly spend twenty-three hours offering zealous sacrifices to my impassioned idols! . . . Discussions of vain, worldly matters, ignoble subjects for the soul, stimulate and give me pleasure, while thoughts of God leave me arid, bored, and lazy. Even if others unwittingly draw me into discussions about divine matters, I quickly strive to change the subject to matters that flatter my passions. I am tirelessly curious for news, about civil appointments, about political events. I greedily strive to gratify my inquisitive nature about the secular sciences, the arts, acquisition of material things, while religious instruction[7], learning about God and religion, make no impression on me, they do not nourish my soul. And I consider this not only a nonessential activity for a Christian, but almost a foreign subject, one of secondary consequence, which I must study only at my leisure, in my spare time. In short, if one's love of God is proved by fulfilling His commandments—"If anyone loves me, he will keep my word" [John 14:23], says the Lord Jesus Christ—and not only do I not observe His commandments, I hardly exert myself at all—then in all truth, the only possible conclusion is that I do not love God. . . . Saint Basil[10] the Great also confirms this when he says, "The proof that man does not love God and His Christ lies in not keeping His commandments."

2. *I have no love for my neighbor.* For not only am I unable to decide to lay down my soul for the good of my neighbor (according to the Gospel), but I won't even sacrifice my honor, happiness and peace for the good of my neighbor. If I loved him as myself, according to the Gospel, then his misfortune would distress me too, and his good fortune would delight me. Yet on the contrary, I am more curious to hear unfortunate accounts about my neighbor, and instead of distress, I feel indifference—or, worse yet, I seem to take pleasure in this. And I do not bear my brother's bad actions in silent love, but am judgmental and publicize them. His well-being, honor, and happiness do not delight me as if they were my own. Instead, they are alien to me and not only do they bring me no joy whatsoever, but in a subtle way, they even generate a kind of envy or contempt.

3. *I have no faith in any spiritual realities.* Not in eternal life. Not in the Gospel. If I were firmly convinced and believed steadfastly in an eternal life beyond death, with recompense for how one's life was lived, then I would continuously reflect on this. The very thought of immortality would overawe me, and I would pass through this life as a stranger preparing to return to his homeland.

Yet, on the contrary, I do not even think about eternity, and I see the end of this life as the limit of my existence. A secret thought nestles within me: Who knows what happens after death? If I even do say that I believe in eternal life, I do so only in my mind, but my heart is far from being convinced of this, and my actions and endless worries about satisfying my sentient needs clearly prove this. If my heart believed that the Holy Gospel contains the words of God, I would continually study it. I would delight in it and would look upon it with deep reverence. The wisdom, the goodness, and the love concealed therein would bring me great joy. I would delight in studying it day and night, and it would nourish me as if it were my only source of food. And I would genuinely strive to fulfill its commandments, while nothing in this world could ever make me abandon it.

Yet it is quite the reverse. If sometimes I happen to read or to listen to readings from the Scriptures, both of which happen either by necessity or out of curiosity, without even any deep concentration, I experience aridity and boredom. And, as from ordinary reading materials, I gain nothing and feel eager to read something secular instead, which satisfies me more and offers newer and more enticing subjects.

4. *I am filled with pride and sensual self-love.* All my actions confirm this: If I see any good in me, I want to display it, or else I brag about it to others, or I admire my own self. Although I am outwardly humble, inside I give myself all the credit for everything and consider myself either superior to others or, at the very least, not any worse than they. If I detect a vice within me, I try to make excuses for it, to justify it as an unavoidable or ingenuous action. I become angry with those who show me no respect and consider them incapable of assessing the worth of others. I am vain about my talents and view any failure as a personal insult. I murmur about and rejoice over the misfortunes of my enemies. If I even strive to do any good, I do so either for praise or for my personal spiritual advantage or social standing. In a word—I constantly create a personal idol of myself, whom I serve unceasingly, as everywhere I seek sensual satisfaction and nourishment for my wanton passions and lusts.

From all the above, I see myself as proud and lustful, lacking in faith, having no love for God, and despising my neighbor. What state could be more sinful? The spirits of darkness are in better shape than I am: Even though they do not love God, despise man, thrive on and are nourished by pride, at least they believe and tremble in the face of that faith. And I? Is there any fate worse than mine? What could possibly be judged and punished more severely than a careless and foolish life, such as I realize I have lived? . . .

After reading this confession given to me by the priest, I was horrified, and I reflected, "My God! What hideous sins lurk inside me, and I had never even been aware of them!" Now that I knew the cause of all these evils, a desire to cleanse myself of them compelled me to seek guidance from this great spiritual Father about how to find a way to heal myself. And he began to explain it all to me.

"You see, dear brother, the reason for not loving God is a lack of faith, and the reason for lacking faith is a lack of conviction. And the reasons for lacking conviction are a failure to seek pure and true knowledge and an indifference toward spiritual enlightenment. In a word: Without faith, it is impossible to love; without conviction, it is impossible to believe. And to acquire conviction, it is necessary to obtain complete knowledge of a given subject. Then, through reflection, studying the Scriptures, and learning to observe, one must rouse in the soul a thirst and a desire or, as others call it, an 'awe,' which gives birth to an insatiable desire to know things more intimately, more deeply, and to penetrate the essence of their nature.

"One spiritual writer explains it this way, 'Love,' he says, 'usually grows from knowledge; the deeper and more profound the knowledge, the greater the love, and the more easily a soul opens itself and becomes disposed to divine love, as it diligently contemplates the exceedingly perfect and exceedingly gracious essence of God and His boundless love for man.'

"Now you can see that the sins on the list you read are rooted in a laziness for reflecting on spiritual matters, which extinguishes the very need for such reflection. If you also want to know how to overcome this evil, then you must always strive for spiritual illumination. Acquire it by diligently studying the Scriptures and the Holy Fathers, and through reflection and spiritual guidance or discussions with those who possess wisdom about Christ. Ah, dear brother, how many calamities befall us because we are lazy about illuminating our soul with the words of truth; because we do not study, day and night, the law of the Lord and do not pray about this diligently and persistently! This is why our inner man is hungry, and cold, and exhausted, and he lacks the strength to pursue vigilantly the way of truth that leads to salvation.

"So as to derive profit from these methods, beloved one, let us resolve as often as possible to occupy our minds with reflection on heavenly matters, and the love that is poured into our hearts from on high will grow and will become a burning fire within us. Along with this, let us pray more often, as much as this is possible, for prayer is the primary and the most powerful means for our renewal and for advancing in the spiritual life. Let us pray with the supplication that the Holy Church teaches us, 'Lord, grant me to love You now, as I once loved sin itself!' " After listening attentively to all this, I fervently asked this Holy Father to hear my confession and to give me Holy Communion.

After being granted to partake of Communion, I wanted to return to Kiev, taking with me the abundant guidance that I had received. Yet my good Father had made plans to visit a large monastery for a few days, during which time he let me stay in his hermit's cell, so that I could immerse myself in prayer without distraction and in silent solitude. Truly, I spent all those days as if in heaven: through the prayers of my starets, I, though unworthy, delighted in perfect tranquility. Prayer flowed from my heart with such delight and ease that during this time, it seemed as if I forgot about all else, even about my own self—my only thoughts were on the one and only Jesus Christ!

Finally the confessor returned, and I asked his advice and guidance about where I should now continue with my pilgrimage. He gave me this blessing, "Why don't you go to Pochaev, and there you can venerate the icon of the Miraculous Footstep of the All-Pure Mother of God? She will guide your steps on the way of peace." I accepted his guidance in faith and left for Pochaev three days later.

I walked about 132 miles feeling somewhat bored, for the road took me past taverns and Jewish *slobody*,* and I seldom encountered any

Christian dwellings. When I saw a Russian Christian coaching inn in a small village, I was overjoyed and went to ask for lodging for the night and for some bread for my journey, as my reserve of bread crusts was dwindling. Inside, I saw the host, a seemingly prosperous old man, and I learned that he was from the same Orlovsk district as I. The moment I walked into the main room, his first question to me was, "What faith do you belong to?"

I replied that I was an Orthodox Christian.

"Oh, and what is that Orthodoxy of yours!" he sneered. "Your Orthodoxy is nothing but words, because you behave like superstitious infidels. Oh, yes, my friend, *I* know that religion of yours! I myself was once lured and led into temptation by some educated cleric, and I joined your church. But after half a year, I returned to our ways. What temptations there are in attending your church: The readers barely manage to mutter through the services, they skip over parts, and their reading is incomprehensible. While the choirs in the villages are no better than tavern singers, and the people stand in church any old way—the men together with the women. They talk during services, they fidget; they look and walk around and don't give you a chance to pray quietly. What kind of church service is that? It's a sin, that's all it is!

"Our services, on the other hand, are devout: Everything is read distinctly, nothing is skipped over. The singing moves you, and, for that matter, the people stand quietly—the men by themselves, and the women by themselves. And everyone knows when and what kind of prostration to make according to the Holy Church's statutes. Indeed, when you walk into our church, you feel that you are present at a service of worship to God; but when one walks into your church, you can't even figure out where you are: in a temple or in a marketplace!"

As I listened to all this, I realized that this old man was an Old Believer[8], but since his words rang true, I could not argue with him or change his mind. I only thought to myself that Old Believers could not be converted to the true Church until our liturgical services were corrected and an example was set, especially by the clergy. The Old Believer knows nothing of interior realities; he relies on the externals, which we *are* careless about.

And so, I decided to leave this place. I had already walked out into the vestibule, when unexpectedly I looked through a door that opened into a very small room. There a man, who did not look like a Russian, lay on a bed reading a book. He motioned me to come in, asked me who I was, and I told him. Then he said, "Listen, kind one, do you think you'd agree to help out a sick man like me, even for a week—until with God's help I get better? I am Greek, a monk from holy Mount Athos, and I'm here in Russia to collect money for our monastery. And wouldn't you know it, on my return trip I fell ill, so that I can't even walk from the pain in my legs. That's why I rented this room here. Don't refuse me, servant of God! I'll pay you."

"I don't need any payment, I'll be glad to take care of you, as best I can, in the Name of God."

And that's how I ended up staying with him, and I learned much from him that was spiritually enlightening. He spoke about the holy Mount Athos, about the great ascetics and the many hermits and anchorites living there. He had a Greek-language *Philokalia* and a book by Saint Isaac the Syrian. We read it together and compared the Slavonic translation of Paissy Velichkovsky[9] with the Greek original. Incidentally, he was of the opinion that there could not be a truer or more accurate translation of the *Philokalia* from the Greek into the Slavonic than the one done by Paissy. I had noticed that he prayed unceasingly and was experienced in the interior prayer of the heart (as well as speaking Russian fluently), so I questioned him about it. He was eager to talk about this, and I listened attentively and even wrote down much of what he said. For example, this is what he said about the superior excellence and the greatness of the Jesus Prayer:

"The greatness of the Jesus Prayer," said he, "is evident even in its very format, which consists of two parts. The first of these—that is, *Lord, Jesus Christ, Son of God*—guides the mind into the history of the life of Jesus Christ, or, as the Holy Fathers say, *it contains within itself the entire Gospel*. The second part—that is, *Have mercy on me, a sinner*— represents the history of our weakness and sinfulness. What is remarkable here is that an impoverished, sinful, and humble soul could not express its desire and supplication more wisely, fundamentally, and clearly than with the words: *Have mercy on me!* No other expression could suffice or be as comprehensive as this one.

"For example, if one were to say: *Forgive me! Release me from my sins! Absolve my trespasses! Wipe out my transgressions!*, all these would merely be the frightened pleas of a fainthearted and negligent soul to be spared from punishment. However, the expression *have mercy on me* represents not only a desire for forgiveness that is prompted by fear, but also the genuine cry of a child's love that hopes for God's mercy and humbly acknowledges its own powerlessness to break its will and to maintain spiritual vigilance over itself. It is a cry for compassion, that is, for the mercy that is expressed through God's gift of the spirit of fortitude, the spirit that strengthens one to resist temptation and to conquer sinful inclinations. Just as a poor debtor asks a merciful creditor not only to forgive him his debt, but also to have mercy born of compassion for his extreme poverty, so these deep words *have mercy on me* are saying: *Merciful Lord! Forgive my sins and help me to mend my life. Awaken deep within my soul a tireless striving to keep Your commandments. Show mercy by forgiving my sins and by turning my dissipated mind, will, and heart to You alone*."

I was amazed by the wisdom of his words and thanked him for edifying my sinful soul, but he explained yet another remarkable thing to me.

"If you want," he said, "I can tell you more about inflections that occur in reciting the Jesus Prayer." (And he used some technical term here, for he had told me that he had studied at the Academy of Athens.)

"Now listen: I often had the opportunity to hear many God-fearing Christians pray the Jesus Prayer out loud as prescribed by God and by the Holy Church; and they do this not only when praying at home, but also in God's churches. If one listens carefully, and even with pleasure, to the quiet recitations of this prayer, one can learn something spiritually beneficial by noticing that the vocal inflections that accompany the prayer differ from one person to another. Specifically: some raise the tone of their voice on the very first word of the prayer, that is, when saying *Lord*—while all the words that follow are said uniformly in a lower pitch. Others begin the prayer in a lower tone of voice, and then raise it in the middle of the prayer, that is, on the word *Jesus*, which they emphasize—and then the rest of the words are said in a lower pitch, as in the beginning of the prayer. Still others begin and continue the prayer in a lower, uniform tone of voice, but on the last words, that is, *have mercy on me*, they elevate the pitch to a level of ecstasy. And then there are some who recite the entire prayer—that is, *Lord, Jesus Christ, Son of God, have mercy on me, a sinner*—raising their pitch only at the words *Son of God*.

"Now listen to this: The prayer is one and the same and, as Orthodox Christians, they all profess the same faith. Everyone understands that this sublime and most important of all prayers contains within itself two subjects—the *Lord Jesus* and *His good will toward reconciliation.* Why then do they all not use the same inflections, or, the same manner of reciting the prayer? Why is a soul so moved to express itself by raising and intensifying the pitch of its voice only in specific parts of the prayer that are uniquely personal to it, rather than in one specific part that would be one and the same for all?

"Many might say that perhaps this is the result of habit, or learned from the example of others, or due to different levels of understanding resulting from individual views. Or, finally, it could be simply a question of individual convenience and comfort in reciting the prayer, according to each person's verbal abilities. . . .

"I, however, have very different thoughts on this. I want to discern something more sublime in this—something that is invisible not only to the listener, but even to the very one who is praying. Could there not be a certain mystical activity of the Holy Spirit, *interceding with unutterable groanings*, which guides the inexperienced in what to pray for and how? And, as the apostle teaches, if everyone prays through the Holy Spirit in the Name of Jesus Christ, then by mystically *granting prayer to the one who prays*, the Holy Spirit may also bestow His gifts of grace on each, according to each one's strength: to one, a reverent fear of God; to another, love; to still another, a steadfast faith; and to yet another, profound humility, and so on. This is why the recipient of the gift is filled with reverence and glorifies the power of the Almighty; and in his prayer, he utters the word *Lord* with special feeling and *rapture*, understanding that it signifies the greatness and the power of the Creator of the world. The one who has received this mystical outpouring of love in his heart is, above all, enraptured and permeated with the sweetness of calling on *Jesus Christ*—like the starets who could not hear the name of Jesus pronounced, even in a passing conversation, without experiencing a special ecstasy of love and sweetness.

"It is in the person with an unwavering faith in the divinity of Jesus Christ, that is of one essence with God the Father, that faith is kindled and grows more steadfast as he utters the words *Son of God*. The one who receives the gift of humility, and who deep within his being acknowledges his own powerlessness, is broken and humbled as he says the words *have mercy on me*. And with all his strength, he utters the last words of the Jesus Prayer in a total outpouring of himself, sustaining his hope in God's mercy and abhorring his own sins.

"As I see it, these are the reasons for the differences in inflection used in reciting the prayer in the Name of the Lord Jesus Christ! . . . From this, the listener can discern (to the glory of God and to one's own edification) specific feelings and spiritual gifts in others. In regard to this, there are some who have asked me, 'Why is it that all these signs of mystical spiritual gifts are not revealed together, as a unit? Then it would not only be a single word, but rather each and every word of the prayer that would be imbued with the same rapture and inflection by the one who is praying.'

"I have replied as follows: Since God's grace bestows gifts according to its wisdom and according to each person's abilities, as is evident in Holy Scripture, who with a finite intellect could probe into this and could fathom the dispositions of grace? Is not the clay completely in the hands of the potter, and is it not for him to create from it what he wishes?"

I spent about five days with this starets, and slowly his health began to improve. This time had been so enlightening for me that I had not even noticed how it had flown. For in that small room, we were as in a secluded cell, exclusively concerned with one thing only: We prayed in silence, calling on the Name of Jesus Christ, or we discussed only one subject—interior prayer.

One day, a certain devout man happened to come to us, and he complained bitterly about the Jews, through whose settlements he had passed; and he was aggrieved and scolded them because of the mistreatment and the fraud he had suffered at their hands. He was so embittered that he cursed them and even proclaimed them unfit to live on this earth because of their obstinacy and lack of faith. Finally, he admitted to an insurmountable loathing for them. After hearing him out, my starets tried to explain and to teach him why he was wrong.

"My friend," he said, "you scold and curse the Jews in vain. They, too, are creatures of God, like you and me. You should have compassion and you should pray for them, and not curse them. Believe me, you hate them because you are not firmly grounded in God's love, and because you lack the inner stability that is born of interior prayer. That is why you have no inner peace. Let me read you something about this from the Holy Fathers. Listen to what Mark the Ascetic[11] writes, 'A soul that has attained interior union with God knows an exceeding joy which makes her like a kind-hearted unassuming child, who no longer judges anyone—neither the Greek, nor the pagan; neither the Jew, nor the sinner. Instead, she looks upon all equally with a pure eye, and she rejoices equally for the whole world. And she desires that all Greeks and Jews and pagans glorify God.' And Saint Makarios the Great of Egypt[11] says that *contemplatives burn with such love that, were it possible, they would draw all people into their bosoms, without differentiating between the good and the evil.* You have heard, my friend, what the Holy Fathers say about this, so my advice to you is to lay aside your rage. See everything and everyone as being under the providence of God, Who is over all. And when you endure offenses, first blame yourself for lacking patience and humility."

Finally, after more than a week had passed, the starets' health returned, and I thanked him from my heart for all his good guidance and bid him farewell. He went on his way, and I went in the direction I had decided on.

Soon I was getting closer to Pochaev. After walking about sixty-six miles, some soldier caught up with me. I asked him where he was headed, and he told me he was going home to the Kamenets-Podolsky district. We had walked together in silence for about six and a half miles, when I noticed that he was sighing deeply, as if grieving about something, and he appeared to be very morose. I asked him, "Why are you so sad?" He began to nag me, saying, "My good man! Since you've already noticed my grief, then swear fast and vow to me that you will keep this to yourself, and I will tell you about myself—for my death approaches, and I have no one I can ask for advice."

I assured him that as a Christian, I had no need to tell anyone about anything, and that I was ready to offer him whatever advice I could out of brotherly love.

"You see," he said, "I was drafted into the army from the manorial peasantry. After serving for five years, it became unbearably difficult for me. They even beat me frequently for being so incorrigible, and, well, for drunkeness too. So I decided to escape, and this is already my fifteenth year of desertion. For about six years, I sought shelter and hid wherever I could. I stole from sheds and barns. I took horses, broke into shops, and did all this on my own. I sold what I stole to different swindlers, and I spent my money on drinking, gave myself over to debauchery, and committed every kind of sin. The only thing I didn't do was to cause anyone to lose their soul. Everything was going well until, finally, I landed in jail for vagrancy without a passport; but, at the first opportunity, I managed to escape even from there.

"Then one day, you see, I unexpectedly met a soldier, who had been given an honorable discharge and was on his way home to a remote province. He was ill and could hardly walk, so he asked me to help him get to the nearest village where he could find a comfortable apartment. I took him there. The village policeman let us spend the night on some hay in the barn, and that's where we lay down to sleep. I woke up early in the morning, looked, and saw that my soldier had died and was already stiff. I quickly searched his pockets—to find his discharge papers, that is—and when I found them, there was also a considerable amount of money. Since everyone was still sleeping, I quickly beat it out of the barn, through the backyard, and into the forest. . . . And that's how I got away. When I looked through his passport, I noticed that he resembled me closely enough in age and physical characteristics. This made me happy, and I boldly set out in the direction of the remote Astrakhan province.

"I settled down there and found work as a laborer. Then, I hooked up with an old man, a commoner, who had his own house and traded in livestock. He was single and lived only with his widowed daughter. After living with them for a year, I married his only daughter, and then the old man died. We didn't know how to run a trading business, and I started drinking again, and so did my wife. In a year, we spent everything that the old man had left us. Finally, my wife also took ill and died. I sold the last of everything, including the house, and in no time I squandered all the money. I had nothing left to live on or to eat. So then, I went back to my old ways; and, well, I started earning a living by stealing again—only now even more brazenly, because I had that passport. So, once again, I lived a corrupt life for about a year.

"At one point, I had a long streak of bad luck. I stole an old, skinny mare from a poor peasant and went and sold it for fifty kopecks to the knacker's yard. I took this money, went to the bar, and drank some wine. Then I got the idea to go to a village where a wedding was going on, so that after the banquet, when everyone was asleep, I could steal whatever valuables I could get my hands on. Since the sun hadn't yet set, I went into the forest to wait until midnight.

"There, I lay down and fell fast asleep. And I dreamt that I saw myself standing in a beautiful, big meadow. Suddenly, a huge cloud passed overhead, followed by such a loud thunder clap that the earth opened up under my feet. I felt an immense pressure on my shoulders as if I were being pushed into the ground, which was pinning me in from all sides—only my head and hands were left uncovered. Then the menacing cloud descended to the ground, and my old grandfather, who had died twenty years earlier, came walking out of it. He had been a devout man and had been the church warden in our village for about thirty years. He approached me with an angry, menacing look on his face, and I began to tremble in fear. I looked around and saw nearby several piles of things that I had stolen over the years. And I became even more frightened.

"My grandfather was now standing next to me, and he pointed to the first pile and said in a menacing tone, 'What is *this*? Crush him!' And suddenly, the earth began to close in around me and to crush me with such pressure that I couldn't bear the pain, the anguish, and the desperation. And I began to moan and to scream, 'Have mercy!', but the torment continued. . . . Then my grandfather pointed to another pile and said again, 'And what is *this*? Crush him even harder!' And again I felt such an intense pain and anguish that no torment on earth could compare to it. Finally, that grandfather of mine led to me the mare that I had stolen yesterday, and he screamed, 'And *this*? Crush him so that his pain is excruciating!' I was so cruelly crushed from all sides that I can't even describe my agony and terror and despair. It felt as if my very sinews were being ripped out my body, and I was suffocating from the pain. It was so unbearable that I would have fainted if the torment had continued a moment longer. But the mare that stood nearby kicked and grazed my cheek, cutting it open. In the instant that I was kicked, I woke up filled with horror and trembling uncontrollably. I looked around me and it was light, the sun was rising. I touched my cheek and there was blood running from it, and those parts of my body that had been pinned under the earth in my dream felt numb, as if crawling with tiny insects. In my panic, I barely managed to get up, and I went home.

"My cheek hurt for a long time, and you can see that there's a scar now that wasn't there before. After that vision, I was frequently haunted by fear and horror. Each time I remembered the torment in my dream, I was overwhelmed with anguish and despair. My torment was so great that I didn't know what to do with myself. . . . As time passed, this happened more frequently, until finally, I began to be afraid of people and to feel ashamed—as if everyone knew all my past crimes. Eventually, I couldn't drink or eat or sleep anymore from that melancholy, and I stumbled around like a mere shadow of my former self. At one point, I even considered returning to my regiment and confessing to everything; maybe if I were punished, there just might be a chance that God would forgive my sins. But I was a coward—terrified because I knew they'd make me run the gauntlet.

"And so, unable to stand it any longer, I wanted to hang myself. But then I thought that since I didn't have long to live anyway, and I'd soon die because I had no strength left to go on, I decided to go back home, to bid my farewells—I have a nephew there—and to die.

So now, it's half a year that I'm on my way there, but the sorrow and the fear still torment me. . . . What do you think, good man—what should I do? I really can't take it anymore!"

After hearing all this, I was silently amazed, and I praised the wisdom and the grace of God for the multitude of diverse ways in which it converts sinners. Then I said to him, "My friend! It is precisely when you are overcome with fear and anguish that you should pray to God. That is the only antidote to all our griefs."

"But that's not possible," he said to me. "I keep thinking that if I start praying, God will strike me down on the spot."

"That's nonsense, man! The devil is filling your head with these thoughts. God is infinitely merciful and compassionate toward sinners, and He is quick to forgive those who repent. Surely you know the Jesus Prayer—*Lord, Jesus Christ, have mercy on me, a sinner*. Well, you just pray it unceasingly."

"How could I not know that prayer! Even when I used to go out to steal, I'd sometimes say it to bolster my courage."

"Then listen to me: God did not strike you down even when you were saying this prayer while on your way to commit crimes. Do you really think He would strike you down when you pray it on the road to repentance? Can you see now that your thoughts are coming from the enemy? . . . Believe, friend, that if you recite this prayer, in spite of whatever thoughts may assail you, you will find joy. All your fears and burdens will pass, and in the end, you will find peace. And you will become a devout man, and all the sinful passions will disappear. I can assure you of this, because I have personally seen it happen many times."

Then I told him about several examples of how the Jesus Prayer had exhibited its miraculous power in sinners, and I urged him that before continuing on his journey back home, he should come with me to venerate the icon of the Pochaev Mother of God, Refuge of Sinners. There, he could go to confession and receive Communion. My soldier listened to all this attentively, and, it seemed to me, with joy, and he agreed to everything.

We set out to Pochaev, having agreed that we would not speak along the way, but would unceasingly pray the Jesus Prayer. We walked thus in silence for an entire twenty-four hours. The next day, he told me that he felt better, and he also seemed much calmer than before. On the third day, we arrived in Pochaev, and I again encouraged him to pray unceaseasingly, day and night, until he fell asleep, assuring him that the Most Holy Name of Jesus, although unbearable to the enemy, had the power to save him. I then read to him from the *Philokalia*, where it said that although we should recite the Jesus Prayer at all times, we should pray it with particular diligence when preparing to receive the Communion of the Mystical Gifts of Christ.

He took my advice and immediately went to confession and then received Communion. Although thoughts continued to assail him from time to time, they were easily banished by the Jesus Prayer. So as to get up on time the next morning for matins, he went to bed early, unceasingly praying the Jesus Prayer. I sat in a corner by a night lamp and read my *Philokalia*. He fell asleep after an hour, and I began to pray. About twenty minutes later, he suddenly stirred, awakened, and jumped up. He ran up to me with eyes full of tears, and in a voice filled with great joy, he said, "Ah, my friend, what I just saw! I am filled with such bliss and joy! I do believe that God does not torment but is merciful to sinners. Glory to Thee, O Lord, Glory to Thee!"

I was amazed and overjoyed by this, and I asked him to tell me everything that had happened to him.

"Well, here's what happened: As soon as I fell asleep, I saw myself in that same meadow, where I had been tormented. At first, I was afraid; but then, I saw that instead of the cloud, a bright sun was rising. A beautiful light illuminated the entire meadow, and there were beautiful flowers and grass. Suddenly, my grandfather came up close to me, so handsome that I couldn't take my eyes off him. And with much warmth and affection, he quietly said to me, 'Take yourself to Zhitomir, to the Church of Saint George the Conqueror, and they will hire you as a church watchman there. Live out the rest of your days there, pray unceasingly, and God will be merciful to you!' After saying this, he made the sign of the cross over me and vanished. I was filled with such joy that I have no words to describe it! It felt as if some burden had been lifted from me and I had flown up to heaven. . . . At that moment, I suddenly woke up, filled with such bliss that my heart was beside itself from all that joy. So what should I do now? I'll go to Zhitomir immediately, like my grandfather directed me to. Even getting there won't be hard with the prayer!"

"Mercy, good man! And where do you think you're going in the middle of the night? At least go to matins, pray, and then go with God."

And so, we did not get any sleep, but after we finished talking, we did go to church. He prayed attentively and tearfully through all of matins and said that he felt such inner bliss and joy as the Jesus Prayer flowed sweetly from him. Then he received Communion at the Divine Liturgy. After lunch, I accompanied him as far as the road that led to Zhitomir, where we parted joyously and tearfully.

Afterward, I thought about myself and wondered where I should go next. I finally decided to return to Kiev, for I felt drawn there by thoughts of the wise guidance that I had received from my spiritual father, who was there. Then, too, while I stayed with him, he just might find some Christ-loving benefactors who could send me on to Jerusalem, or, at least, to Mount Athos. Thus, after spending another week in Pochaev reminiscing about the enlightening experiences I had encountered in my travels and recording certain edifying moments, I prepared to leave. I put on my knapsack and decided to go to church to venerate the icon of the Mother of God, as a parting gesture, and then to pray at the Liturgy and be on my way.

I was standing in the back of the church when a man came in who looked to be a member of the nobility, although he was somewhat shabbily dressed. He asked me where the candles were sold, and I showed him. When the Liturgy ended, I stayed to pray awhile before the icon of the Miraculous Footstep of the Mother of God, then went on my way. A short way down the street, in one of the houses, I saw an open window next to which sat a *barin** reading a book. Since I had to walk past that window, I saw that the man sitting there was the one who had asked me in church about the candles. I tipped my hat to him in passing and he called me over and said, "You must be a pilgrim, am I right?" Then he invited me in and asked about me and where I was headed. He served me tea and said, "Listen, friend! I suggest you visit the Solovetsky Monastery; there's a very secluded and peaceful skete there called Anzersky. What a place—it's like another Athos—and everyone is welcome there. All they ask is that you take turns reading the Psalms in church, for about four hours a day. I'm on my way there, and I made a vow to travel on foot. We *could* go together, and that would be safer for me, because they say the road is deserted. I've got money, so I'll feed you during the entire trip. We could even walk about seven yards apart, so that we wouldn't bother each other while we recite the prayer. Think about it, friend—say you'll do it! It'll be good for you too."

I took this unexpected invitation as a sign from the Mother of God about where I should go next, for I had asked Her to guide me in the right direction. So, without hesitation, I immediately agreed.

Thus we set out the next day, and for three days, we walked as agreed, one behind the other. He read a book, which he never put down, day or night. At times, he would be deep in thought about something. Finally, we stopped to eat, and the book lay open before him as he ate, and he frequently turned to look in it. I noticed that it was the Bible, and I said to him, "If I may be so bold as to ask, Batyushka, why is it that you never put down the Bible? Day and night, you never let it out of your hands."

"Because," he replied, "I almost continually study only from that."

"What is it that you are studying?" I asked.

"About the Christian life, which consists of prayer. I consider prayer to be the main thing that is necessary for salvation and the primary obligation of each Christian. Since prayer is both the first step toward and the ultimate pinnacle of a pious life, the Bible commands us to pray at all times and unceasingly. While other devout acts each have their own time, prayer is not prescribed only for specific times. No good deed can be done without prayer, and true prayer cannot be learned without the Bible. That's why anyone who has attained salvation by living the interior life—prophets who spoke the words of God, and hermits and ascetics, and even all God-fearing Christians—was taught to do this only by constantly and regularly studying the deepest meaning of the words of God; and reading the Bible was their most important task. Many of them never let the Bible out of their hands, and to those who sought their guidance on salvation, they replied, 'Sit in the silence of your cell and read, and reread, the Bible."

I was delighted by his thoughts and his attraction to praying, and I asked him another question, "From which of the specific scriptural texts did you glean your knowledge about prayer?"

"From all four Gospels," he replied. "In a word, from the entire New Testament, starting from the beginning and reading it in order. After reading it for a long time and understanding the text, it was revealed to me that there is a gradual progression and a real connection between all the Gospels in their teaching on prayer, beginning with the first Gospel and progressing in an ordered and methodical manner (as in a system). For example: At the very beginning, an approach or an introduction to the teaching on prayer is presented, followed by the teaching on its form or external verbal expression. Then the conditions necessary for prayer are given—the method for how to learn to pray, along with examples. Finally, you have the mystical teaching on the spiritual, unceasing interior prayer in the Name of

Jesus Christ, which is presented as being more sublime and more beneficial than formal prayer. Then comes the part about why it is necessary to pray, about its fruits, and so on. In a word, everything is provided in detail. Everything that one needs to learn in order to pray is presented methodically, in a systematic order in the Gospels, from the very beginning to the end."

After hearing this, I decided to ask him to show me everything in detail, so I said to him, "There is nothing I love more than to hear and to talk about prayer. So I would like very much to see for myself this mystical connection and progression in the teachings on prayer, in as much detail as possible. For the sake of the Lord, please show me exactly where I can find all this in the Gospels."

He eagerly agreed and said to me, "Open your New Testament, look in it and mark everything I say to you (he even gave me a pencil)." (Kindly refer to the notes I make.[13])

"Now, first of all," he began, "find Matthew, chapter 6, and read verses 5 to 8 [Matt. 6:5–8]. Find where it speaks about how to prepare for praying, or the introduction to prayer, which teaches that one should pray neither from vanity, nor in noisy surroundings, but in a secluded, peaceful place, and that one should pray only for forgiveness of sins and for union with God and should not make up excessive and superfluous petitions about worldly things, as the pagans do.

"Then, further on in the same chapter, read verses 9 to 13 [Matt. 6:9–13]. Here, the formula for prayer is given, that is, what words must be used when praying. It wisely includes everything that is needful and necessary in our lives. Continue, then, and read verses 14 and 15 in the same chapter, and you will see the conditions that must be observed to make prayer genuine; for unless we forgive those who have offended us, the Lord will not forgive our sins either. Moving on to chapter 7, you'll read in verses 7 to 12 about the right way to pray, and you'll find the encouragement *to ask, to seek, and to knock* with steadfast hope. This intensified expression addresses the repetitive aspect of prayer and the primary need to practice it in such a way that the prayer will not only accompany all your activities, but will eventually become your priority.

"This constitutes the most important characteristic of prayer. You will see an example of this in the Gospel of Mark, chapter 14, verses 32–40, where Jesus Christ Himself prays the same prayer several times. The Gospel of Luke [Luke 11:5–14] also presents a similar example of constant prayer in the parable about persistence in asking something of a friend; and also in the parable of the widow's wearisome, annoying pleas to the judge [Luke 18:3–7]. Here Jesus Christ bids us to pray at all times and in all places and not to become despondent, that is, not to grow lazy.

"In addition to so many detailed lessons, the Gospel of John reveals yet another essential teaching on the mystical interior prayer of the heart. We see this first in the wise account of Jesus Christ's conversation with the Samaritan woman, which teaches that interior worship of God must be in spirit and in truth, as God desires it to be, and that this is true unceasing prayer that flows like living water into eternal life [John 4:5–26]. Further on, in chapter 15, verses 4 to 8, the power, the might, and the necessity of interior prayer is revealed even more clearly, that is, it is the soul dwelling in Christ, in the eternal remembrance of God. Finally, read chapter 16 of the same Gospel, verses 23 to 25. See the mystery that is revealed there!

"Do you now see what tremendous power lies in praying constantly and regularly in the Name of Jesus Christ, or in the so-called Jesus Prayer—*Lord Jesus Christ, Son of God, have mercy on me, a sinner* and how easily it opens the heart and illumines it? We can see a concrete example of this with the apostles: They had not yet been his disciples for a full year, when the Lord Jesus Christ had already taught them the Lord's Prayer—that is, the Our Father (which they passed on to us). And yet, before the end of His earthly life, He revealed to them still another mystery about what was still missing in their prayer to make it fully effective. He said to them: 'Until now, you have asked for nothing in my Name . . . whatever you ask of the Father in my Name, He will give you.' [John 16:23–24] And that is precisely what happened. For after learning to pray in the Name of the Lord Jesus Christ, how many wondrous miracles did the apostles perform, and how abundantly were they themselves enlightened! . . . Do you now see the interconnections and the fullness contained in the teachings on prayer that are presented with such sublime wisdom in the Holy Gospels? If you go on to read the Epistles of the Apostles, you will find additional teachings on prayer.

"To continue with what I've already discussed, I will point out for you several sections that teach us about what must accompany prayer. In the Acts of the Apostles, we find a teaching on praying, that is, the diligent and continual way it was practiced by the first Christians who were enlightened by coming to believe in Jesus Christ [Acts 4:31]. We also learn about the fruits or the benefits of praying unceasingly, which is the outpouring of the Holy Spirit and His gifts on those who pray. You will see something similar in chapter 16, verses 25 and 26. Then, read on, in order, the epistles of the Apostles and you will see: (1) how vital prayer is for all aspects of life [James 5:13–16]; (2) how the Holy Spirit helps one to pray [Heb. 1:20–21 and Rom. 8:26]; (3) how one must always pray in the Spirit [Eph. 6:18]; (4) how necessary tranquility or inner peace is for praying [Phil. 4:6–7]; (5) how important it is to pray unceasingly [I Thess. 5:17]; and finally, (6) that we should pray not only for ourselves, but for all men [I Tim. 2:1–5].

"Thus, by spending much time diligently reading the texts, one can discover even more revelations of mystical knowledge that are hidden in the words of God, which would be lost with infrequent or cursory reading. Now, from what I have pointed out to you, have you noted the wisdom and the consistency (that is, in the systematic, mystical interconnections) with which the New Testament reveals the teaching of our Lord Jesus Christ on the subject that we just went through step by step, along with the wonderful ordered progression in how the teaching unfolds in all the four Gospels? For example: In Saint Matthew, we see the preface or the introduction to prayer, to its form, its conditions, and so on. Then in Saint Mark, we are given examples of it; in Saint Luke, the parables; and in Saint John, the mystical practice of interior prayer—even though all this is contained in all four of the Gospels (in greater or lesser detail). The practice and the fruits of prayer are discussed in Acts. In the epistles of the Apostles, as well as in Revelation, many conditions are inseparably linked to praying! . . . This, then, is why I accept only the Bible for learning all the ways that lead to salvation."

During the entire time that he was explaining everything to me, I was marking in the New Testament portion of my Bible all the references that he was citing. It all seemed so remarkable and so edifying, and I thanked him profusely for this.

Then we walked in silence for about five more days. My companion's feet began to hurt terribly, probably because he was unaccustomed to walking long distances. As a result, he hired a cart with a pair of horses and took me along with him. And that is how we arrived here, and we will stay for three days to rest. Then we will head straight to the Anzersky Skeet, where he is impatiently eager to go.

STARETS: "What a remarkable companion you have! Judging by how devout he is, he must be highly educated. I would like to meet him."

PILGRIM: "We are sharing an apartment. If you like, I will bring him to you tomorrow. Now, it's too late. . . . I'm sorry!"

The Sixth Meeting

"Brother helped by brother is like a city, strong and tall; it is fortified as a firmly established kingdom."

—Prov. 18:19[14]

PILGRIM: "As I promised and gave my word yesterday, when I saw you, I brought along my esteemed travelling companion, the one who made my journey more pleasant with his illuminating conversations, and whom you wanted to meet."

STARETS: "I am very pleased, as, I hope, are my honored guests, to see both of you and to enjoy the benefit of hearing about your experiences. Here are my guests: This is a venerable skhimnik, and this is a Reverend Father. And so, where there are two or three gathered in the name of Jesus Christ, there He Himself also promised to be. Since there are already five of us gathered in His Name, then certainly His Grace will be poured out on us all the more abundantly!

"Good friend, the story that your travelling companion told me yesterday about your ardent devotion to the Holy Gospel is remarkable and enlightening. I would be curious to hear how this great devout mystery was revealed to you."

PROFESSOR: "In His great mercy, the abundantly loving Lord, who desires that all be saved and come to the knowledge of truth, revealed this knowledge to me in a wondrous manner, without any human intervention. I was a professor at the Lyceum* for five years, living a degenerate life swept away by vain secular philosophies, but not according to Christ. I might have totally perished if not for some positive influence from my devout mother and my sister, a serious, unmarried young woman, with whom I lived. . . .

"One day, while strolling along the main boulevard, I met and made the acquaintance of a wonderful young man. He told me that he was a Frenchman, with a degree, and had recently come from Paris to seek a tutoring position. I was very impressed by his high level of education. Since he was new in town, I invited him to my home, and we became friends. For two months, he often visited me, and sometimes we went out together, amused ourselves, and went to places that were, as you may imagine, frequented by less-than-moral people.

"One day, he invited me to one such place and, to convince me to go, he carried on about the special attractions that this place had to offer. After a few moments, he suddenly stopped talking and asked if we could leave my study, where we had been sitting, and go to the drawing-room. This seemed strange to me, and I mentioned that this was not the first time that I had noticed his unwillingness to be in my study. I asked, 'What is the reason for this?' I was also trying to detain him, because the drawing-room was next to my mother's and sister's rooms, and it would be inappropriate to hold a conversation such as ours there. He offered several pretexts to get me to leave, until finally, he honestly admitted, 'Among the other books on your shelf, there's a New Testament. I respect it so much that I find it difficult to discuss our immoral affairs in its presence. Please, take it out of here, and then we can talk freely.'

"In my own foolishness, I smiled at his words, took the New Testament off the shelf, and said, 'You should have told me this a long time ago!' I handed it to him and said, 'Here, you put it in the other room!' . . . The moment the Holy Testament came into contact with him, he immediately began to tremble and—*disappeared*. I was so shocked and terrified by this that I fell to the floor in a dead faint. The servants heard the noise and came running into the study. For half an hour they tried but could not revive me. Finally, when I came to, I was overwhelmed with terror. I trembled and was filled with anxiety, and my hands and feet were so numb that I couldn't move them. The doctor was summoned, and he diagnosed the illness as paralysis resulting from some powerful shock or fright.

"For an entire year after this incident, and despite the excellent care of many physicians, I lay in bed with no relief from the illness. Subsequently, I had to resign from my teaching position. My elderly mother died during this time, and my sister decided to enter a monastery. All these events only aggravated my illness. Only one thing brought me any joy during this period of illness—it was reading the New Testament, which was never out of my hands from the onset of the illness and was a reminder of my strange experience.

"One day, an unknown hermit unexpectedly came to me, collecting money for his cloister. He urged me not to rely only on medicines, which have no power to help without the help of God, but to ask God and to pray diligently about this, for *prayer is the most powerful means for healing all illnesses, both physical and spiritual.*

"Bewildered, I objected, 'But how can I pray in this position, when I can't even do prostrations or raise my hands to make the sign of the cross?'

"He replied, 'At least try to pray somehow!' And he couldn't explain anything more about how to pray. . . .

"After this visitor left, my thoughts unwittingly turned to prayer, to its power and effects, and I remembered theology lectures that I had heard long ago in school, when I was still a student. It made me glad to recall these enlightening religious truths, and it warmed my soul. I immediately began to feel a certain relief from my illness. The New Testament was always at my side, and, since I believed in it after that miraculous incident, and I remembered that the lectures I had heard about prayer were based entirely on New Testament texts, I decided that it would be best to learn about prayer and Christian piety from the teachings in the New Testament. As I read it carefully and painstakingly, it became an abundant spring, from which I drew knowledge about the complete way to salvation and true interior prayer. I carefully marked all the passages on this subject, and ever since then, I try regularly to study this divine teaching and to put it into practice, as best I can, although this is difficult. During the time I was doing this, my illness gradually subsided, until finally, as you can see, I was completely healed. Since I was now alone, I decided that in gratitude to God for His Fatherly mercy, for His healing and guidance, I would follow my sister's example and the urgings of my own soul and would consecrate myself to an ascetic life, so that unhindered I could seek and acquire those very sweet words of eternal life that were revealed to me in the Scriptures.

"So, now, I am making my way to the secluded skete at the Solovets Monastery by the White Sea, the one called Anzerskiy, which I heard, from a reliable source, is a most suitable place for the contemplative life. I'll tell you even more: Although it's true that the holy New Testament comforts me on my journey and abundantly illumines my immature mind and even warms my cold heart, yet in acknowledgement of my weakness, I can tell you honestly that I am frightened both by the weakness and the damaged state of my heart, and by the magnitude of the conditions required for doing good works and attaining salvation—which demand complete self-sacrifice, valiant spiritual struggles, and a profoundly humble wisdom, as taught by the New Testament. And so, as I now find myself standing between despair and hope, I don't know what will become of me!" . . .

SKHIMNIK: "After receiving such a binding token of the special and miraculous mercy of God, and given your education, it is unforgivable for you not only to despair, but to permit even a shadow of doubt into your soul about God's providence and His help! Do you know what the 'Golden-Mouth,'[15] enlightened by God, says about this? 'No one must despair,' he teaches, 'and proclaim the Gospel decrees to be unattainable or impossible to fulfill! In appointing the way for man's salvation, God certainly did not decree commandments intending them to be so impossible to fulfill that man would turn to sin. No! It was done so that through their holiness and their beneficial necessity, we would be blessed both in this life and in eternity.'

"Of course, the steadfast and regular fulfillment of God's decrees seems extremely difficult for our nature and, subsequently, salvation appears difficult to attain. Yet the very same words of God, which decreed these commandments, also provide the means not only for fulfilling them easily, but even consolation in the process of doing so. If, at first glance, this is shrouded in mystery, it is, of course, to guide the beginner more perfectly to humility and to draw him more easily into union with God by teaching him that his closest refuge lies in prayer and in asking for His Fatherly help. Therein lies the mystery of salvation, and not in relying on one's own efforts."

PILGRIM: "Weak and powerless as I am, how I would love to know this mystery, so I could use it as a means to improve my lazy life, at least to some degree, to the glory of God and for my salvation!"

SKHIMNIK: "You do know this mystery, beloved brother, from your book the *Philokalia*. It consists of unceasing prayer, which you have learned so well, and which you practice so fervently and find such comfort in. . . ."

PILGRIM: "I would fall down in gratitude before your feet, Reverend Father! For God's sake, grant me to hear from your own mouth some insights into this mystery of salvation and this sacred prayer, which, above all else, I long to hear and love to read about for strengthening and comforting my very sinful soul."

SKHIMNIK: "Although I cannot fulfill your wish with my own thoughts on this sublime spiritual activity, because I have little personal experience with it, I do have a very instructive work written by a spiritual writer specifically on this subject. If it pleases the others here, I will bring it right now, and, if you wish, I can read it to you. If you will be so kind as to agree!"

EVERYONE: "Do be so kind, Reverend Batyushka! Do not deprive us of such knowledge for our salvation!"

The Mystery of Salvation as Revealed through Unceasing Prayer

"How can you save yourself?" This pious Christian question naturally arises in everyone's mind after experiencing fallen and weak human nature and the remains of its original proclivity for truth and righteousness. When anyone with even some degree of faith in immortality and in the recompense of eternal life turns his gaze toward heaven, he unwittingly confronts the question of how to save himself. . . . Unable to find the answer on his own, he turns to wise and knowledgeable people, who advise him to read instructive books by spiritual writers on this subject, and he strives steadfastly to conform to the truths and the rules that he hears and reads about. In all these manuals, he finds the following conditions prescribed as necessary for salvation: a devout life; valiant spiritual battles; and inner struggles to achieve a complete self-renunciation that will guide him to perform good works and to keep faithfully all the commandments of God, which is proof of a firm and steadfast faith. . . .

"Then, he is taught that all these conditions for salvation must be fulfilled together and with profound humility. For just as all the virtues depend on each other, so they must support each other, must perfect and must inspire each other. This is similar to the rays of the sun, which display their power and ignite a flame only when concentrated through glass onto one focal point. Apart from this, *he who is unfaithful in little things is also unfaithful in big ones.*

"In addition, so that he is more convinced of the need to perform all these complex activities in their entirety, he hears high praise of the excellence of the virtues and condemnation of the baseness and the wretchedness of the vices. And all this is indelibly imprinted on his mind with truthful promises of either great rewards and bliss or tormenting punishment and suffering in eternal life.

"Such is the unique nature of preaching in modern times!

"Armed with such guidance, the ardent seeker of salvation happily sets out to follow these instructions and to put into practice all that he has heard and read about. But alas! With his very first attempt, he is unable to achieve his goal. He had anticipated, and has now experienced, the reality that his damaged and weakened nature is taking the upper hand over the convictions of his mind; that his free will is constrained, his intentions impure; and that the strength of his spirit has been exhausted. After experiencing such personal powerlessness, he naturally begins to wonder if there may be any other means to help him fulfill the decrees of God's law and the requirements of Christian piety, which were fulfilled by all who were made worthy to receive salvation and holiness.

"And so, in order to reconcile within himself the demands of reason and conscience with his inability to satisfy them, he once again asks the preachers of salvation: *How can I be saved? How can I justify my inability to fulfill the conditions for salvation? And can the preacher himself faithfully do all that he preaches?*"

"Ask God! Pray to God for His help!"

"So, the seeker concludes: Would it not be more profitable at first, or even always and at all times, to learn about prayer as being the power for achieving all that is required by Christian piety and the means for attaining salvation?

"With this in mind, he begins to study about prayer—he reads, he reflects, and he considers the teachings of those who have written on this subject. Indeed, he discovers many enlightened ideas, profound knowledge, and powerful pronouncements. One offers excellent discourses on the need to pray; another, on its powers, benefits, one's duty to pray; on the fact that prayer requires diligence, attention, and warmth of spirit, pure thoughts, reconciliation with one's enemies; on humility, contrition, and everything else that must accompany prayer. . . .

"*Yet, what is prayer, in and of itself? How does one pray correctly?* Although these questions are so fundamental and essential, it is very rare to find answers to them that are comprehensive and that can be understood by everyone. So, once again, the zealous student of prayer finds himself shrouded in mystery. From his general reading, he will remember only the external, albeit pious, side of prayer and, subsequently, will arrive at the following conclusion: In order to pray, he must attend church; he must make the sign of the cross over himself, do prostrations, kneel, recite psalms, *kanons, akathists*. . . .*

"And this is the common understanding of prayer among those who are not familiar with the literature on interior prayer and with the contemplative works of the Holy Fathers.

"Finally, the seeker finds a book called the *Philokalia*, in which twenty-five Holy Fathers clearly present their teaching on the art of the true and essential prayer of the heart. There, the veil of the mystery that had once surrounded salvation and prayer begins to lift, and he sees that true prayer consists of focusing the mind and the memory on the unwavering remembrance of God; of walking in His divine presence; of rousing one's self to His love by thinking of Him; and of learning to repeat God's name in rhythm with one's breathing and the beating of the heart. And all this is guided by verbally invoking the Most Holy Name of Jesus Christ or praying the Jesus Prayer—unceasingly, at all times, in all places, and during all manner of activity. . . .

"These clear truths enlighten the seeker's knowledge and reveal the way for him to learn to pray correctly; and they succeed in convincing him to begin immediately to put these wise instructions into practice. However, in spite of this, he still encounters difficulty in his intermittent attempts, until an experienced guide (using that same book, the *Philokalia)* clarifies for him that the fullness of the mystery lies solely in *constancy,* or in the unceasing, repetitive aspect of prayer (no matter how it is recited at first)—and that this is the only powerful means for achieving both perfect interior prayer and salvation of the soul. Constancy in praying is the basis or the foundation for everything done to attain salvation, as Saint Simeon the New Theologian confirms, 'The one who prays unceasingly,' he says, 'has included everything that is good in this one activity.'

"And so, in order to present the truth of this revelation in all its fullness, the guide develops it in the following manner:

"First of all, genuine faith is necessary for the salvation of the soul. Holy Scripture says, '. . . for without faith, it is impossible to please Him . . .' [Heb. 11:6]—*For he who has no faith will be judged.*

"Yet in the same Holy Scripture, one can see that on his own, a man cannot produce faith even the size of a mustard seed; that faith does not come from us but is a gift from God; and that being a spiritual gift, faith is granted by the Holy Spirit.

"What then should one do? How can man's need for faith be reconciled with his inability to produce it on his own? The means for this is revealed in the same Holy Scripture, along with examples: *Ask and you will receive.* On their own, the apostles could not produce perfect faith within themselves, so they asked Jesus Christ: 'Lord, grant us faith.' This is an example of acquiring faith, and from this, it is clear that faith is acquired through prayer.

"Along with genuine faith, good works—acts of virtue—are also necessary for the salvation of the soul, *for faith without works is dead.* 'For a man is justified by works and not by faith alone.' And, 'If you want to enter into life, keep the commandments. . . . You shall not murder, You shall not commit adultery, You shall not steal, You shall

"For this reason, constancy and regularity are attributed only to prayer. While there is a time for each of the other virtues, we are commanded to pray constantly—'pray unceasingly.' It behooves us to pray always, at all times and in all places.

"True prayer requires its own conditions. It must be offered with a pure mind and heart, with ardent zeal and undivided attention, with tremulous awe and profound humility. Yet, who would not agree, in all good conscience, that he is far from the aforementioned conditions for true prayer, that he offers his prayer from a sense of obligation, by forcing himself, and not from feeling inclined to and delighted by prayer, from a love of praying? Holy Scripture also asserts that on his own, man is not able to cleanse and empty his mind of inappropriate thoughts—*Man's thoughts are evil from his youth*—and that only God can give us a new heart and create a new spirit within us, *for both the willing and the doing are from God.* The Apostle Paul himself says: 'My spirit (i.e., my voice) prays, but my understanding is unfruitful' [I Cor. 14:14]; and he adds this emphasis, 'For we do not know what we should pray for as we ought. . . .' [Rom. 8:26]. From this, it follows that in praying on our own, we cannot discern the most essential characteristics of prayer!

"In the face of such powerlessness, what is left to each man's will and personal abilities to save his soul? He cannot acquire either faith or good works without prayer. In the end, even true prayer is beyond his powers. What, then, is left for him to do on his own? What is left to his free will and powers to avoid perishing and to save himself?

"Since each action possesses its own unique *quality* or value, the Lord reserved this for Himself, to grant it as a gift according to His will. And to emphasize man's dependence on the will of God, He left only the *quantity* or practice of prayer to man's own will and abilities, commanding him to pray unceasingly at all times, in all places. In this are revealed the mystical means to achieving true prayer, and, along with it, faith, keeping the commandments, and salvation. Thus, *quantity* was left up to man, and constancy of prayer to his will. . . . The Fathers of the Church specifically teach this. Saint Macarius the Great says, 'To pray in any manner (as long as it is constantly) is within our will; but true prayer is a gift of grace.' The Venerable Hesychius[15] says that constancy in prayer turns into habit, which then becomes as binding as second nature, and that it is impossible to purify the heart without constantly calling on the Name of Jesus Christ.

"The Venerable Callistus and Ignatius advise uninterrupted, constant prayer in the Name of Jesus Christ before performing any ascetic feats or acts of virtue, because constancy purifies even an impure prayer. The blessed Diadochus insists that if man would call on the Name of God more constantly (would pray), he would not sin. How full of experience and wisdom are these practical directives from the Fathers, and how close to the heart they are! With a simplicity born of their own experience, they shed light on the ways and the means for perfecting the soul. What a sharp contrast between their teaching and the moral directives of theoretical reason! Reason dictates: Do this and that which is good; be courageous; use your will power; bolster yourself by believing in the fruits of virtue—for example, cleanse your mind and heart of empty daydreams and occupy them with instructive meditation. Do good, and you will be respected and will have peace. Live according to the dictates of your reason and conscience. . . . But alas! Despite the best efforts, even all this does not achieve its goal without constant prayer and the help of God that it invokes.

"Now, let us look further in the teachings of the Fathers, and let us see what they say, for example, about purifying the soul. Saint (John) of the Ladder writes, 'When the soul is darkened by unclean thoughts, flog the foes with the Name of Jesus, repeating it constantly. You will find no stronger weapon than this in heaven or on earth.'[17] Saint Gregory of Sinai teaches, 'Know that no man is able to control his mind on his own; so in the face of unclean thoughts, call on the Name of Jesus

Christ with greater frequency, and the thoughts will subside on their own.' What a simple and convenient method this is, yet experience proves that it works; and how contrary it is to the advice of theoretical reason that strives single-mindedly to achieve purity by its own actions! And so, after understanding this experienced teaching of the holy Fathers, we arrive at this veritable conclusion: that the only principal and most convenient method for working toward salvation and spiritual perfection lies in the frequency, in the uninterrupted activity of prayer, however weak it may be.

"O, Christian soul! If you find not within yourself the strength to worship God in spirit and in truth; if your heart still knows not the warmth and the sweet delight of mental and interior prayer, then offer up in prayerful sacrifice whatever you are able to, whatever lies within the power of your will, whatever is within your strength. First, let your humble lips become accustomed to the constant and persistent supplications of prayer. Let them continually, constantly, uninterruptedly call on the mighty Name of Jesus Christ. This does not require great effort, and it is possible for everyone. This, too, is what the Holy Apostle urges us to do from his own experience: '. . . let us (continually) offer the sacrifice of praise to God, that is, the fruit of our lips, giving thanks to His name' [Heb. 13:15].

"The constancy of prayer will surely turn into habit and will become a natural thing to do. In time, it will create a suitable and appropriate disposition of mind and heart. Imagine if man would steadfastly fulfill this one commandment of God about praying—in this one action, he would fulfill all the commandments. For if he prayed uninterruptedly, at all times and during all manner of activity and work, calling on the divine Name of Jesus Christ in the innermost secret place of his heart—even if this is done initially without spiritual warmth and zeal; even if it is done by sheer will power—this of itself would leave no time for sensual, sinful pleasures. Each sinful thought of his would meet with resistance before it could take root; no sinful act would seem worthwhile, as it does to an idle mind. Long-windedness and idle talk would diminish or completely vanish, and the power of grace contained within the Name of God, when constantly invoked, would instantly wipe out each transgression.

"The practice of constant prayer would constantly distract the soul from sinful acts, and it would draw the soul to what it knows to be the most essential thing of all—union with God! Do you now see how important and how necessary *quantity* is in praying? Constant praying is the only means to achieving pure and true prayer. It is the best and the most authentic way to prepare for praying and the most reliable path toward achieving the goal of prayer and salvation!

"So as to further strengthen your conviction in the necessity and the benefits of constant prayer, be aware of this: (1) each stirring, each thought about prayer results from the activity of the Holy Spirit and the voice of your guardian angel, (2) the Name of Jesus Christ invoked in prayer contains self-existing and self-acting beneficent powers within itself; and because of this, (3) do not be troubled by the impurity or the aridity of your prayer, but patiently await the fruits of your continuous calling on the Name of God. Do not listen to the inexperienced and thoughtless suggestions of a vain world, which argue that even a single lukewarm supplication, though it be persistent, is useless and long-winded. . . . No! The power of the Name of God and calling on it unceasingly will bear their own fruit, in their own time!

"One spiritual writer presents this in a wonderful way. 'I know,' he says, 'that for many seemingly spiritual pseudo-wise philosophers—who seek false grandeur everywhere, and who act in a manner that is noble in the eyes of reason and arrogance—the simple, vocal, and singular, but constant, practice of prayer seems an insignificant or lowly activity, or even a mere trifle. But, O, unfortunate ones—how they deceive themselves by forgetting the teaching of Jesus Christ, '. . . unless you . . . become like little children, you will by no means enter the Kingdom of God' [Matt. 18:3]. They invent for themselves some sort of a science of prayer based on the shaky foundations of natural reason. Does it really take that much education, intelligence, or knowledge to say with a pure heart, 'Jesus, Son of God, have mercy on me!'? Is this not the kind of regular prayer that our Divine Teacher Himself praised? Were not miracles entreated and performed precisely through such brief but constant prayers?

"O, Christian soul! Take courage and do not silence the unceasing invocations of your prayers! And if your prayer cries out from a heart that is still dissipated, still even partly filled with worldly concerns, it does not matter! You need only to forge on—do not give up, do not be anxious—for that prayer will purify itself by virtue of its constancy. Never forget that '. . . He who is in you is greater than he who is in the world' [I John 4:4]. *For God is greater than your heart, and He knows all,* says the Apostle.

"Thus, after all these convincing arguments that unceasing prayer is so powerful, in spite of any human weakness, and that it is undoubtedly accessible to man and fully in the scope of his will, make up your mind to spend if only a day, at first, in being vigilant over yourself and in praying constantly, so that this invocation of the Name of Jesus Christ in prayer would take up the greater part of your day than any other activity. By giving prayer priority over worldly activities, it will eventually and certainly prove to you that the day was not lost, but was used toward your salvation and that on the scales of divine justice, unceasing prayer by far outweighs all your weaknesses and sins and erases the sins of that one day from the pages of the book of life. It sets you on the path of righteousness and bestows the hope that you will receive illumination even in life eternal." (From the author's manuscript that was given by the Dobry monastery to Father Ambrosius.)

PILGRIM: "I thank you, Holy Father, with all my heart! You have delighted my sinful soul with this reading. For the Lord's sake, and with your blessing, permit me to make a copy of this manuscript for myself. I can do it in just a few hours. Everything you read is so wonderful, so comforting; and it is just as clear to my dense mind as are the writings of the Holy Fathers on these subjects in the *Philokalia*. Take, for example, John of Karpathos, in part 4 of the *Philokalia*, who also says that if you have no strength for abstinence and great ascetic spiritual feats, then know that the Lord wants to save you through prayer. And all this is so wonderfully and clearly presented in your manuscript. I first thank God, and then you, for the honor of having listened to this!"

PROFESSOR: "Most esteemed Father, I, too, listened to your reading with great pleasure and attention! According to the highest logic, all the conclusions are correct, and I find them remarkable. Still, it seems to me that unceasing prayer essentially depends on favorable conditions and peaceful solitude. I do agree that constant or unceasing prayer is powerful, that it is the only means for acquiring the help of grace in all good works and for illuminating the soul, and that these means are within the measure of man's abilities. Yet they can be applied only when a man has the opportunity for peace and solitude. In the absence of work, cares, or distractions, he can pray constantly or unceasingly, and then, his only struggle will be with laziness or tedious thoughts. However, if he is burdened with endless responsibilities, with matters that require his constant attention, and if he must be in the noisy company of people, then despite his ardent desire to pray constantly, he would not be able to because of unavoidable distractions. Consequently, a method for constant prayer that requires favorable conditions cannot be accessible to all and is not meant for everyone."

SKHIMNIK: "Your conclusion is unfortunate! Setting aside the fact that a heart that has learned interior prayer is able to pray unhindered and to invoke the Name of God during any manner of activity (both physical and mental) and in any noisy surroundings (he who has done so, knows this; but he who has not, needs to be taught gradually)—one can state with certainty that no external distractions can interrupt the prayer of one who desires to pray. For man's innermost hidden thoughts are sovereign and are not bound by anything external. They are always accessible to him and can always be focused on prayer. Even the tongue can silently recite the words of prayer in the presence of others and during external activities. For that matter, our activities are not so important and our conversations not so interesting that while engaged in them, we cannot find at least some time to call on the Name of Jesus periodically but constantly, even if the mind has not yet acquired the habit of unceasing prayer. Of course, isolation from people and distractions does constitute the primary condition for attentive unceasing prayer. However, if this is not possible, one must not make excuses for not praying constantly. *Quantity* and constancy are possible to all, within each one's ability—to both the healthy and the infirm—and they are within man's will power.

"This has been proved by examples of people burdened with responsibilities, distracting obligations, cares, woes, and work, who not only continuously invoke the divine Name of Jesus Christ, but learn and attain, through this, the unceasing interior prayer of the heart. Patriarch Photius is one of them. Elevated from the rank of senator to the position of Patriarch, and while administering the vast diocese of Constantinople, he unceasingly invoked the Name of God, which even helped him to acquire the self-impelled prayer of the heart. Callistus of holy Mount Athos also learned in this manner to pray unceasingly, while performing the distracting and busy duties of a kitchen chef. Also, the simple-hearted Lazarus, burdened with never-ending work for the brethren, recited the Jesus Prayer during all his noisy activities and was comforted. And so it was with many others who practiced continual invocations of the Name of God. If it were impossible to pray during distracting activities or among people, then, of course, the impossible would not have been prescribed.

"Saint John the Golden-Mouth says the following in his teaching on prayer, 'No one should say that it is impossible for him who is occupied with worldly activities, or him who cannot attend church, to pray always. Wherever you may be, you can offer sacrifice to God in your mind through prayer. Thus, one can conveniently pray at the marketplace, while travelling, while selling wares and working at one's trade. One can pray anywhere and everywhere. Indeed, if only man would practice watchfulness over himself and would become convinced that prayer must be the chief activity among all his obligations, he would find it convenient to pray anywhere. Then he would certainly arrange his affairs more purposefully and would limit his conversations with others only to what is necessary. He would observe silence and would refrain from idle chatter; and he would not be overly burdened by cares and woes, thus allowing himself to find more time for quiet prayer. When this becomes his goal, the power of calling on the Name of God would crown all his activities with success. In the end, he will have trained himself to invoke unceasingly the Name of Jesus Christ in prayer. Experience will then teach him that as the only means to salvation, constant prayer is within man's ability and will power; that one can pray at all times, in all places and in all situations; and that one can progress easily from verbal prayer to mental prayer, which then leads to the prayer of the heart that opens up the Kingdom of God within us."

PROFESSOR: "I agree that with routine activities, it is possible and even convenient to pray constantly and even uninterruptedly, because they do not require intense concentration and alertness and, thus, allow my mind to immerse itself in unceasing prayer and my mouth to recite it. However, if something requires mental concentration, such as careful reading or deep reflection or writing something, how can I do that and simultaneously pray with my mind and my mouth? And since prayer is chiefly a mental activity, how can I simultaneously focus my one mind on more than one task?"

SKHIMNIK: "There is a very simple answer to your question, if we consider that those who pray unceasingly are divided into three categories: (1) the beginners, (2) those who are still progressing, and (3) the proficient in prayer. Given this, there are even cases of beginners who, although otherwise mentally occupied, can feel their minds and hearts being drawn to God and to reciting verbally a short prayer—constantly, but for shorter periods of time. Those who are still progressing and those who have acquired prayer as a permanent state of mind can be immersed in reflection or in writing something and can simultaneously and uninterruptedly remain in the presence of God, which is the very foundation for prayer.

"Here is an example of this: Imagine that an austere and exacting king orders you to write a treatise on a complex subject of his choice—while you are in his presence and right before his throne. However concentrated you may be on your task, the presence of the emperor, who holds your life in his hands, controls you; and it will not allow you for a moment to forget that you are not concentrating, thinking, and writing in solitude, but, rather, in a place that demands special reverence, respect, and decorum. This feeling, this immediate sense of the king's close presence, serves as a very clear example of how unceasing interior prayer can be practiced even during other mental activities.

"As for those who have progressed from the prayer of the mind to the prayer of the heart, either through long practice or by God's mercy, they pray unceasingly not only during other intense mental activity, but even while they sleep. The Wise One[18] bears witness to this: 'I sleep, but my heart is awake' [Song of Sol. 5:2]. . . . In those who are proficient in prayer, the heart acquires such an ability to invoke the Name of God that it stirs itself to pray, and it draws the mind and the entire soul into an outpouring of unceasing prayer no matter what situation the one who prays happens to be in, no matter what other mental activity he may be occupied with."

PRIEST: "Venerable Father, permit me my own turn to express my thoughts. The article you read states wonderfully that the only means to salvation and perfection is through constant prayer—'however it may sound'. . . . This is hard for me to understand, and so I wonder: What's the point of my praying continually and calling on the Name of God only verbally, if my attention is not focused on this, and I don't understand what I am saying? That would simply be empty words! The only result of this would be an over-exerted tongue. And the mind, which resisted this exercise with its own thoughts, would also suffer in its ability to function properly. God does not require words, but an attentive mind and a pure heart. Is it not better, even infrequently, or only at prescribed times, to recite even a brief prayer, but to do so with attention, zeal, warmth of spirit, and appropriate understanding? Otherwise, you can recite the prayer day and night; but without a pure spirit and good works, you won't acquire anything for your salvation. If you persist with only verbal babbling, you'll end up tired and bored, and you'll lose all faith in prayer and will give up this fruitless exercise. Moreover, even Holy Scripture stresses that verbal prayer alone is useless. For example, 'These people . . . honor Me with their lips, but their heart is far from Me' [Matt. 15:8]. 'Not everyone who says to Me, *Lord, Lord*, shall enter the Kingdom of Heaven. . . .' [Matt. 7:21]. '. . . I would rather speak five words with my understanding . . . than ten thousand words in a tongue' [I Cor. 14:19]. And so on. All this is saying that inattentive verbal prayer is useless."

SKHIMNIK: "Your conclusion could have some basis, were it not for the advice that is given for verbal prayer—constancy and regularity—and if prayer in the Name of Jesus Christ did not have its own self-impelled power, and if attention and diligence were not acquired gradually through practicing prayer. But since the issue is one of frequency, length of time, and constancy in prayer (though initially it may be inattentive and arid), your incorrect conclusions do not hold.

"Let's look at this more carefully. After defending the immense benefits and the fruitful results of constant prayer which involves repeating the same words, one spiritual writer concludes, 'Although many pseudo-enlightened people consider that verbal and constant recitation of one and the same prayer is useless and even trivial and consider it a mechanical and mindless exercise for simple people, unfortunately they do not know the mystery that is revealed through this routine exercise. They do not know how this verbal but constant calling imperceptibly unites with the genuine calling of the heart, how it delves into the depths of the interior man and becomes exceedingly pleasant—becoming, as it were, the most natural activity for the soul, and enlightening it, nourishing it, and leading it to union with God.

"It seems to me that these critics are like little children, to whom one decides to teach the alphabet and how to read. Eventually the lessons bore them, and they cry out, 'Isn't it a hundred times better for us to go fishing, as our fathers do, than to spend the day endlessly repeating the ABCs or scribbling on paper with a quill pen?' The profit and the education from reading that they should have acquired from this boring repetition of the alphabet remains a mystery to them. In a similar way, the simple but constant calling on the Name of God remains a hidden mystery for those who lack knowledge and conviction in its immense resulting benefits. By assessing faith on the basis of their inexperienced and shortsighted reason, they forget that man is both body and spirit. . . . For example, when you want to purify your soul, why do you first cleanse your body? Why do you fast and deprive your body of nourishing and stimulating food? You do this, of course, so it would not interfere with—or, more precisely, so that it would assist in—purifying the soul and enlightening the mind—so that the body's constant hunger would serve to remind you of your resolve to seek interior perfection and spiritually beneficial exercises, which you so easily forget about. . . . And experience teaches you that through bodily abstinence, you attain interior refinement of the intellect, peace in your heart, a weapon for subduing the passions, and a constant reminder to practice spiritual exercises. Thus, by applying exterior measures, you acquire interior spiritual benefits.

"Understand that this also applies to unceasing and constant verbal prayer, which gives rise, through long practice, to the interior prayer of the heart, and which guides and assists in the union of the intellect with God. It is a mistake to imagine that constant repetition damages the tongue, and that boredom from arid incomprehension makes us abandon this useless verbal exercise of prayer. No! Experience shows quite the opposite. Those who practice unceasing prayer insist that he who resolves unceasingly to invoke the Name of Jesus Christ or to recite the Jesus Prayer uninterruptedly (which is the same thing) will certainly experience initial difficulty and will struggle with laziness. But the longer he persists, the more imperceptibly he becomes one with this exercise, so that in the end, his mouth and lips acquire a life of their own, and they function effortlessly and unrestrained, of their own accord, and silently recite the prayer. At the same time, the laryngeal muscles develop in such a way that the one who is praying begins to feel as if the repetition of the prayer is something that was always a natural part of him; and when he stops praying, he feels as if something is missing inside. This is why the mind surrenders and begins to listen to this involuntary recitation of the lips, which commands its attention and ultimately becomes the very source of sweet delight in the heart and of the genuine prayer of the heart. These are the true and beneficent results of unceasing or constant verbal prayer, and they are completely contrary to the conclusions drawn by those who have no experience or understanding of this matter!

"With regard to the texts you cited from Holy Scripture to support your objections, a careful examination will clarify them. Jesus Christ condemned hypocritical verbal worship of God and flaunting it—or deceitful invocations of 'Lord, Lord!'—because the arrogant Pharisees professed their faith in God only with lip service and did not justify it by their actions or acknowledge it in their hearts. This was directed at them and has nothing to do with praying, for which Jesus Christ gave a clear and definite or explicit directive, *It is fitting to pray always and not to grow indifferent* (that is, not to become discouraged). Similarly, the holy Apostle Paul attributes more value to five words spoken meaningfully than a multitude of empty words spoken thoughtlessly or in foreign tongues in a church. He was referring to teaching people in general and not specifically to prayer, about which he asserts the following, '. . . I desire that (Christians) pray everywhere' [I Tim. 2:8]; and in general, his advice is: '. . . Pray without ceasing. . . .' [I Thess. 5:17]. Now do you see how fruitful constant prayer is, for all its simplicity—and what sober perception is required to understand Holy Scripture correctly?"

PILGRIM: "That is so true, honorable Father! I have seen many people who practiced the unceasing Jesus Prayer on their own—simply and without human guidance and unaware of the importance of being attentive. And yet, they achieved a state where their mouths and tongues could not refrain from reciting the prayer, which subsequently brought them such delight and illumination and transformed them from weak and negligent people into heroic ascetics and champions of virtue. . . ."

SKHIMNIK: "Yes! It is as if a man is somehow born again through prayer. Its power is so great, that nothing, not the strongest of passions can withstand it. If you like, friends, in parting, I will read to you a short but interesting article that I brought along with me."

EVERYONE: "We would be delighted to hear it!" . . .

SKHIMNIK: *On the Power of Prayer*

"Prayer is so powerful and so dynamic that you can pray and do whatever else you wish, and the prayer will guide you to act properly and righteously.

"Only love is needed to please God—*Love and do whatever you wish*, says the blessed Augustine, *for he who truly loves cannot even desire to offend his beloved*. . . . Since prayer is the outpouring and the activity of love, the following can also certainly be said about it: nothing more is necessary for salvation than unceasing prayer. Pray and do as you will, and you will fulfill the goal of prayer, and through it, you will acquire illumination!

"For a more thorough understanding of this, let us clarify it with examples:

1. Pray and think any thoughts you wish, and your thoughts will be purified by prayer. Prayer will illumine your mind, and it will silence and will drive away all inappropriate thoughts. Saint Gregory of Sinai confirms this with his advice: 'If you wish to drive away thoughts and to purify your mind,' he advises, 'then drive them away with prayer; for only prayer can control thoughts.' Saint John of the Ladder also speaks of this, 'Banish hostile thoughts with the Name of Jesus; you will find no other weapon than this.'

2. Pray and do as you will, and your deeds will be pleasing to God, as well as beneficial and redemptive for you.

Constant prayer, no matter what its subject, will not be barren [cf. Mark the Ascetic], for it contains within itself the power of grace. 'Holy is His name . . . (and) . . . everyone who calls on the Name of the Lord will be saved' [Acts 2:21]. For example, There was one who prayed with no success and without devotion; but through his prayer, he was enlightened and was called to repentance. Resolving to change her wanton life, an unmarried woman prayed; and prayer showed her the way to a life of chastity and obedience to the teachings of Jesus Christ.

3. Pray and do not overly exert yourself in trying to defeat the passions. Prayer will destroy them in you. Holy Scripture says, '. . . He

who is in you is greater than he who is in the world' [I John 4:4]. And Saint John of Karpathos teaches that if you lack the gift of abstinence, do not grieve; but know that God requires your diligence in prayer, and that the prayer will save you.

This is proved by the example of the starets in the *Lives of the Fathers*, who had "failed to overcome," that is, when confronted with the stumbling block of sin and who did not despair but turned to prayer, which restored his inner peace.

4. Pray and be not anxious about anything; do not fear misfortune and disasters; prayer will protect you and will ward them off. Remember the drowning Peter of little faith; Paul, praying in prison; the monk rescued from temptation by prayer; the young woman rescued by prayer from the ill-intentioned soldier; and similar other cases. These affirm the power, the strength, and the all-encompassing ability of prayer in the Name of Jesus Christ.

5. Pray, at least in some manner, but pray always, and let nothing dismay you. Rejoice in your spirit and be at peace: prayer will take care of everything and it will teach you. Remember what the Saints John the Golden-Mouth and Mark the Ascetic say about the power of prayer. The first one asserts that 'though in all our sinfulness we utter prayer, it will instantly cleanse us.' . . . And the second one says: 'Even the least form of prayer is within our ability; but pure prayer is the gift of grace.' And so, offer whatever is within your ability as a sacrifice to God. Begin by offering at least the *quantity* of prayer (as much as you can) as a sacrifice to Him, and the strength of God will fill your weakness. Prayer that is arid and distracted—as long as it is frequent and constant and becomes a habit that is as second nature—will be transformed into pure, illumined, fervent, and righteous prayer.

6. And finally, if your ascetic efforts are accompanied by prayer, there certainly would be no time left, not only to sin, but even to think about sinning.

"Do you now see how many levels of profound meaning are contained in this wise saying, 'Love and do as you will. Pray and do as you will!'. . . . What joy and comfort all this brings to a sinner weighed down by weakness—to the one who groans beneath the burden of his warring passions!

"Prayer—this is all that we are given as the all-encompassing means for salvation and for perfecting the soul. . . . This is true! Yet prayer is also inextricably bound to its own condition: God commands us to 'pray unceasingly.' It follows then that prayer will reveal its all-encompassing power and will bear fruit only when it is practiced constantly, unceasingly. For just as constant prayer is undoubtedly within our will power, so purity, zeal, and perfection in prayer are the gifts of grace.

"And so, let us pray as often as possible. Let us devote our entire lives to prayer, though initially it be distracted! Constant praying will teach us to be attentive, and *quantity* will certainly lead to *quality*. As one experienced spiritual writer said: In order to learn to do anything well, one must do it as often as possible."

PROFESSOR: "Indeed, prayer is a great thing! And the zeal to pray constantly is the key to opening its beneficent treasures. And yet, how often I find myself struggling between zeal and laziness! How I desire to find the means and the help to achieve victory, to acquire conviction and to rouse myself to constant diligence in prayer!"

SKHIMNIK: "Many of the spiritual writers offer various means based on sound reasoning for encouraging diligence in prayer. For example, they counsel us to:

1. think seriously about the necessity, the superiority, and the benefits of prayer for saving the soul;
2. acquire conviction that God absolutely requires us to pray, and that these words of His are preached everywhere;

3. remember always that laziness and carelessness in praying will not bring success in good works and in attaining peace and salvation and will inevitably result both in punishment in this life and suffering in eternal life;
4. bolster our resolve through the examples of God's saints, all of whom attained illumination, salvation, and so on, through unceasing prayer.

"Though all these means have their own merit and originate from a true understanding, a wanton, negligent soul rarely sees their value when it applies and utilizes them. It rarely sees their efficacy, because these healing techniques are bitter to its pampered tastes and weak for its deeply damaged nature. For which Christian does not know that one must pray constantly and diligently; that God requires this; that we will be punished for laziness in praying; and that the saints prayed zealously and unceasingly? And yet, all this knowledge so rarely produces any positive results! Each person knows within himself that the convictions of his reason and conscience are either rarely or never justified by actions; and, because he rarely remembers this, he continues to live a bad and lazy life. . . .

"This is why the Holy Fathers, filled with divine wisdom and experience, focused on this—because they knew well the weakness of the human will and the denseness of the lustful human heart. As doctors who mask a bitter medicine with sweet syrup and sweeten the rim of a medicine vial with honey, they prescribed the simplest and the most authentic methods, rooted in hope and in God's help, for combating laziness and negligence in prayer, and for achieving perfection and joyful trust through loving prayer to God.

"They counsel us to contemplate as often as possible such a state in our souls and to read attentively the teaching of the Fathers on this subject. With reassurance, they assert how simple and easy it is to attain these delightful interior experiences during prayer, and also—should one long for them—a sweetness that issues from the heart; a delightful warmth and light that radiate from within; an unspeakable ecstasy; joy and inner freedom; profound peace and abundant bliss; as well as contentment in life, which are all bestowed through the activity of prayer in the heart.

"By deeply reflecting on all this, the weak and indifferent soul is warmed, strengthened, and encouraged that it can succeed in prayer. It is, as it were, enticed to the experience of praying. On this subject, Saint Isaac the Syrian says, 'The enticement for the soul is joy, which is born of hope that blossoms in the heart; and the heart flourishes in meditating on its hope and trust.' He goes on to say, 'From the beginning and to the end of this exercise, one hopes and assumes that there is a way to accomplish this, which motivates the mind to set a goal for itself. By focusing on that goal, the mind is comforted while performing the exercise.' In writing about laziness as a stumbling block to prayer and about realizing the need to renew one's zeal for praying, the Venerable Hesychius openly concludes the following, 'We desire the inner stillness of the heart for no other reason than the sweet consolations and joy that it brings the soul.'

"It follows, then, that this Father teaches that the incentive for prayer should be 'its sweet consolations and joy.' . . . Similarly, Saint Makarios the Great[19] teaches that 'we must perform our spiritual exercises (prayer) with the goal and in the hope of attaining its fruits, that is, of enjoying delight in our hearts.'

"Clear examples of the powerful means of this method can be found in numerous parts of the *Philokalia* that provide detailed descriptions of the spiritual delights of prayer. He who struggles with the affliction of laziness or aridity in prayer must read these passages as often as possible. At the same time, he must see himself as unworthy of these delights and must endlessly reproach himself for his laziness in praying."

PRIEST: "Would not such considerations lead an inexperienced person into spiritual gluttony—or what the theologians call that striving of the soul that thirsts for excessive consolations and spiritual gifts of grace, and that is not satisfied with performing good works only from obligation and duty without expecting any reward?"

PROFESSOR: "I think that in this case, the theologians warn against excessiveness or lusting after spiritual consolations, but they do not completely reject seeking sweetness and consolations while practicing the virtues. Although desiring rewards is not a sign of perfection, God does not forbid man to contemplate rewards and consolations. He, Himself, uses the idea of rewards to encourage man to keep the Commandments and to attain perfection. 'Honor your father and your mother. . . .' Now there's a commandment! And it is followed by the promise of a reward that encourages one to fulfill it: '. . . and it (will) be well with you. . . .' [Deut. 5:16]. 'If you want to be perfect, go, sell what you have and give to the poor. . . .'—this is what perfection demands, and this, too, is followed by a reward to encourage attaining perfection: '. . . and you will have treasure in heaven. . . .' [Matt. 19:21].

" 'Blessed are you on that day when men (will) hate you . . . and (will) cast out your name as evil, for the Son of Man's sake' [Luke 6:22]—this is the great demand of a heroic act, which requires unusual strength of spirit and unshakeable patience. It is for this that great rewards and consolations are promised, which are capable of rousing and supporting an unusual strength of spirit: '. . . for great is your reward in heaven' [Luke 6:23]. This is why I think that a certain desire for sweet consolations in the prayer of the heart is necessary, and that it constitutes the principal means for acquiring both diligence and efficacy in prayer. And so, all this indisputably corroborates the Father Skhimnik's reflections on the subject we have just heard about." . . .

SKHIMNIK: "Saint Macarius of Egypt, one of the great theologians, very clearly says the following on this subject, 'Just as in planting a vineyard, when much effort and labor is expended so that it bears fruit, the lack of which makes the work all in vain, so it is with prayer—if you do not see in yourself the spiritual fruit, that is, love, peace, joy and so on—your labors will have been in vain. This is why we must perform our spiritual exercise of prayer 'either with the goal or in the hope of acquiring its fruit, the delight of sweet consolation in our hearts.'

"Do you see how clearly this Holy Father resolved the issue of needing consolations during prayer? . . . By the way, this reminds me of another spiritual writer's views that I recently read, about the fact that man is drawn to pour himself out in prayer because it is so natural for him. For this reason, a study of this innate aspect of prayer could also serve as a powerful means for rousing diligence in prayer—the very means that the gentleman professor is so earnestly looking for.

"Now, I will summarize briefly for you what I can remember as being of note in that article. For example, this spiritual author writes that reason and nature both lead man to a knowledge of God. The first (reason) concludes that there can be no action without cause; and by ascending the ladder of physical creation, from the lowest form to the highest, it finally arrives at the primary cause—God. The second (nature) reveals at each step of the way a marvelous wisdom, harmony, order, and gradual progression, through which it provides sound building blocks for a ladder that starts from finite causes and ascends to the infinite one. In this way, natural man can innately attain a knowledge of God.

"This is why there never has been, and is not now, a single nation or a single primitive tribe of people that has not had at least some sort of concept of God. As a result of this concept, the most primitive islander turns his gaze to heaven, almost unwittingly and with no external inducement. He falls on his knees, as a sigh escapes from him not bear false witness, Honor your father and your mother, and You shall love your neighbor as yourself' [Matt. 19:17–19]. And one must keep all these commandments. 'For whoever shall keep the whole law, and yet stumble in one point, he is guilty of all' [James 2:10]. This is what the holy Apostle James teaches.

"And in speaking of human weakness, the holy Apostle Paul says that '. . . by the deeds of the law no flesh will be justified . . .' [Rom. 3:20]. 'For we know that the law is spiritual, but I am carnal, sold under sin. . . . For to will is present in me . . . (but) the good I will to do, I do not do; yet the evil I will not to do, that I practice. . . . For in my mind, I delight in the law of God, but in my flesh I delight in the law of sin' [Rom. 7:14–23]. When man is powerless and unable to justify himself through keeping the commandments, how can he fulfill the necessary works of the law of God? He is unable only for as long as he does not ask for this and does not pray about this. The reason given for this by the holy Apostle is, '. . . you do not have because you do not ask' [James 4:2]. Even Jesus Christ Himself says: '. . . without me you can do nothing' [John 15:5]. And this is what He teaches about working with Him: 'Abide in Me, and I in you. . . . He who abides in Me . . . bears much fruit' [John 15:4]. To be in Him means continually to know His presence and unceasingly to ask in His Name: 'If you ask anything in My name, I will do it' [John 14:14].

"Thus, it is through prayer that one acquires the ability to perform good works! You can see an example of this in the Apostle Paul himself, who prayed three times to overcome his temptations; who knelt before God the Father, that He would confirm his inner man; and who preached, in the end, that prayer must come before all else and that one must even pray unceasingly about everything. From all the above, it follows that man's spiritual salvation depends on prayer, and this is why prayer is necessary above all else. For it gives life to faith, and through it, all the virtues are acquired. In a word, everything can be achieved through prayer; without it, no works of Christian piety can be performed.

that is incomprehensible and yet natural for him. And he experiences firsthand something that is special, something that draws him upward, something that impels him toward the unknown. . . . All the natural religions have their origins in such a basic concept. And the most remarkable thing is that everywhere, *mystical prayer* constitutes the essence or the soul of each religion and manifests itself in the form of various external expressions and distinct sacrificial acts, which are more or less distorted by the ignorance of the crude and primitive understanding of pagan peoples! . . . The more the mind is amazed by this, the more insistently it demands to understand the mystery behind such a phenomenon that manifests itself in a natural inclination to pray.

"Psychology's response to this is a simple one: The source, the guiding force and the strength behind all human passions and actions is an inherent love of self. The fundamental and universal concept of self-preservation clearly corroborates this. The goal of each human desire, undertaking, and action is to satisfy this love of self and the pursuit of personal gain, and natural man must satisfy this need throughout his life. Yet the human spirit cannot be satisfied with anything tangible, and the inherent love of self will never deviate from its objectives. As a result, the desires grow deeper and deeper, and the search for personal gain intensifies, as they flood the imagination and incite the emotions to participate in this activity.

"The effusion of these interior feelings, and the self-impelled desire, constitute the natural stimulus to pray. They are the demands of self-love, which achieves its own goals with great difficulty. The less successful man is, and the more intensely focused on his own personal gain, the more he desires, and the more intensely this desire pours itself out in prayer. And he appeals to the Unknown Source of All Being to fulfill his desire. In this manner, the inherent love of self—the prime element of life—is the fundamental cause that rouses natural man to pray!

"The all-wise Creator of life instilled in human nature the capacity of self-love precisely as an inducement, as the Fathers call it, to entice and to elevate fallen humanity to heavenly communion.

" Oh! If only man would not distort this capacity, if only he would preserve its excellence for his spiritual life! He would then possess the powerful encouragement and resources that he needs on his journey toward moral perfection. But, alas! All too often does man transform this noble capacity into the corrupt passion of self-love, making it an instrument of his lower nature!"

STARETS: "My dearest visitors, I thank you from the bottom of my heart! Your discussions, so redemptive for my soul, delighted me immensely and were most instructive for one as inexperienced as I. May the Lord reward you with His grace for your edifying love. . . ."

All present bid their farewells.

The Seventh Meeting

"*. . . pray one for another that you may be healed.*"

—James 5:16

PILGRIM: "My devout traveling companion the professor and I could not depart without fulfilling our mutual desire to bid you a final farewell and to ask you to pray for us. . . ."

PROFESSOR: "Yes, we have understood your sincerity and those redemptive conversations which delighted us in your home and in the company of your friends. This memory will forever remain in our hearts, as a pledge of communion and Christian love in the distant country where we are headed."

STARETS: "Thank you for remembering me and for your love. By the way, you came just at the right moment! There are two travelers staying with me: a Moldavian monk and a hermit who has been living in solitude in a forest for twenty years. They would like to meet you—I'll go get them. . . .

"Here they are!"

PILGRIM: "Ah! How blessed is the life of a hermit! And how conducive it is to bringing a soul undistractedly to union with God! The silence of the forest is like the Garden of Eden, where the sweet tree of life grows in the prayerful heart of a hermit! If only I had some money to feed myself, I think that I would always live as a hermit."

PROFESSOR: "For us, everything always appears exceptionally good from a distance. Yet experience convinces us that every place with advantages also has its disadvantages. Of course, for the melancholy personality that is inclined to solitude, the hermit's life is attractive. Yet how dangerous it can be to live such a life! The history of asceticism contains numerous examples of how hermits and ascetics who abandoned all contact with people fell into megalomania and deep delusion."

HERMIT: "It amazes me how frequently one hears in Russia, not only in monasteries, but even among certain God-fearing lay people, that those who desire to live a hermit's life or to practice interior prayer are deterred from pursuing this because of fear that they will perish from delusion. Those who insist on this offer examples to substantiate the conclusions of their own minds; because they themselves shun the interior life, they urge others to avoid it as well. . . . I think that this originates from either a lack of understanding and spiritual illumination, or from one's own laziness in regard to the valiant spiritual efforts required to live a contemplative life. And they envy others who are not as enlightened as they, yet who might surpass them in attaining to higher levels of knowledge. . . .

"It is very unfortunate that those who are so convinced do not grasp what the Holy Fathers say on this subject, when they openly and firmly state that one must have no fears or doubts in calling on God. If certain people actually did succumb to self-deception and mental aberrations, this was the result of pride, of not having spiritual guidance, and of mistaking certain visions and thoughts as being from God. They go on to say that when such temptations do occur, they could lead to experience and a crown of glory, because God swiftly provides help in such struggles. Dare to try! 'Fear not, for I am with you!' says Jesus Christ (Saint Gregory of Sinai).

"It follows from this that it is useless to fear and to avoid the interior life on the pretext of a risk of falling into self-deception because a humble realization of one's own sins; baring one's soul to a spiritual guide; and *pure prayer*—free from all thoughts and images—provide a sure and safe defense against the delusion that so many fear and that causes them to avoid the contemplative life. Incidentally, they are the ones who are in delusion, according to Saint Philotheus of Sinai, who says the following from his own experience, 'Many monks do not understand the delusions of their own minds with which the demons torture them; that is, they diligently focus their efforts on one thing only—practicing external acts of virtue. Yet they neglect their intellects, that is, the interior contemplative life, for they are not enlightened and have no knowledge of it.' Saint Gregory of Sinai corroborates this: 'If others even tell them that they have experienced grace at work within themselves, they become envious and call it a delusion.' "

PROFESSOR: "Permit me to ask you the following: certainly the realization of one's own sins is easy for anyone who attends to his interior life, but what should you do when you have no spiritual director who can guide you in the interior life from experience; and who, after you have bared your soul to him, could offer you correct and reliable guidance for living the spiritual life? In such a case, is it surely not better to avoid the contemplative life, rather than to attempt it on one's own, without a guide? . . . Furthermore, it is hard for me to understand how, by placing one's self in God's presence, one can maintain perfect *freedom from all thoughts and images*. This is not natural, because our souls or minds cannot imagine anything without any shape, in absolute *formlessness*. And in focusing one's mind on contemplating God, why not imagine Jesus Christ or the Most Holy Trinity, and so on?"

HERMIT: "The guidance of an experienced and knowledgeable director in spiritual matters or of a starets—to whom one can easily, trustingly, and profitably bears one's soul, thoughts, and experiences each day on the path of learning to live the interior life—does constitute the main condition for practicing interior prayer by one who has taken the vow of silence. However, in cases when such a guide cannot be found, the same Holy Fathers, who stress the need for one, grant an exception. The Venerable Nicephorus the Solitary clearly teaches the following on this subject: 'A true and knowledgeable guide is necessary for practicing the interior activity of the heart. If there is none, then one must be sought diligently. If you cannot find one, then appeal to God, with a broken heart, to help you find instruction and guidance in the teachings of the Holy Fathers and to verify this, and check yourself against the words of God contained in Holy Scripture.'

"At the same time, one must also take into consideration that he who seeks with genuine and ardent desire can learn something beneficial and instructive even from simple people. For the Holy Fathers assure us that if you turn to a Saracen for guidance, but do so with faith and the right intention, even he could offer valuable advice. Yet if you seek guidance from a Prophet, without faith and true intentions, even he could not satisfy you. . . . Saint Macarius the Great of Egypt is an example of this; a simple peasant once taught him something that helped him to overcome a passion.

"On the subject of *no thoughts or images*, that is, not imagining or accepting any visions—of any light, any angel, of Christ or any of the saints—and rejecting all thoughts while practicing contemplation, the Holy Fathers certainly command this from their own experience, because the imagination can easily produce or, as it were, bring forth concepts or thoughts in the mind. For this reason, someone without experience can be enticed by such thoughts, can mistake them for revelations of grace, and can fall into self-delusion, especially since Holy Scripture says that 'even Satan can present himself as an angel of light.' The mind can easily and naturally be in a state that is *free of any thoughts or images*, and it can maintain this state even while placing itself in the presence of God. This is because the power of the imagination can clearly envision something *formless*, and it can maintain this while perceiving things that are invisible to the physical eye and that are without physical shape or form.

"Take, for example, how we perceive and experience our own souls—or air, warmth, and cold. When someone is cold, he can easily imagine warmth in his mind, even though it is without shape or form and is not visible to the eye or tangible to the one who is experiencing the cold! Similarly, the presence of the spiritual and unattainable Being of God can be perceived by the mind and can be known by the heart in the perfect *absence of thought and image*."

PILGRIM: "During my travels, I also happened to hear from godly people in search of salvation that they were afraid to attempt any practice of the interior spiritual life because of warnings about falling into delusion. Some were helped by what I read to them from the teachings of Saint Gregory of Sinai in the *Philokalia*, who said that 'the activity of the heart cannot be the work of delusion (not as mental activity can). For even if the enemy wanted to transform the warmth of the heart into his own irritating heat, or to substitute sensual pleasure for the joy of the heart—time, experience and the very sensation of it would expose this deceit, these tricks of his, even to those who are not so familiar with his deviousness."

"I also met others, who even after experiencing the life of silent solitude and the prayer of the heart, unfortunately fell into despair and abandoned the interior prayer of the heart that they had learned, because they encountered some kinds of obstacles or experienced the weakness of sinning!"

PROFESSOR: "Well, but that's very natural! It has happened to me, too, that sometimes I am inclined to let myself get carried away by distractions or to commit some sin. . . . Since the interior prayer of the heart is a holy activity and represents union with God, then is it appropriate, and not an impertinence, to introduce a holy activity into a sinful heart, without first cleansing it with silent humble repentance and with suitable preparation for communion with God? Better to stand mute before God than to utter *senseless words* from a heart that is distracted and filled with darkness."

MONK: "How very unfortunate that you think this way! Thoughts of *despair*, which is more abominable than any other sin, are the main weapon that the realm of darkness has against us. . . . Our Holy Fathers, who had great experience, teach something very different in this case. The Venerable Nikitas Stithatos says that even if you were to fall into the depths of the evil abyss of hell, you must not despair, but quickly turn to God, and He will restore your fallen heart and give you a strength greater than you had before.

"Thus, after each fall and after each time sin wounds your heart, you must immediately place yourself in the presence of God to be healed and cleansed. This is similar to something that is contaminated and which becomes less contagious after a certain amount of exposure to the rays of the sun. Many spiritual teachers speak strongly on this subject. While waging war against the enemies of salvation—our passions—one must never abandon any life-giving exercises, that is, calling on Jesus Christ, Who dwells within our hearts! Not only must our sinful actions never turn us away from walking in the presence of God and from interior prayer—which only causes anxiety, despair, sorrow—they must also be instrumental in turning us as quickly as possible toward God. A child who is guided by his mother when he first starts to walk will quickly turn and firmly cling to her when he stumbles."

HERMIT: "What I think is that the spirit of despair and tumultuous, doubtful thoughts are more easily roused in a distracted mind and in the absence of guarding silence in one's self. In peaceful, silent solitude and isolation, the ancient Fathers, who were filled with the Wisdom of God, achieved victory over despair and were granted interior illumination and the strength to place all their hope in God. They even passed on to us some profitable and wise advice about this: 'Sit in the silence of your cell, and it will teach you everything.' "

PROFESSOR: "Since I trust you, I would very much like to hear your opinion of my thoughts on silence and on the benefits of a solitary life, which you praise so highly and which is so loved by the hermits. Here is what I think about it: Since the Creator designed human nature in a way that makes people necessarily depend on each other, and subsequently they are obligated to help each other in life, to work for each other, and to contribute to each other's well-being, this social aspect forms the basis for the well-being of all humanity and for the love of one's neighbor. Yet by isolating himself from contact with people, how can a solitary hermit be of any service to his neighbor by living an idle life, and what could he contribute to the well-being of human society? He is completely breaking within himself the Creator's law regarding loving communion with others of his own kind and being a positive influence on his fellow man!"

HERMIT: "Since your opinion of the silent solitary life is not correct, your conclusions are also wrong. Let's look at this more closely.

1. Not only does a hermit living in silent solitude *not* live an idle or empty life, but he is far more active than if he were living in society. He tirelessly functions on the level of his higher rational nature; he observes, he understands, he keeps vigil over the state and the progress of his moral life. This is the true goal of the silent solitary life! And as much benefit as he derives from this for his own perfection, that much does his neighbor derive from it, who does not have the opportunity to work undistractedly on himself to develop his moral life. For in sharing his inner experiences, either by speaking of them (in rare instances) or by passing them on in writing, the observant solitary contributes to the spiritual well-being and the salvation of his brethren. And he accomplishes this far better than if he were to per-

form social or private charitable work, because the private and humane charitable work of lay people is always limited by the small numbers of philanthropists. While he who performs works of 'moral charity,' gaining from experience the knowledge and the means for perfecting the spiritual life, becomes a philanthropist for entire nations. His experience and teaching are passed on from generation to generation, for we ourselves know this and it has helped us since ancient times. In no way is this different from the good works done for the sake of Christ and out of Christian love—it even surpasses them in its far-reaching effects.

2. The good and highly beneficial influence of a hermit on his fellow man is evident not only in the sharing of his instructive observations on the interior life. The very example of his solitary life also benefits the diligent lay person by leading him to self-knowledge and awakening in him a reverential attitude. . . . After hearing about a pious hermit or walking by his solitary abode, a person living in the world is roused to living a devout life. He remembers who man was meant to be in this life and how possible it is for man to return to the original contemplative state in which he was created by the hands of the Creator. The hermit teaches through his very silence. Through his very life, he gives much. He edifies and persuades us to seek God. . . .

3. The benefits mentioned above originate from a true solitary life of silence, one that is illumined and sustained by grace. Yet even if a hermit did not have these gifts of grace to become a beacon for the world, even if he embarked on a life of silent solitude only to avoid contact with others, because his laziness and carelessness would make him a temptation and a bad example, even then he would have a positive influence on people around him, as a gardener who trims dry and barren branches and uproots harmful plants to encourage the growth of better and healthier ones. In itself, this is a great thing and beneficial to society—that through his ascetic life, a hermit shuns tempta-

tions. This would be impossible in a life among people, which is full of temptation, and would corrupt the morality of those around him.

"Saint Isaac the Syrian says the following about a life of silent solitude: 'If we gather all worldly activity on one side, and place silence on the other, we will find that the latter tips the scales. Do not compare those who perform signs and miracles, and who are powerful, with those who live a true life of solitary silence. Love the inactivity of silence more than feeding the hungry of the world and converting many nations to God. It is better to free yourself from the bonds of sin than to free slaves from bondage.'

"Even the most ancient wise men knew the value of silence. Under the tutelage of the philosopher Plotinus, the Neo-Platonic school of thought, with its many renowned followers, emphasized developing the contemplative interior life, which is attained primarily in the silence of solitude. . . . One spiritual writer said that even if a government achieved the highest level of education and morality, it would need not only civil servants, but also contemplatives to perpetuate the spirit of truth—to inherit it from past generations, to preserve it and to pass it on to future generations. Such people in the Church are its hermits, ascetics, and anchorites."

PILGRIM: "It seems to me that no one has assessed more correctly the superiority of silent solitude than Saint John of the Ladder: 'Silent solitude,' he says, 'is the mother of prayer; a return from the prison of sin; imperceptible progress in virtue; and a perpetual ascent to heaven.' There were times when even Jesus Christ stopped teaching the people and went off by Himself to pray and to find peace, in order to teach us the value of and the need for silence and solitude.

"Contemplative solitaries are like pillars that support the pious spiritual life of the Church with their unceasing prayers. Even in ancient times, we know that many devout lay people, even the tsars and their dignitaries, visited hermits and anchorites to ask for their prayers, so they would be spiritually strengthened and saved. It follows then that a solitary hermit can serve his fellow man and contribute to the well-being of others by praying in solitude."

PROFESSOR: "Now this is another issue that I have trouble understanding: We Christians are all accustomed to asking for each other's prayers, to desiring that another prays for me, especially someone whom I view as a trusted member of the Church. Is this not merely a requirement of our self-love, an acquired habit of repeating what we have heard from others, or something our mind has devised without giving it any serious thought? Does God really require man's petitions, when He already foresaw and ordered everything according to His all-good providence, and not according to our desires, and knew and determined everything before we ask for it, as it is written in Holy Scripture? Can the prayers of many really sway His decisions more powerfully than the prayers of one individual? Wouldn't God be biased in that case? Can someone else's prayers really save me, when it is our own actions that either honor or shame us? This (I think) is why asking for another person's prayers is only the devout product of a pious courtesy, which is a sign of humility and a desire to please one another in a respectful manner—and nothing more!"

MONK: "It could appear to be so, if you look at it superficially and from the viewpoint of elemental philosophy. However, spiritual reason that is sustained by the light of religion, and that is taught through the experience of living the interior life, probes more deeply, contemplates in a more illumined manner, and mystically reveals something that is completely contrary to what you have just presented! . . . So that we can understand this more quickly and more clearly, let's use an illustration, and we'll verify it in Scripture. Take, for example, the student who went to a teacher to learn. His limited abilities, not to speak of his laziness and lack of concentration, prevented the student from making progress in his studies and labeled him as lazy and a failure. This made him sad, and he didn't know what to do or how to overcome his deficiencies. One day he ran into another student, a classmate, who was more capable, more diligent, and a better student, and he told him about his problem. The other student empathized with him and suggested that they work together: 'Let's study together,' he said, 'it will encourage us and will be more fun, so we'll learn much more.'

"So they began to study together, sharing what each one learned. And what do you think happened after a few days? The poor student became diligent; he acquired a love of learning, and his carelessness was replaced by zeal and an ability to comprehend what he was learning. All this had a positive influence on his personality and moral character, while his more capable friend became even better and more industrious. By influencing each other, they acquired mutual benefit. . . .

"But that's very natural, because man is born into a community of people. He learns to think and to understand through other people, from whom he acquires his habits, emotional development, and goals. In a word, he learns everything from the examples of others like himself. Since people's lives are tightly interwoven and powerfully affect each other, a person will take on the customs, the traditions, and the moral code of the society he lives in. Consequently, a dispassionate person can become impassioned; a dull-witted person, clever; and a lazy person can become industrious through interacting with other people. A spirit can pass from one person to another and can exert a positive influence on the other. It can inspire the other to pray, to be vigilant; it can encourage the other in times of despair and can discourage the other from a sinful life by encouraging him to live a devout one. As a result, the one who helps others can become more devout can perform greater ascetic feats and can become more pleasing to God. . . . This is the mystery of praying for others, which explains that devout custom among Christians of praying for one another and asking the brethren for their prayers!

"From this it is obvious that it is not God who is satisfied by a multitude of prayers and petitions (as are powerful earthly leaders). It is the very spirit and power of prayer that cleanse and rouse the soul for whom prayers are offered and render it capable of union with God. . . . If praying for each other is so productive, then it is obvious that prayers for the departed are as mutually beneficial, because of the deep bonds that exist between this life and the next, and that these prayers can bring the souls of the Church Militant into communion with the souls of the Church Triumphant or with the departed, which is the same thing.

"Although everything that I have said is psychological reasoning, we can still be certain of its truth by reading Holy Scripture!

"(1) This is what Jesus Christ said to the Apostle Peter: 'But I have prayed for you, that your faith should not fail. . . .' [Luke 22:32]. In this case, the power of Christ's prayer strengthens Peter's spirit and encourages him when his faith is tested; (2) When the Apostle Peter was in prison, the Church diligently prayed for him. Here we learn how communal prayer can help during difficult times in life . . . ; (3) But the command to pray for one's neighbor is expressed most clearly by the apostle James: 'Confess your trespasses to one another, and pray for one another, that you may be healed. The effective, fervent prayer of a righteous man avails much' [James 5:16]. The conclusions of psychology that I mentioned above are definitely corroborated here. . . .

"And what can we say about the Apostle Paul who is given to us as an example of praying for one another? One writer observes that this example of the Apostle Paul should teach us just how necessary it is to pray for one another—when even such a holy and strong spiritual champion admits that he needs the help of the prayers of others. In his Epistle to the Hebrews, he expresses this request in the following manner: 'Pray for us; for we are confident that we have a good conscience, in all things desiring to live honorably' [Heb. 13:18].

"After hearing this, how foolish it would be to rely solely on one's own prayers and accomplishments, especially when such a humble man, so holy and so filled with grace, asks his brethren (the Hebrews) to join their prayers to his own. Given this, with what humility, sincerity, and loving communion should we strive not to reject, not to scorn the help that comes through the prayers of the weakest of the brethren—when the wise spirit of the Apostle Paul did not discriminate in such cases, but asked for the prayers of the entire community, knowing that the power of God is revealed in the weak and, consequently, could even sometimes be revealed in those whose prayers may appear weak. . . .

"Once we are convinced by this example, let us also note that praying for one another sustains the unity of Christian love that is commanded by God, that it is proof of the humility and the spirit of the one who prays; and that it inspires mutual prayer."

PROFESSOR: "Your analysis and everything that you presented in support of it are wonderful and precise, but I would be curious to hear from you about the very method and formula for praying for others. For I think that if the benefit of prayer and the enticement to pray depend on an active relationship with one's neighbors, and primarily on a continually exerted influence by the spirit of the one who is praying on the spirit of the one who needs to be prayed for, then would not such a concentrated effort by the soul distract it from unceasingly placing itself in the invisible presence of God and from pouring itself out to God as a result of its own need to do so? Yet, if you show concern for your neighbor only by remembering him once or twice a day and by asking God to help him, will this be enough to strengthen the soul of the person you are praying for and to draw him into communion? In other words, I'd like to know how, by what means, I can pray for others."

MONK: "When offered to God, and no matter what it is about, prayer should not, indeed it even cannot, distract one from placing one's self in the presence of God—because if prayer is an outpouring to God, then inevitably this would have to happen in His presence. . . . Regarding the question of how to pray for one's neighbor, it should be noted that the power of such prayer resides in a sincere Christian relationship with him and that the influence it exerts on his soul depends on the level of that relationship. For this reason, when you remember someone (your neighbor) or when you set aside a specific time to do this, you should turn your mind to God and offer your prayer as follows: 'Merciful Lord! Your will be done, that desires all men to be saved and to be brought to the knowledge of the Truth! Have mercy on and save Your servant (give his name). Accept this, my wish, as a cry of the love that You command for us!'

"Usually, these words are said at times when the soul experiences special stirrings or when one is praying with chotki. I have personally seen what positive effect such prayer can have on the one who is being prayed for."

PROFESSOR: "I must forever remember this instructive conversation and the enlightening knowledge that I have gleaned from listening to your opinions and discussions, and I must extend my respect and my gratitude to all of you from my beholden heart."

PILGRIM AND PROFESSOR: "And so, the time has come for us to depart. In parting, we sincerely ask for your prayers, so they may accompany us in our travels!"

SKHIMNIK: "Now may the God of peace Who raised our Lord Jesus Christ from the dead, that great Shepherd of the Sheep, through the blood of the everlasting covenant, make you complete in every good work to do His will, working in you what is well pleasing in His sight, through Jesus Christ, to Whom be glory forever and ever. Amen" [Heb. 13:20–21].

Appendix

THREE KEYS TO THE INTERIOR TREASURE HOUSE OF PRAYER

Found in the Wealth of the Spiritual Teachings of the Holy Fathers

Your word I have hidden in my heart. . . .

—Ps. 119:11

It behooves the mind to be on guard against every deception and to strive for the sublime.

—Kataphigiota, ch. 19

Since each person possesses his own unique characteristics, predispositions, and abilities, he will use different ways and means to achieve one and the same goal. In like manner, there are many ways to achieve the goal of the interior activity of prayer, as can be seen from reading the insights of the Holy Fathers.

Among these, the only universal methods for succeeding both in prayer and in living a Christian life are *unconditional obedience*, according to Simeon the New Theologian—the labor of good works and of valiant ascetic spiritual struggles, as the Church expresses in its hymns: *Inspired by God, you dedicated yourself to good works and were raised to the pinnacle of contemplation* (*troparion* to a holy martyr); *formal prayer*, as a supplication for attaining interior prayer: "Lord, teach us to pray" [Luke 11:1]; *special acts of grace*, as, for example, Kapso Kalivitis, who after two years of persistent prayers to the Mother of God, once venerated her icon and suddenly experienced sweetness and warmth that filled his heart; and the young George, whose simple prayers unexpectedly enlightened him and granted him the unceasing self-acting prayer; and other similar examples.

There are other essential methods for achieving interior prayer, which are, as it were, directly related to it. The following three are given by the Holy Fathers:

1. *constancy* in invoking the Name of Jesus Christ;
2. *attention* while invoking His Name;
3. *entering one's self*, or, as the Fathers of the Church say, *the mind entering the heart.*

Since these methods open the Kingdom of God within us and the treasure chest of interior spiritual prayer in our hearts in the fastest and most convenient manner, it is highly appropriate to call them the *keys* to this hidden repository.

The First Key

If *quantity* leads to *quality*, then *constant*, almost uninterrupted calling on the Name of Jesus Christ, though initially done in a distracted manner, can also lead to attentiveness and warmth of the heart, insofar as human nature is capable of acquiring a specific disposition through constant repetition and habit. One spiritual writer said that to learn to do something well, one must do it with great frequency. Saint Hesychius says that constancy engenders habit, which then becomes as second nature (Text 7). As seen from the observations of experienced people, this occurs in relation to interior prayer in the following manner: The one who desires to achieve interior prayer resolves to invoke the Name of God constantly, almost uninterruptedly—that is, verbally to recite the Jesus Prayer: *Lord Jesus Christ, Son of God, have mercy on me a sinner*—or, sometimes, in its abbreviated form, *Lord Jesus Christ, have mercy on me*, as Saint Gregory of Sinai teaches. He also adds that the abbreviated invocation is more convenient for the beginner, although he does not refute either form; he merely advises that using fewer words in prayer facilitates becoming accustomed to the invocation.

In order to rouse one's self increasingly to unceasing prayer, the one who prays sets a rule for himself: Within a given period of time, he will recite the prayer a specific number of times, that is, so many hundred or thousand times during the day and the night, using his chotki; and he will not rush, but will exert his tongue and lips to pronounce the words clearly. After a certain time, the lips and the tongue will become so accustomed to this, they will pronounce the Name of God with little effort, as if self-driven, and even silently. The mind then begins to listen to the words pronounced by the tongue and is gradually drawn away from its distractedness and turns its attention to the prayer. In the end, as the Fathers describe this, the mind could even descend into the heart. That is, by returning into the heart, the mind warms it with the radiance of divine love, and then the heart itself—freely, without any coercion and with unspeakable sweetness—begins to call on the Name of Jesus Christ, as it pours itself out to God in an unceasing stream of tenderness, "I sleep but my heart is awake. . . ." [Song of Sol. 5:2]. Saint Hesychius spoke splendidly of the benefits of constant mental invocation of the Name of Jesus Christ: *As heavy rains soften the earth, in the same manner our joyful invocation of Christ's name creates and gladdens the soil of our hearts, the more frequently it is invoked.*

Although this method, rooted in the experience and the insights of the holy Fathers, is sufficient to guide one to attaining interior prayer, there are other, more superior methods, such as *attention* and the *mind entering the heart*. The first of these is more appropriate for those who have not yet learned attention and are not yet able to work effectively on their hearts; or it can serve to prepare and to lead them on to subsequent methods. But then, as Nicephorus the Solitary says, given the variety of talents and abilities, each one must choose what suits him best.

The Second Key

Attention is safe-keeping (guarding) the mind, as Nicephorus the Solitary said; or, attention is collecting the mind within one's self and focusing it exclusively on a given subject, while cutting off all unrelated thoughts and imaginings. Citing the words of the Venerable Nilus, Saints Callistus and Ignatius assure us how important this is for prayer: "Attention which seeks prayer will unfailingly find it. For prayer is the result of attention more than of anything else, and thus we should guard our attention" (*Dobrotolyubiye*, part II, chapter 24).

Saint Hesychius writes something similar: "The more you guard your mind against thoughts, the stronger will be the desire with which you pray to Jesus" (Text 90);[20] and also: ". . . the *air* of the heart is filled with joy and stillness . . . as a result of intense attention. . . ." (Text 92),[21] which ". . . is as necessary to prayer . . . as a candle is to a lantern . . ." (Text 102).[22]

In his teaching on interior prayer, Nicephorus the Solitary concludes that if what he describes does not help one to enter the heart, then one should pray with as much attention as possible, and this will undoubtedly open the door to the heart and give rise to interior prayer. He assures us that this knowledge has been derived from experience. And Holy Scripture confirms the truth that union with God is not possible without attention: "Be still and know that I am God" [Ps. 46:10].

And so, the one who desires through attention to attain interior prayer must remain in solitude as much as possible and must avoid conversations with people. He must not rush through his prayers or attempt too much right away; rather, he must pace himself and focus his mind on the words of prayer as when carefully reading a book. As far as possible, he must chase away thoughts and must do his utmost to heed Jesus, Whom he invokes, and His good will, which he supplicates. At times, having recited a prayer, he must be silent for a time, as if awaiting a response from God, and must strive to remain attentive even when distracted. Always remember that it is for the sake of the Lord that you have resolved to practice continuous attention to prayer, while emptying your mind of thoughts.

The Third Key

The third key is entering one's self or into the heart. Instead of putting forth our own thoughts on this, let us present what the Holy Fathers describe and teach about entering the self and entering the heart, along with the methods that their own experience showed to be reliable guideposts to true spiritual interior prayer. We will present here the teachings of the Holy Fathers in their own words, and for the sake of convenience, we will classify them by dividing them into three categories and will arrange them in the following order:

The *First Category* will consist of the following Fathers who have passed on to us their complete teaching on the Jesus Prayer: (1) Simeon the New Theologian, (2) Gregory of Sinai, (3) Nicephorus the Solitary, and (4) the Monks Ignatius of Xanthopoulos and Callistus.

The *Second Category* will consist of the following Fathers who have passed on to us brief sayings about interior prayer: (1) Hesychius, (Priest) of Jerusalem, (2) Philotheus of Sinai, (3) Theoleptus, Metropolitan (of Philadelphia), and (4) Barsanuphius and John.

The *Third Category* will consist of *The Most Edifying Narrative of Abba Philemon*, which presents the complete way of a valiant, ascetic, spiritual life.

THE TEACHINGS OF THE HOLY FATHERS ON THE INTERIOR PRAYER OF THE HEART

A. First Category

(1) The Teaching of Saint Simeon the New Theologian

Saint Simeon the New Theologian presents the way for entering the heart in his third method of prayer (in article 68, page 163, Russian translation, 2nd edition):

"The third method of prayer is truly splendid and difficult to explain. For those who have not experienced it firsthand, it is not only hard to comprehend, but also appears inconceivable. In fact, there are few in our time who practice this form of prayer, even though it destroys whatever traps and wiles that demons use to entice the mind toward numerous and varied thoughts. For only when the mind is free from everything it is able, unhindered and in a timely manner, to examine thoughts suggested by the demons; to repel them easily, and to offer its prayers to God with a pure heart."

After listing the conditions for successfully practicing this form of prayer—namely, perfect obedience and preserving a clean conscience in relation to God, people, and things—and after encouraging us to do everything as if we were standing before the Face of God—he goes on to say:

"By doing this, you will pave for yourself a true and reliable path to the third method of prayer, which is the following: while the heart prays, the mind must guard it and must steadfastly circulate its attention within; and it must offer up prayers to God from the depths of the heart.

"Everything is contained in this: work at it until you experience and partake of a relationship with the Lord. When the mind is finally established in the heart, and when it tastes and experiences with the heart how good the Lord is, it will not want to leave the place of the heart. Then, the mind will say as did Saint Peter: '. . . it is good for us to be here. . .' [Matt. 17:4]; and it will always gaze into the heart and always commune with it there, while driving off all thoughts sown by the devil.

"To those who do not understand this activity and who have no experience of it, it mostly appears somewhat difficult and burdensome. Yet those who have tasted the sweetness which it brings, and who have been delighted by it in the depths of their hearts—they cry out with Saint Paul and say, 'Who shall separate us from the love of Christ? . . . [Rom. 8:35]. Therefore, after hearing the Lord say that '. . . out of the heart proceed evil thoughts, murders, adulteries, fornication, thefts, false witness, blasphemies . . .' and that 'these are the things which defile a man. . . .' [Matt. 15:19–20]; and after reading elsewhere in the Gospels that we are commanded to cleanse '. . . the inside of the cup and the dish, that the outside of them may be clean also . . .' [Matt. 23:26], our Holy Fathers renounced all other spiritual activity and gave themselves over entirely to doing this one thing—that is, guarding the heart. For they were convinced that by practicing this, they would easily attain every virtue; whereas without this, they would not attain a single one.

"They all practiced this above all else and wrote about it. Let him who wishes read their works; let him read what Mark the Wrestler wrote about this; what John of the Ladder said; the Venerable Hesychius (of Jerusalem); Philotheus of Sinai; Abba Isaiah; Barsanuphius the Great; and others.

"If you wish to learn the right way to do this (that is, to enter the heart and to abide there), I will tell you about it.

"Before all else, you should observe three things: *freedom from all cares*, not only the good, but also the bad and vain ones, or, in other words, be dead to all things; a *clear conscience* in everything, so that it does not denounce you in anything; and *absolute dispassion*, so that your thoughts do not incline toward anything. Then sit by yourself in a special, quiet place and close the door. Draw your mind away from thoughts of any temporal and vain things; bend your head to your chest and focus your attention inside (not in your head, but in your heart); turn both your mind and your physical eyes on that place and regulate your breathing. With your mind there, try every possible means to find the place of the heart, so that when you have found it, your mind will remain exclusively there. At first, you will find a certain darkness, and a hardness inside; but afterward, if day and night you continually exercise your attention in this manner, you will acquire a certain unending joy. By compelling the mind to practice this, it will find the place of the heart; and there, inside, it will instantly see things that it had never before seen or known. From that moment on—no matter where any thought may arise or appear from, and before it can come inside, be entertained, or envisaged—the mind will instantly drive it from that place and destroy it with the Name of Jesus—that is, *Lord, Jesus Christ, have mercy on me.* Also, from that moment, the mind acquires an anger toward the demons and begins to drive off and to vanquish them. Regarding other results derived from this exercise, with God's help, you will learn them from your own experience through guarding the attention and clinging to Jesus, that is, to His prayer: *Lord, Jesus Christ, have mercy on me!*"

(2) The Teaching of Saint Gregory of Sinai

Saint Gregory of Sinai presents his teaching on the interior prayer of the heart, and on how it can become a habitual practice, in three of his texts on silence and prayer, found in the *Dobrotolyubiye*, part I, pages 112–119. We present here a synopsis.

Having taken on the Spirit of life in Jesus Christ, we should do as the cherubim and converse with the Lord through the pure prayer of the heart. Yet because we do not understand the magnificence, the honor, and the glory of the grace of rebirth, and because we do not attend to our spiritual growth by keeping the commandments, so that our intellect attains to contemplation, we give in to negligence, through which we succumb to impassioned habits and descend into the abyss of insensitivity and darkness. It also happens that we seldom remember if God even exists, and we don't know anything about how we should act as God's children by grace. We believe, but our faith is not active, and though we are reborn in the Spirit through Baptism, we continue to live according to the flesh. If sometimes we repent and begin to keep the commandments, we do so only superficially and not in a spiritual manner, and we grow so detached from the spiritual life that seeing others living it appears to us as something blameworthy and as delusion. Thus we live until we die—with a dead spirit—not living and acting in Christ and according to the definition that what is born of the Spirit must be spiritual.

Moreover, we do not destroy what we accept through Holy Baptism in Christ, but only bury it as some treasure in the ground. Yet wisdom and gratitude demand that we uncover and reveal it. How can we do this?

There are two methods for doing this: (1) this gift is discovered through great effort to keep the commandments, so that to the degree that we keep them, to that degree will this gift reveal its brilliance and splendor, and (2) it is uncovered and revealed by unceasing invocation of Jesus Christ or by constant remembrance of God, which is the same thing. While the first method is powerful, the second is more so; thus the first method acquires its full strength from the second. Therefore, if we sincerely desire to discover this blessed seed within ourselves, we must not delay in acquiring the habit of this second method or rule for the heart, and we must attain only this unseen and formless activity of prayer in our hearts, until it warms our hearts and ignites in them an inexpressible love for the Lord.

The activity of this prayer in the heart can occur in two ways: sometimes the mind leads the way, clinging to the Lord in the heart through constant remembrance, and sometimes the activity of the prayer, rousing itself ahead of time with the flame of joy, draws the mind down into the heart and constrains it to call on the Lord Jesus and to stand devoutly before His presence. In the first case, the activity of prayer begins to reveal itself as the passions diminish through keeping the commandments, and by the warmth in the heart that results from intense invocation of the Lord Jesus. In the second case, the Spirit draws the mind into the heart; and it joins the mind to the heart in the depths of the heart, thus restraining the mind from its accustomed wandering. With these two forms of prayer, sometimes the prayer of the mind is active and sometimes contemplative: through action, and with God's help, it conquers the passions; through contemplation, it gazes upon God, as much as this is accessible to man.

Active mental prayer of the heart is practiced in the following manner: Sit on a small stool up to about seven inches high. Draw your mind down from your head into your heart and hold it there. Then call out with your mind and heart, *Lord, Jesus Christ, have mercy on me!*, while regulating your breathing so that it is not uncontrolled, for this can scatter your thoughts. If you notice that thoughts are appearing, ignore them—even the simple and good ones, not only the vain and impure. By confining the mind in the heart and constantly, patiently calling on the Lord Jesus, you will soon vanquish and banish these thoughts, conquering them invisibly with God's Name. Saint John of the Ladder says: *With the Name of Jesus flog the foes, for there is no surer weapon against them, either in heaven or on earth.*

If the mind becomes exhausted during such an exercise, and if the body and the heart ache from the exertion of joining with the mind and the constant invocation of the Lord Jesus, then get up and chant the psalms or reflect on a certain passage from Scripture or on death, or else read something, or do some manual work or occupy yourself with something else.

When you undertake this exercise of prayer, it is appropriate for you to read only books on teachings about the interior life, about sobriety and prayer—namely, by John of the Ladder, Isaac the Syrian, the ascetical works of Maximus the Confessor, Simeon the New Theologian, Hesychios, Philotheus of Sinai, and other similar works. For a time, set aside any books on other subjects, not because they are bad but because it is not appropriate for you to read them while you are involved in this pursuit, and because they can distract your mind from prayer. Do not read too much, but concentrate on what you are reading and master it.

Do not abandon prayer books. Some people strictly adhere to many rules of prayer; some completely abandon prayer books and pray to the Lord only with the prayer of the mind. You, however, should find a middle ground: do not opt for too many prayers, for this will confuse you, but neither abandon them completely in moments of sickness or weakness. If you see that the prayer is acting within you and continues in your heart on its own, do not abandon it and turn to a prayer book. This would mean that you are leaving God inside your heart, going outside of it and striking up a conversation with Him from outside the heart. Those who have not yet acquired this self-acting prayer should recite numerous prayers, even to an excess, so that they would remain constantly immersed in reciting these many and varied prayers, until this exhausting exercise warms the heart and sparks the prayer of the heart. The Fathers teach that he who finally experiences this gift of grace should recite formal prayers in moderation and give more time to the prayer of the mind. At times of inner weakness, one should recite prayers or read the writings of the Fathers. There is no need to use oars when the wind has filled the sails, they are necessary only when the wind dies down and the boat comes to a stop.

He who sheds tears of contrition during prayer possesses a great weapon against his enemies and against falling from the joy of prayer into self-conceit. He who safeguards this joyful sorrow will be safe from all harm. Genuine interior prayer that is free of prelest* radiates a warmth which is generated by the Jesus Prayer and which produces a fire that ignites the soil of our heart and scorches the passions like weeds. It envelops the heart in joy and peace, which originate not from the left or the right, nor even from above, but issue from the heart like a spring of water from the life-giving Spirit. Love only this kind of prayer—guard it zealously in your heart—and guard your mind against fantasies and daydreams. Fear nothing when you are in the company of this prayer; for He Himself—Who said, *Have courage, it is I, be not afraid!*—is with us.

(3) The Teaching of Nicephorus the Solitary

Nicephorus the Solitary presents his teaching on entering into the heart in his *Discourse on Sobriety and the Guarding of the Heart* (*Dobrotolyubiye*, part II, pages 36–43).

"You, who desire tangibly to perceive the divine fire in your heart and to experience firsthand the Kingdom of God that is within you, draw near and I will teach you the science or, better yet, the art of eternal life, which leads its practicer without toil or sweat to the haven of dispassion. Through our Fall we went outside that refuge; let us now return to our selves and turn our backs in aversion to what lies outside. We cannot be reconciled with God and enter into union with Him unless we first return to our selves and come back inside our selves from the outside. The interior life is the only true Christian life. All the Fathers bear witness to this.

"A brother once asked Abba Agathon, 'Which is more important, physical labor or guarding the heart?' The starets replied, 'Man is like a tree. His physical labor is like the leaves, and guarding the heart is the fruit. Insofar as according to Scripture "every tree which does not bear good fruit is cut down and thrown into the fire" [cf. Matt. 3:10], it is clear that you must concentrate on the fruit—that is, on guarding the heart. However, we also need the garb of the leaves—that is, of physical labor.' "

FROM SAINT JOHN OF THE LADDER

Saint John of the Ladder says, "Close the door of your cell to the body, the door of your lips to conversation, and the interior door of your soul to evil spirits. When you are in control (that is, when your attention is firmly focused on your heart), observe, if you know how, what kind of and how many thieves try to enter into the vineyard of your heart to steal the clusters of grapes. When a guard gets tired (that is, the one who is guarding the heart), he gets up, prays, and then sits down again and courageously returns to the same task (that is, to guarding the heart and to prayer)."

FROM SAINT MACARIUS THE GREAT

Saint Macarius the Great teaches, "The most important work of valiant ascetic spiritual struggles consists of entering into one's heart, of hating Satan and of waging war against him by rejecting his thoughts."

FROM SAINT ISAAC OF SYRIA

Saint Isaac of Syria writes, "Try to enter the innermost secret repository of yourself, and you will see the treasures of heaven. The ladder to the Kingdom of God is hidden within you—that is, within your heart. And so, cleanse yourself of sin and collect yourself inside your heart, there you will find the rungs by which you can ascend on high."

FROM SAINT JOHN OF KARPATHOS

This is what Saint John of Karpathos says, "Great ascetic effort and labor in prayer are required to achieve an unconfused state of mind—that other heaven of the heart wherein Christ dwells—and, as the Apostle says, 'Do you not know . . . that the spirit of God dwells in you?' [I Cor. 3: 16]."

FROM SAINT SIMEON THE NEW THEOLOGIAN

These are the words of Saint Simeon the New Theologian: "From the time when man was banished from Paradise and alienated himself from God, the devil with his demons was given the freedom, day and night, invisibly to agitate the reasoning powers of all men. There is no other way for the mind to protect itself against this than through constant remembrance of God. He who has the remembrance of God engraved within himself is able to protect his reasoning powers from turmoil."

All the Holy Fathers teach this.

BY NICEPHORUS HIMSELF

"Almost everyone learns this greatest spiritual activity of all through being taught by others. Rare are the individuals who because of their fervent faith, received and still receive this gift directly from God, without being taught by others. Thus, it is necessary to seek a guide with experience. If there is not such a one, then turn to God with a broken heart and with tears; ask for His help, and do what I tell you.

"You know that breathing through our lungs brings air to the heart. And so, sit down, collect your mind, and draw it down, inside, along the passages through which air travels as it is inhaled. Force your mind to enter your very heart along with the air you inhale and keep it there; do not let it escape as it would wish to. As you keep the mind there, do not leave it empty, but fill it with the following words: *Lord, Jesus, Christ, Son of God, have mercy on me!* And let the mind repeat these words day and night. Make an effort to become accustomed to residing in this inner place through this specific prayer and guard your mind so that it does not leave that place too soon. For in the beginning, the mind will be very despondent from such constrained internal imprisonment. Yet, when the mind becomes accustomed to this, it will be happy and joyful to be there and will want to remain there of its own accord. Like a man who has come home from a foreign land is beside himself with joy at seeing his wife and children again, so the mind when joined to the heart is filled with unspeakable joy and gladness.

"If you succeed in entering the place of the heart by the method that I have shown you, give thanks to God and always continue in this exercise; it will teach you things that you never even thought of. If after much effort you are not able to enter the place of the heart by using the method which I have shown you, then do what I will now tell you, and with God's help, you will find what you seek.

"It is known that man's faculty of speech (the internal words, words with which he speaks to himself) resides in his bosom, for there within the bosom, when the lips are silent, we speak with ourselves; there we pray (when we recite prayers silently in our minds); there we chant psalms and conduct all other conversations with ourselves. It is this faculty of speech that you must always use to repeat unceasingly, *Lord, Jesus Christ, Son of God, have mercy on me*, without allowing any thoughts to intrude; and you must compel yourself to cry out only these words and none other. Persist patiently in this exercise for but a while, and without fail, it will open for you the door into the heart, as we ourselves have found through our own experience.

"Together with this exceedingly desirable and joyful entering into the heart and guarding it with the attention, you will receive the full complement of the virtues: love, joy, peace, patience, meekness, and so on."

(4) The Teachings of the Monks Ignatius of Xanthopoulos and Callistus

The Monks Ignatius of Xanthopoulos and Callistus present their teaching on the interior activity of the heart in a full one hundred chapters in the *Dobrotolyubiye* (part II, pages 56–31). For us, the following points are the most important.

The beginning of living a life in God lies in zeal and diligent care to live according to the life-saving commandments of Christ. The end is the perfection of that which was intended for us by divine grace in baptism or, which is the same thing, "putting off the old man with his former conduct and lusts and putting on the new spiritual man" [Eph. 4:22–24], that is, in the Lord Jesus Christ, as the divine Paul says, "My little children, for whom I labor in birth again until Christ is formed in you" [Gal. 4:19].

Saint John Chrysostom says that when we are baptized, our soul, cleansed by the Holy Spirit, shines more brightly than the sun. As polished silver illumined by the rays of the sun radiates its own light, not because this is its natural property, but because of the sun's illumination, so a soul cleansed in baptism is illumined by rays emanating from the glory of the Spirit and radiates its own inner beauty. But, alas! This indescribable and awesome glory dwells within us but a day or two, and then we extinguish it with the storm of life's cares and woes and acts of passion.

We accept this perfect divine grace in the divine womb—that is, in the holy baptismal font. If later we bury it under the obscurity of life's cares and passions, we can restore it again, cleanse it again through repentance and by fulfilling the divine commandments, so we can see its original inherent splendor. This occurs according to each man's degree of faith and the fire of his zeal to live according to that faith, but most effectively by the blessing of the Lord Jesus Christ. Saint Mark says, "Christ, as perfect God, bestowed the perfect grace of the Holy Spirit on the baptized, which requires nothing on our part, and which is revealed and manifested in us according to the degree that we keep the commandments, until we achieve *the measure of the stature of the fullness of Christ*" [Eph. 4:13].

And so, since the beginning and the root of the work of salvation consist of living according to the Lord's commandments, and the end and the fruits are the restoration of the perfect grace of the Spirit, which was originally bestowed on us through Baptism, which is within us, but obscured by the passions, and which is revealed through keeping the commandments of God, it behooves us to become zealous about keeping the commandments in order to cleanse again the gift of the Spirit that is within us and to see it more clearly. The Apostle John, who laid his head on the Lord's bosom, said that he who keeps the commandments of the Lord abides in the Lord and He in him. The Lord Himself states this more fully, "He who has My commandments and keeps them, it is he who loves Me. And he who loves Me will be loved by My Father, and I will love him and manifest Myself to him. . . . If anyone loves Me, he will keep My word; and My Father will love him, and We will come to him and make Our home with him" [John 14:21, 23].

It is impossible for us to fulfill perfectly these redemptive commandments without the Lord Jesus Christ, for as He Himself says: ". . . for without Me, you can do nothing" [John 15:5]; and as the Apostle (Peter) preached: "Nor is there salvation in any other. . . ." [Acts 4:12]. For us, He is *the Way and the Truth and the Life*. It is for this reason that those glorious guides and teachers of ours, in whom the All-Holy Spirit dwelt, so wisely teach us that before undertaking anything, we must pray to the Lord, lay aside all doubts, and ask Him for mercy; and we must constantly keep and carry His All-Holy and Most Sweet Name in our hearts, in our minds, and on our lips; and we must continually live with it, when sleeping or in wakeful vigilance, while walking, eating, or drinking. For when we fail to invoke His Name, we are filled with all that is bad and destructive; whereas when His Name abides in us, all evil is banished, everything good flows abundantly, and there is nothing that we cannot accomplish, as the Lord Himself said, "He who abides in Me, and I in him, bears much fruit. . . ." [John 15:5].

And so, after acknowledging our weakness and placing all our hope in the Lord—after acquiring a love for the commandments so great that we would lay down our lives rather than transgress against any of them—we must focus all our efforts to accustom and firmly to establish ourselves in this act of unceasingly invoking the life-saving Name of the Lord, which destroys all evil and creates all good. To help us with this effort, the Holy Fathers prescribe a specific exercise, which they call an *art* or even the *art of arts*. We offer here the natural *art* of the excellent Nicephorus on how to enter into the heart in harmony with the breathing, which is a very helpful method for collecting one's thoughts.

This is his rule: Sit in solitude, collect your mind and draw it down into your heart along the passageway that air travels as you inhale. Hold it there with the power of your attention, as you continually invoke *Lord, Jesus Christ, Son of God, have mercy on me!* Do this until this invocation becomes one with the beating of your heart and flows unceasingly. This is what all the Holy Fathers taught.

Saint John Chrysostom says, "I implore you, brothers, never to abandon the rule of this prayer." Elsewhere, he says, "Whether eating or drinking, sitting or officiating in church, traveling or doing anything else, everyone must cry unceasingly, *Lord, Jesus Christ, Son of God, have mercy on me*! And the Name of the Lord Jesus Christ will descend into the depths of the place of the heart, it will subdue the evil serpent and will save the soul and will breathe life into it. Continue to invoke unceasingly the Name of the Lord Jesus, so that your heart embraces the Lord within itself and the Lord embraces your heart, and the two become one." And further: "Do not let your heart retreat from God, but guard in it the remembrance of our Lord Jesus Christ, until the Name of the Lord immerses and firmly roots itself in the heart; and think of nothing else but that Christ is glorified in you."

Saint John of the Ladder says, "May the remembrance of Jesus unite with your breathing." And Saint Hesychius writes, "If you want to shame the thoughts that are extraneous and alien to you and unceasingly to guard your heart, may the prayer to the Lord Jesus intertwine with your breathing; and in a few days, you will obtain the fulfillment of your desire."

Let it be known that if we teach the mind to descend into the heart in harmony with our breathing, we will also notice that once there, the mind can feel lonely and exposed while it concentrates on remembering only one thing and invoking the Lord our Jesus Christ. Conversely, when it goes out of that place and scatters its attention on external things, its attention is unwittingly divided by many thoughts, ideas, and memories. To preserve a guileless and collected mind, the Fathers, who have experience in this matter, instruct the one who zealously desires to acquire the habit of guarding the mind in the heart to sit in a silent and dimly lit place, especially when first embarking on this good and valiant spiritual exercise. For seeing external objects naturally causes our thoughts to disperse and to scatter. When a silent and dimly lit place shuts out the external world, our thoughts are no longer distracted and are more easily collected, as Saint Basil the Great says, "A mind that is not focused through the senses on the external world will return into itself."

Note carefully that the significance of this great effort lies in the single-minded, pure, and undistracted calling of the heart on the Lord our Jesus Christ with faith, and not solely in the exercise of descending into the heart in harmony with the breathing and of sitting silently in a dimly lit place. The Fathers devised all this and similar techniques for no other reason than they saw in them a certain method for collecting the thoughts and bringing them back inside the mind from their usual dispersion. The habit of being collected and watchful over one's self gives birth to the habit of the pure and undistracted prayer of a mind joined with the heart.

Know, too, that all such exercises for positioning the body are prescribed and determined by precise rules and are considered necessary only until the pure and undistracted prayer of the heart is attained. When you achieve this through the benevolence and the grace of the

Lord our Jesus Christ, then set aside the many and varied exercises, and you will silently remain united with the only Lord in the pure and undistracted prayer of the heart, and you will have no further need of any of those techniques.

And so, if you wish to make an effort to be deemed worthy of a life in Christ, try to pray to the Lord in your heart in a pure and undistracted manner, at all times and at every hour, and during all manner of activity; so that through this, you may mature from infancy into ". . . a perfect man, to the measure of the stature of the fullness of Christ . . .' [Eph. 4:13]. Remember also that if at times you are granted the self-acting pure prayer, under no circumstances must you destroy it with your own rule of reciting prayers. Philemon teaches the following: "If either by day or by night the Lord deems you worthy to grant you pure and undistracted prayer, then set aside your own rule of prayer and strive with all your strength to cling to the Lord God; and He will illumine your heart about the spiritual life."

When you are deemed worthy of being granted the unceasing prayer of the heart, then, as Saint Isaac of Syria says, you have attained to the pinnacle of all the virtues and have become the abode of the Holy Spirit. Then, whether you are sitting or walking, eating or drinking, or doing anything else, even in the depths of sleep, the sweet fragrance of prayer will waft effortlessly from your heart. Even if it is silent while you sleep, it will always mystically and uninterruptedly perform its sacred activity in the innermost secret place.

B. Second Category

(1) The Teaching of Saint Hesychius (Priest) of Jerusalem

1. Attention is the constant silence of the heart, unbroken by any thoughts—a stillness in which the heart uninterruptedly and unceasingly ever breathes only Jesus Christ, Who is the Son of God and is God Himself, and Him alone—in which it calls on Him and bravely

fights with Him its enemies and confesses its sins to Him Who has the power to absolve them (Text 5, *On Watchfulness and Holiness).*

2. Watchfulness is a fixed positioning of the mind as it stands guard at the door of the heart, from where it observes the approach of predatory alien thoughts, those thieves and robbers. From there it hears what these destroyers say; it observes what they do and what images the demons devise and construct for the thoughts that they use to entice the mind into considering them in order to seduce it. If we apply ourselves industriously to this exercise, it will be very instructive in teaching us the art of warfare against thoughts (Text 6).

3. Types of watchfulness: The first type consists of carefully scrutinizing every mental image or deceptive provocation. The second type consists of keeping the heart profoundly silent, still, and free from all thoughts, and of praying. The third type consists of continually and humbly calling on the Lord Jesus Christ for help. The fourth type consists of the soul preserving a constant remembrance of death. The fifth type is the most effective of all—fixing your gaze exclusively on heaven and regarding as nothing all that is of this world (Texts 14–18).

4. The one who engages in spiritual warfare at every moment must practice the following: *humility,* perfect *attention, refutation of thoughts, and prayer. Humility*—because his warfare is with arrogant adversarial demons, so that the arm of his heart may always embrace the help of Christ, for the Lord despises the arrogant. *Attention*—in order to keep his heart always free from all thoughts, even though they appear to be good. *Refutation of thoughts*—so that the instant his sharp-sighted mind recognizes the comer, he angrily and immediately repels this deceiver—as it is written, "So shall I have an answer for him who vilifies me. . . ." [Ps. 119:42], "Truly my soul silently waits for God. . . ." [Ps. 62:1]. *Prayer*—so that after resisting evil, he immediately calls to Christ from the depths of his heart with cries that

cannot be uttered. Then the one who struggles will see how the venerable Name of Jesus scatters the enemy and his imaginings like dust in the wind or makes them vanish like smoke (Text 20).

5. The one whose prayer is not free of all thoughts does not have weapons for battle. I speak of the kind of prayer that acts unceasingly in the innermost secret place of the soul and that battles and scorches the enemy and his secret onslaughts by calling on the Lord Jesus Christ (Text 21).

6. You must look inward with a sharp-sighted and concentrated mind to identify the invading demons. The moment you recognize them, immediately crush the head of the snake through refutation and call out to Christ with those same cries that cannot be uttered. Then you will experience the invisible divine intercession (Text 22).

7. If you always humbly strive to keep your attention inside your heart, to reflect on death, to reproach yourself, to refute thoughts, and to call on Jesus Christ—and if armed with these weapons you daily travel the narrow but sweet and joyous road of the mind—you will attain to the contemplation of the Holy of Holies and will be illumined in the knowledge of profound mysteries by Christ, ". . . in Whom are hidden all the treasures of wisdom and knowledge" [Col. 2:3]. For through Christ Jesus you will feel and will know that the Holy Spirit has descended into your soul, Who illumines man's intellect so that it beholds ". . . with unveiled face . . . the glory of the Lord" [2 Cor. 3:18] (Text 29).

8. With his army, the devil ". . . walks about like a roaring lion, seeking whom he may devour" [I Peter 5:8]. May we never relax the attention of our hearts, our watchfulness and refutation of thoughts, as well as our prayer to Christ Jesus, our God. In your entire life, you will never find greater help than from Jesus, for being the One Lord,

He alone, as God, knows the snares, the subtle guile and the deceit of the demons (Text 39).

9. As salt seasons bread and other food and preserves meat from spoiling to keep it fresh for a long time, understand that in a similar manner, the attention of the mind protects and preserves the spiritual delight of the intellect and the wondrous activity within the heart. For in a divine manner, it, too, seasons and sweetens the inner and the outer man, dispelling the stench of evil thoughts and preserving us in a constant state of goodness (Text 87).

10. The more closely attentive you are to your mind, the warmer the desire with which you pray to Jesus; and again, the more carelessly you watch over your mind, the further will you distance yourself from Jesus. As attentiveness brilliantly illumines the mind, so carelessness—that is, deviating from watchfulness and from delightful invocations of Jesus—usually darkens it completely (Text 90).

11. The sweet, unceasing invocation of Jesus, accompanied by a certain warm desire, and filled with sweetness and joy, fills a heart that is intensely watchful with a soothing tranquility. It is also Jesus Christ, Son of God and God Himself, Cause and Creator of all that is good, Who completely purifies the heart. For He Himself says, "I am God who makes peace" [Isa. 45:7] (Text 91).

12. A certain divine inner state is produced by the unceasing remembrance and invocation of the Lord our Jesus Christ, provided that you do not neglect constant mental supplications to Him and resolute watchfulness, regarding these as the only pressing and necessary activities. Indeed, there is but one task that we must hold before us and must always perform in the same manner—to call on Jesus Christ, our Lord, entreating Him with a burning heart that He would grant us to partake of and to taste the blessings of His Holy Name. For constancy is the mother of habit for both virtue and vice, and habit eventually

takes over as second nature. After attaining such a state, the intellect begins to seek out its enemies of its own accord, as a hound searches for a hare in a thicket. But the hound searches only to get food, while the mind seeks in order to strike and to drive away (Text 97).

13. The great spiritual master David said to the Lord, "I shall preserve my strength through You" [Ps. 59:9]. And so it is with us, we depend on the Lord's help to preserve the strength of the heart's and the intellect's stillness, from which all the virtues are born. For He gave us the commandments, and, when we constantly invoke Him, He expels from us that foul forgetfulness which, above all else, destroys the stillness of the heart as water extinguishes fire. Therefore, do not surrender from negligence to the sleep which is unto your destruction [Ps. 13:3] and flog the enemies with the Name of Jesus. May this sweetest Name of all adhere to every breath of yours, and then you will learn the value of stillness (Text 100).

14. When unworthy we are granted to receive, with fear and awe, the Communion of the Divine and Most-Pure Mysteries of Christ our God and King, we should demonstrate the highest degree of sobriety, watchfulness over the mind, and strict attention, so that this divine fire—the Body and the Blood of the Lord our Jesus Christ—may consume our sins and our iniquities, both great and small. For when He enters into us, He instantly banishes the cunning spirits of evil from the heart and absolves us of our past sins; and then our intellect is freed from the bothersome annoyance of evil thoughts. If after this you stand guard at the door of your heart and vigilantly watch over the intellect, you will again be honored to receive the Communion of the Holy Mysteries, and the Divine Body will increasingly illumine your intellect and make it to shine like the stars (Text 101).

15. Diligent care must be taken to protect that which is precious, and the only truly precious thing for us is that which safeguards us from

all evil that enters through both the senses and the mind. This is the guarding of the intellect while invoking Jesus Christ: a continual looking into the depths of the heart; a constant state of stillness of the mind—which is, I would say, unbroken even by thoughts that appear to be good—and making an effort to keep the mind completely empty of any thoughts in general, so that the demons cannot hide behind them undetected (Text 103).

16. The Name of Jesus Christ must always be repeated in the heart just as flashes of lightning reappear in the sky before it rains. Those who have experience in interior spiritual warfare know this well. This warfare must be waged in the same way as regular war. We begin with the attention; then, when we notice a hostile thought approaching, we strike at it with angry curses from the heart. The third step is to direct our prayer against it, by concentrating the heart on invoking Jesus Christ, so that the demonic presence may instantly be dispelled, and so the mind may not pursue this thought as a child who is lured away by some cunning sorcerer (Text 105).

17. This is the great gain that the intellect derives from stillness: All the sins that originally attacked it only in the form of thoughts—which if accepted by the heart would turn into the crude sins of outward sensory acts—are all excised in the inner man by the intellect's virtue of watchfulness. And, with the support and the intercession of the Lord our Jesus Christ, this virtue of watchfulness does not permit thoughts to come inside and to turn into sinful acts (Text 111).

18. As valleys produce abundant wheat, so the Jesus Prayer will produce an abundance of blessings in your heart; or, rather, the Lord our Jesus Christ will grant you this Himself, for without Him we can do nothing. At first, you will see prayer as a ladder, then as a book which you read, and finally, as you advance further and further, you will see it as the heavenly Jerusalem, the city of the King of Hosts, Who is

together with His Father—with Whom He is of one Essence—and with the venerable Holy Spirit (Text 117).

19. When a soul is released in death and rises to the gates of heaven, even there it will not be disgraced by its enemies if Christ is on its side. Instead, it will then, as now, confront them boldly. But let the soul not tire day and night in calling on the Lord Jesus Christ, the Son of God, until its time has come to leave this mortal life. And He will swiftly avenge the soul, both in this life and after it departs from the body, according to the true and divine promise which He Himself made in the parable of the unjust judge: "I tell you that He will avenge them speedily" [Luke 18:8] (Text 149).

20. If we strive to be watchful over our mind and if we combine sobriety with humility and refuting thoughts with prayer, we will be traveling the right spiritual road together with the venerable and holy Name of Jesus Christ as with a lantern to guide our way. Yet if we rely only on our own sobriety and watchfulness, we will fall under the first attack of the enemy and be cast down. And then these crafty deceivers will set out to overpower us in every way and will increasingly entangle us in the webs of their evil desires; or else they will easily and completely slaughter us, because we do not carry within us the victorious sword of the Name of Jesus Christ. For only this glorious sword, when constantly on guard in a heart that is free of all thoughts, knows how to flog and to turn back the enemy, to scorch and to devour him as fire does dry straw (Text 152).

21. The task of constant watchfulness, so beneficial and productive for the soul, is to observe imaginary thoughts as soon as they begin to take shape in the mind. The task of refuting thoughts is to expose and to expel in shame a thought that attempts to infiltrate the space of our mind by presenting itself as an image of some material object. It is the invocation of the Lord that instantly extinguishes and disperses each

plan of the enemy, each word, each fantasy, each idol and pillar of evil. And through our intellect, we can observe firsthand how mightily they are overcome by Jesus, our great God, and how He defends us, who are humble, poor, and good for nothing (Text 153).

22. A ship will not go far where there is no water; guarding the mind will not succeed without attention that is combined with humility and without the unceasing Jesus Prayer (Text 168).

23. Unceasing prayer of the mind creates in us a state that is clear of dark clouds and the tempests of evil spirits. When the heart is pure, then nothing will prevent the divine light of Jesus from shining therein—unless we are filled with self-esteem and doubts, and unless we reach for the unreachable, thus depriving ourselves of the help of Jesus. For Christ abhors all this, because He is the perfect example of humility (Text 175).

24. Just as words should be inscribed on a solid surface and not in the air, so that they can be preserved for a long time, so our great efforts to be watchful must be combined with the Jesus Prayer so that the splendid virtue of being watchful together with Him would remain intact, and that through Him, it would forever be preserved inviolable in us (Text 183).

25. When guarding the intellect with God's help is done solely for the sake of the one and only God, and this becomes established in the soul, it imparts to the mind a wisdom that guides it to perform valiant, ascetic, spiritual struggles according to God. It also enables its spiritual warrior to act and to speak according to God's will with impeccable discernment (Text 194).

26. Truly blessed is he whose mind becomes as one with the Jesus Prayer and whose heart cries out to Him unceasingly, as air becomes one with our bodies and a flame with a burning candle. The rising sun

brings daylight to the earth, and the holy and praiseworthy Name of the Lord Jesus shining constantly in the soul gives birth to infinite contemplations that are as radiant as the sun (Text 196).

27. Dispersing clouds clear the air, and when Jesus Christ, the Sun of Righteousness, disperses the fantasies of passion, then contemplation as brilliant as the sun and radiant as the stars is born in the heart because Christ has illumined it (Text 197).

(2) The Teaching of Philotheus of Sinai

1. The one who strives toward righteousness should resolve that the goal of his mind will be to cherish fully in his heart the remembrance of God, as if it were a priceless pearl or a precious jewel. He should set aside all else, disregarding even his body and scorning his very life in this world, in order to acquire only God in his heart (Text 1).

2. One must begin each day with his mind bravely and steadfastly standing guard at the door of the heart with an unwavering remembrance of God and the unceasing prayer of Jesus Christ in his soul. With an attentive mind, he must slay all the sinners of this world. In other words, for the sake of the Lord, he must behead the powerful and must thwart the onslaught of emerging thoughts with the steadfast, resolute, and uplifting remembrance of God (Text 2).

3. Watchfulness is correctly called both a *way*—for it leads to the kingdom that is within us and the one that is yet to come—and a *workplace of the mind* (a spiritual workshop), because it fashions and hones (polishes) spiritual habits and transforms passion into dispassion. It is also similar to a small window through which God gazes and reveals Himself to the intellect (Text 3).

4. God's dwelling-place or the *heaven* of the heart is where humility, sober and watchful remembrance of God, and constant prayer directed against evil are present; and the hosts of demons fear to tread there because God dwells in that place (Text 4).

5. The wise silence of the lips is the first door into the *Jerusalem* of the mind or the watchfulness of the mind, even though the mind itself is not yet silent. The second door is temperate moderation in eating, drinking, and sleeping. The third door, which purifies the mind and the body, is the constant remembrance of and reflection on death (Text 6).

6. The delightful remembrance of God—that is, Jesus Christ—together with sincere wrath and righteous hatred (against all sin) usually destroys all the temptations of thoughts; of various suggestions, words, and fantasies; of shameful imaginings; and, in brief, every weapon brazenly used by the life-destroying enemy in his attempts to devour our souls. When invoked, Jesus easily vanquishes them all, for we have no salvation in anyone except Jesus Christ. The Savior Himself said: "Without me you can do nothing" [John 5:5] (Text 22).

7. And so each hour and at every moment, let us zealously guard our heart against thoughts that obscure the mirror of the soul which should reflect none other than the holy image of Jesus Christ, Who is the Wisdom and the Power of God the Father. Let us constantly seek the Kingdom of Heaven within our hearts; and in the end, if we but purify the eye of our intellect, we will mystically acquire within ourselves the seed, the pearl, the leaven, and everything else. This is why the Lord our Jesus Christ said: "the Kingdom of God is within you" [Luke 17:21], referring to the Deity that dwells within our hearts (Text 23).

8. Interior spiritual warfare should be conducted in the following manner: Combine prayer with watchfulness, and the watchfulness will strengthen prayer, and the prayer, watchfulness. By constantly overseeing all that transpires within, watchfulness will observe how the enemy tries to gain entry, and while doing everything in its power to prevent this, watchfulness will simultaneously call on the Lord Jesus Christ to banish these evil warriors. In doing so, watchfulness ob-

structs their entry through refutation, while Jesus Who is invoked chases away the demons and their fantasies (Text 25).

9. Guard your mind with extreme watchfulness. As soon as you notice a hostile thought, immediately refute it, but also hasten to call on Christ the Lord to work vengeance. While you are still calling on Him, the most delightful Jesus will reply: *Here I am with you, to defend you.* However, after all these enemies have been subdued by your prayer, you must again continue diligently to guard your mind. For waves of thoughts, more numerous than before, will head in your direction, one after another, so that the soul will feel as if it is engulfed by them and about to perish. But Jesus, as God, to Whom the disciples cried out, again rebukes the evil winds of thoughts, and they cease [Luke 8:23–24]. And having been spared, whether for an hour or for a minute, from the attacks of the enemy, you must glorify Him Who saved you and immerse yourself in reflecting on death (Text 26).

10. You must continue in your spiritual struggles with all earnest watchfulness guided by spiritual wisdom. When combined daily, watchfulness and prayer become like the fiery chariot of Elias, raising him who practices them up to heaven. What am I trying to say? The pure heart of one who is established in watchfulness becomes a heaven for the intellect—with its own sun, moon, and stars—and through mystical contemplation and ecstasy (rapture of the intellect), the heart becomes a vessel for the uncontainable God (Text 27).

(3) The Teaching of Theoliptus, Metropolitan of Philadelphia (*Dobrotolyubiye*, part II, pages 44–50)

1. The setting of the sun brings the night, and when Christ departs from the soul, it is enveloped in the darkness of passions, and the beasts of thoughts begin to torment it. When the physical sun rises, the beasts hide in their caves. When Christ rises and shines on the world of the mind that prays, all worldly concerns depart, and the

mind applies itself to its task of acquiring divine knowledge until the setting of the sun (page 45).

2. Refrain from conversations and struggle against interior thoughts until you attain the state of pure prayer and the dwelling-place of Christ, Who illumines and delights you with His knowledge and His presence (ibid).

3. Footprints in the snow will vanish either when the sun melts the snow or when seeping water washes them away. In the same manner, memories of sensual acts are erased by Christ, Who illumines the heart through prayer, and are washed away by the rain of tender tears of contrition (page 46).

4. When accompanied by ardent, tender emotion, constant prayer blots out memories of past actions. The illumination of the soul through constant remembrance of God, together with faith and a broken, contrite heart, cuts away bad memories like a razor (ibid).

5. Find a solitary place and then strive to enter the innermost, guarded, secret chamber of yourself (the *watchtower*), which is the dwelling-place of Christ, and where there is always peace, joy, and stillness. Christ, the Sun that shines on the intellect, bestows these gifts, which emanate from Him like rays, as a kind of reward to the soul that has welcomed and has accepted Him with faith and a love of all that is good (page 46).

6. Remember God as you sit in your cell; take your mind off everything else and concentrate it on the one and only God. Pour out to Him all that is in your heart and cling to Him with love. Remembrance of God is the intellect contemplating God, Who attracts the contemplation and the desire of the mind and illumines it with the light that radiates from Him. When the intellect can turn to God purified of all forms and images of existing things, its contemplation of God is *formless* and *imageless* (ibid).

7. Prayer is the mind conversing with the Lord, simultaneously uttering the words of prayer and focusing its attention on God. When thoughts are focused on constantly repeating the Name of the Lord and the mind clearly listens to this invocation of the Divine Name, the light of divine contemplation envelops a man's entire soul like a radiant cloud (ibid).

8. Believe me, for I speak the truth—if everything you do is inseparably linked with prayer, the mother of all good, it will not rest until it has shown you the way to the bridal chamber and has led you inside, and until it has filled you with inexpressible bliss and joy. Prayer removes all obstacles, it smoothes the path to virtue, and makes it conveniently accessible to those who seek it (page 48).

9. In walking the spiritual path, recite the words of prayer; speak to the Lord crying out unceasingly, and never despair. Pray steadfastly by emulating that importunate widow who moved the unyielding judge. Then (it will mean that) you walk in the Spirit, you ignore the lusts of the flesh, and you do not interrupt your constant prayer with worldly thoughts—but you are a temple of God wherein He is silently praised. In the end, such prayer of the mind will grant you to attain unceasing remembrance of God; to acquire the inaccessible treasures of the intellect; to gaze on the Unseen through mystical contemplation, so that you, alone in your solitude, will worship the one and only God with outpourings of love that only you can comprehend (page 48).

(4) The Teachings of Saint Barsanuphius the Great and Saint John the Prophet

1. Enemies are weakened when the Name of God is invoked. Knowing this, let us not cease to invoke the Name of God for help. This is prayer, and Scripture says, "Pray unceasingly" [I Thess. 5:17].

2. Remember that God knows man's heart and sees into his heart. So call on Him in your heart, for Scripture says, ". . . shut your door

(and) pray to your Father who is in the secret place. . . ." [Matt. 6:6]. Let us seal our lips and pray to Him in our hearts; for he who seals his lips and calls on God or prays to Him in his heart fulfills the aforesaid commandment.

3. Your spiritual efforts in connection with your heart must consist of praying unceasingly to God. If you wish to succeed in this, apply yourself to this task, seek tirelessly and with hope, and God will bless you with success.

4. The constant invocation of the Name of God is healing; not only does it destroy the passions, but also their activity. Just as a doctor determines the appropriate treatment or bandage to heal a patient's wound, and it is effective without the patient even knowing how this happens, so the Name of God when invoked destroys all the passions, even though we do not know how this is accomplished.

5. The Lord said, ". . . ask, and it will be given to you . . ." [Luke 11:9]. So pray to the All-Good God that He will send you the Holy Spirit, the Comforter, Who will teach you everything and reveal every mystery to you. Make Him your guide, and He will not permit illusion or confusion to enter into your heart. He will not let your thoughts turn to negligence, laziness, or lethargy. He will illumine your eyes, strengthen your heart, and uplift your mind. Cling to Him. Believe Him. Love Him.

6. If you notice that the cunning webs woven by the enemy are interfering with your prayer, do not enter into a discussion with him; rather, try to invoke the Name of God, and He will help you and will put a stop to the enemy's wiles.

7. Perfect prayer consists of conversing with God with a mind that has collected its thoughts and feelings and is not distracted by them. A man enters into such a state when he is *dead* to people, to the world,

and to everything that is in it. Such a man thinks of nothing while he prays other than that he is in the presence of God and is conversing with Him.

C. The Most Edifying Narrative of Abba Philemon

1. It was said about Abba Philemon the Hermit that he shut himself up in some cave not far from a lavra called Romyeva and dedicated himself to a life of ascetic spiritual warfare. And, following the example of the great Arsenius, as we are told, he regularly asked himself: *Philemon, why have you come to this place?*

He spent a long time in this cave, where he occupied himself with winding twine and weaving baskets, which he gave to a steward in return for small loaves of bread to feed himself. He ate only bread and salt, and even this not every day. It is clear that he paid no attention to his bodily needs but practiced only the contemplative life, and he lived in a state of divine illumination, which bestowed on him a knowledge of ineffable mysteries and a state of spiritual enlightenment.

On his way to church on Saturdays and Sundays, he always walked in a state of deep self-contemplation allowing no one to approach him, so that his mind would not be distracted from this interior contemplation. In church, he would stand in a corner with his head bowed, as tears streamed down his face from endless sorrow, and his mind concentrated on his heart and on the example of the Holy Fathers, especially Arsenius the Great, in whose footsteps he endeavored to walk.

2. When a heresy sprang up in Alexandria and its suburbs, Philemon left and went to the Nikinarov Lavra, where the God-loving Paulinus welcomed him and relinquished his own secluded abode to enable Philemon to live in complete silence. For an entire year, Paulinus allowed no one to visit Philemon, and he himself did not bother him, except to supply him with bread. Then came the holy Feast of Christ's

Resurrection, and they met one day and struck up a conversation that touched on living the life of a hermit. It was then that Philemon realized that the most devout brother Paulinus also had a noble desire (to live as a hermit), and that the words—both oral and written—that were preached about the ascetic spiritual life had been abundantly sown as seeds in his heart—words that prove to everyone that without complete solitude it is not possible to please God. The divinely inspired Moses philosophized of old that "silence gives birth to great feats of spiritual asceticism, which in turn give birth to tears; and tears give birth to fear, and fear to humility. Humility opens the eyes and then love is born. It is love that makes the soul healthy and dispassioned—and then man knows that he is not far from God."

3. He (Philemon) then said to him, "You should completely purify your mind by living a life of silence and use it exclusively for performing spiritual exercises. As the physical eye that looks at something material marvels at what it sees, so a pure intellect that turns its gaze upon the intangible is so enraptured by what the spiritual eyes see that you cannot tear its gaze away. To the degree that the mind is dispassioned and purified through silence, to that degree will it be granted knowledge (of those spiritual realities). A mind is made perfect when it partakes of divine knowledge and union with God. Enabled with the dignity of royal stature, the mind no longer lacks anything—and were it offered all the kingdoms in the world, it would not be drawn by any earthly desires.

"And so, if you wish to attain such blessings, flee this world as fast as you can and earnestly follow the path of the saints. Stop being concerned about your external appearance; clothe yourself as a poor man and adorn yourself with humility. Let your demeanor be unpretentious, modest; and speak sincerely— do not strut about arrogantly or speak in an affected, pompous manner. Learn to live a life of poverty and to be ignored by all. Above all else, take care to guard your mind and to be watchful; be patient in hard times and do all that it takes to preserve undefiled and resolute the spiritual blessings you have already acquired. Maintain strict watchfulness over yourself and reject every pleasurable delight that secretly tries to sneak its way inside. Although a life of silence subdues the spiritual passions, if you ignite and fan their fires, they will usually rage out of control and will draw him, who has permitted this to happen, more powerfully into sin. So it is with bodily sores—when irritated and lacerated, they cannot be healed. A single word can draw the mind away from the remembrance of God, if the demons compel one to do this and the senses consent. An awesome and extraordinary ascetic effort is required to guard the soul!

"And so, you should isolate yourself completely from the world and divest your soul of any empathy for the body. You must become a man without a city and without a home; without any possessions, money, or desire to acquire anything. You must renounce all cares and companions and keep yourself ignorant of the affairs of the world. You must be humble, compassionate, kind, meek, and with a quiet temperament—prepared to receive the imprint of divine knowledge in your heart. For as Saint Basil the Great teaches us, you cannot write on a wax tablet unless you first erase the letters previously inscribed on it. Such was the assembly of the saints, by renouncing all the ways of the world and by preserving within themselves the tranquil contemplation of heavenly things, they were illumined by divine laws and became shining examples of righteous deeds and words, having *put to death (the) members which are on the earth* [Col. 3:5] through abstinence, fear of God, and love. For through unceasing prayer and learning from divine Scripture, the innermost eyes of the heart are opened and gaze upon the Lord of Hosts with abundant joy. A divine, irresistible, and intense longing is ignited in the soul, which through the action of the Spirit enraptures the body as well—and the entire man becomes spiritual. This is what is bestowed on those who practice blessed stillness and follow the narrow way of the ascetic spiritual life: having renounced all human consolation, they enjoy unceasing conversation—alone with the only Lord in heaven."

4. After hearing this, that God-loving brother's soul was pierced by divine love. He left his abode and went with him (Philemon) to the skete where the greatest Holy Fathers had attained to a righteous life. Together they settled in the Lavra of Saint John Kolobos, and because of their desire to live a life of silence, they entrusted the care for all their needs to the steward of that Lavra. And so, by the grace of God, they lived there in perfect silence, emerging only on Saturdays and Sundays to attend church services and remaining in their cells the rest of the time. Moreover, each one prayed and practiced the monastic rule privately.

5. The holy starets (Philemon) kept the following monastic rule: At night, he slowly and patiently chanted the entire Psalter and all the canticles (the nine included in the Psalter) and then read the beginning of one of the Gospels. Then he sat down and for a considerable time, with total concentration, he silently repeated *Lord, have mercy!* When he could no longer recite these words, he allowed himself to take a nap. At dawn, he chanted the First Hour, after which he sat facing the East and took turns chanting (the psalms) and reading his own selections from the Epistles and the Gospels. Thus he spent the entire day constantly psalmodising, praying, and delighting in divine contemplation. Often, his intellect was so caught up in contemplative ecstasy that he knew not whether he was in heaven or on earth.

6. Seeing how earnestly he prayed and kept the monastic rule, and how sometimes his countenance completely changed while he was immersed in mystical contemplation, a brother once asked him, "Father, is it not difficult for you at your old age to mortify and to exert your body so much?" He replied, "Believe me, God has instilled such zeal

and such love for prayer in my soul that I don't even have the strength to satisfy fully its longings. Love of God and hope for future blessings overcome physical weakness." Thus, his intense longing transported his intellect up to heaven; and this happened even during meals, not only at other times.

7. A certain brother who lived with him once asked Philemon, "What kind of mysteries does mystical contemplation reveal?" Seeing his persistence and that he sincerely sought guidance, Philemon replied, "I tell you, my child, that to him who has completely purified his mind, God grants visions of the Powers and the Ranks (of angels) who serve Him."

8. The same brother then asked him, "Why is it, Father, that you take greater delight in the Psalter than in any other book of Holy Scripture; and why is it that when you are quietly chanting, it looks like you are talking with someone?" To this, he replied, "God has imprinted the power of the psalms in my soul as deeply as in the prophet David, and I cannot tear myself away from delighting in all the mystical revelations that are hidden in them. For they embrace the entire Holy Scripture."

9. A certain brother named John, who had traveled from the coast, came to see this great and Holy Father Philemon. He embraced his feet and said to him, "What shall I do, Father, to save myself? For my mind wanders and drifts everywhere it should not." After a moment of silence, Philemon said, "This (spiritual) sickness occurs in people who are focused on the external, and it afflicts them. You have this sickness, and that is why you have not yet acquired a perfect love of God—you do not yet have an intimate love for and knowledge of Him."

The brother said, "Then what should I do, Father?" Philemon replied, "Go and acquire the hidden secret knowledge of the heart, and it will purify your mind of this (sickness)." The brother did not know what the starets was talking about and asked him, "Father, what is this secret knowledge?" And he replied, "Go and practice watchfulness in your heart, and with attention, fear and trepidation recite *Lord, Jesus Christ, have mercy on me!* This is what the blessed Diadochus teaches beginners to do."

10. The brother left, and with God's help through the prayers of the starets, he found peace and some delight from doing what he had been taught. But then the delight left him, and he could no longer practice watchfulness and pray. So he went again to see the starets and told him what had happened. The starets replied, "Now that you have had the experience of silence and prayer of the mind and have tasted the sweetness that this brings, you must always keep this in your heart—whether you are eating or drinking, having a conversation with someone, traveling, or sitting in your cell—with attentive thought and an undistracted mind, do not stop repeating that prayer, psalmodising, and learning from the prayers and the psalms. Even when attending to your most pressing needs, do not let your mind remain empty, but exert it to study and to pray in secret. In this manner you will understand the profound meaning of Holy Scripture and the power that is hidden there; you will teach your mind to pray unceasingly and will thus fulfill the words of the Apostle that command us to *Pray without ceasing* [I Thess. 5:17]. Diligently practice watchfulness over yourself and guard your heart against accepting any evil, vain, or futile thoughts, but let your heart, in secret, alternate learning from the psalms and praying *Lord, Jesus Christ, Son of God, have mercy on me!* Do this always—when you sleep and when you awaken; when you are eating, drinking, or having a conversation. Then, when you chant the psalms with your mouth, be careful that you do not only mouth the words while your mind wanders elsewhere."

11. The brother then said, "I have many vain dreams while I sleep."

The starets said to him, "Do not be lazy or afraid. Instead, before falling asleep, recite many prayers in your heart; resist thoughts and the devil's attempts to get you to do what he wants, and God will defend you. Do all you can to try to fall asleep with the psalms on your lips and your mind reflecting on what you have learned. Never let your mind become careless by accepting extraneous, alien thoughts, but go to bed with the same thoughts that accompanied your prayers; and let your mind reflect on them, so that they may remain with you while you sleep and converse with you when you awaken. Likewise, before you fall asleep, recite the Creed of the Orthodox Faith, for professing a true and correct faith in God is both the source and the safeguard of all blessings."

12. And again the brother asked, "Father, would you be so gracious as to describe to me the spiritual exercises that you practice in your mind? Teach me, so that I, too, can be saved." He replied, "Why are you so curious to know this?" The brother got up, embraced and kissed the saint's feet, and pleaded with him to tell him. After a considerable time, the starets said, "You are not yet able to endure doing this. To exercise each of the senses in a way that is proper to its functioning is appropriate for a strong man who has experience in living with the blessings of spiritual truth and reality. It is impossible for the one who is not yet completely free of vain, worldly thoughts to be worthy of being granted this gift. Therefore, if you truly desire this, preserve in a pure heart the secret knowledge you have acquired. For if you achieve a state of unceasing prayer and learning from the Scriptures, the eyes of your soul will be opened; and it will be filled with great joy and a certain inexpressible burning feeling accompanied by a warm sensation, even in the body, that is generated by the Spirit—so that the entire man becomes spiritual. And so, should God grant you either by day or night to pray undistractedly with a pure mind, set aside your rule of prayer, and with all your strength make an effort to

reach out and cling to God. And He will illumine your heart in the way of the spiritual life that you have embarked on."

He then added, "A starets once came to me, and when I asked him about the spiritual state of his mind, he said, 'I spent two years praying before God and diligently imploring Him with all my heart that He would grant me the gift of imprinting in my heart the unceasing and undistracted prayer that He gave to His disciples. And the exceedingly generous Lord saw my labors and my patience and granted me my wish.' "

And this is what else he told him: "Thoughts of vain things that occur in the soul constitute the sickness of an idle soul that has become mired in negligence. This is why Scripture teaches us that we must carefully guard our mind, psalmodise intelligently and undistractedly, and pray with a pure mind. And so, brother, God desires that we show Him our zeal, first through our efforts (our ascetic spiritual struggles and good works), and then through our love and unceasing prayer. And He will show us the path to salvation. After all, it is obvious that there is no path that can lead us up to heaven other than complete renunciation of all evil, embracing all good, perfect love for God and communion with Him in reverence and in truth—so that he who attains to this will rise up to join the heavenly choirs.

"However, he who desires to ascend on high must steadfastly *put to death (the) members which are on the earth* [Col. 3:5]. For when our soul delights in contemplating true bliss, it no longer returns to any passions incited by sinful pleasures. Instead, it renounces all bodily, sensual delights and receives the vision of God with pure and undefiled thoughts. And so, we must maintain strict watchfulness over ourselves; we must endure much physical exertion and purification of the soul to welcome God into our hearts. Then we must fulfill His divine commandments without sinning, so that through the grace of the Spirit instilled in us, He Himself would teach us to keep His laws steadfastly, as His illuminating activity in our hearts emanates from Him like the rays of the sun.

"We must work hard and suffer many trials in order to purify in ourselves the image in which we were originally created—as intelligent beings capable of receiving enlightenment and of attaining to the image and the likeness of God—and in order to keep our senses pure and undefiled by purging them in the fiery furnace of trials, so that we are elevated to the dignity of royal stature. God also created human nature as capable of sharing in every blessing and with an intellect that is able to contemplate the unapproachable Light and the exceeding Glory, as well as the ranks of the angels of glory—the dominions, the powers, the principalities, the thrones.

"However, once you purify any of the virtues, be careful lest you think yourself greater than your brother for having done this, while he was careless about it—for this is the beginning of pride. When you are struggling with some passion, do not despair or be afraid because its attack is relentless, but resolve to resist it; then prostrate yourself before the face of God and cry out with your whole heart as did the prophet: 'Plead *my cause*, O Lord, with those who strive with me, for I am powerless against them!' [Ps. 35:1]. Seeing your humility, He will swiftly send you His help. If you are traveling with a companion, do not take part in empty conversation; but keep your mind busy with its usual spiritual exercises so that it keeps up this good habit, forgets about worldly pleasures, and does not leave the safe harbor of dispassion."

After speaking to the brother about these and many other things, the starets let him go.

13. Still, after a short time, the brother returned and said, "What should I do, Father? When I practice my rule of prayer at night, I become so sleepy that I can't continue to pray attentively and to keep a longer vigil, and I want to do some work to keep my hands busy while I psalmodise." To this, the starets replied, "When you are able to pray with attention, do not do any work with your hands; but when

drowsiness overcomes you, struggle a bit with that thought and resist it, and then busy your hands with some work."

Again the brother asked, "Father, don't you get sleepy when you practice your own rule of prayer?" The starets said, "Not that easily. However, if the drowsiness persists and I feel its effects, I read the Gospels from the beginning, starting with John, while I contemplate God with the eye of my intellect, and the drowsiness instantly disappears. I handle thoughts in a similar way—specifically, when one assails me, I quench it like a flame with my tears, and it vanishes. You are not able yet to resist thoughts in this manner; it is better for you to hold fast to your spiritual lessons and to recite zealously the daily cycle of prayers prescribed by the Holy Fathers, such as the Hours—the Third Hour, the Sixth Hour, the Ninth Hour, and Vespers, as well as the night services. With all your strength, avoid doing anything only to please others, and guard yourself against any animosity toward any of the brethren, lest this separate you from your God. Strive also to guard your mind against distractions, so that it can zealously meditate on your inner thoughts. When you are in church and plan to receive the Communion of the Holy Mysteries of Christ, do not leave afterward until you have been filled with perfect peace. Find one place to stand in church and do not move from there until the Dismissal. Inside yourself, reflect that you are in heaven with the holy angels and in the presence of God, preparing to receive Him into your heart. Prepare yourself for this with fear and trembling, lest you end up unworthy to share in the communion of the heavenly host."

After strengthening the brother in this manner and delivering him into the care of the Lord and His Spirit of Grace, the starets let him go.

14. In addition to this, a brother who lived with the starets related the following:

"Once when I was sitting with him, I asked him if he had ever been tempted by the revilement of the demons while he lived in solitary places. He replied, 'Forgive me, brother, but if God permitted you to suffer the same temptations of the devil that I have experienced, I do not think you could endure the bitter sting of that. I am seventy or more years old now and have suffered many temptations living in solitude in various isolated places. It would not help those who have not yet experienced the solitary life to hear about the bitter sting of what I have experienced and have endured from these demons. There was one rule I always followed while suffering those temptations: I placed all my trust in God and made a vow to Him to renounce all else, and He swiftly rescued me from all calamities. For this reason, brother, I am no longer concerned about providing for my needs. Instead, I easily endure the temptations that beset me, because I know that He will provide for me. The only thing I can offer Him from myself is unceasing prayer. And in all this, it is no little thing to trust that the more sorrow and misfortunes befall you, the more they contribute to weaving a crown of glory for the one who suffers, for the Righteous Judge equally balances one against the other.

'Knowing this, brother, do not give in to faintheartedness. If you have stepped into the arena to fight—then fight—and be encouraged by the knowledge that those who fight on our side against the enemies of God far outnumber the enemy hordes. For that matter, how could we even dare to stand up to such a terrible enemy of the human race if the mighty hand of God the Lord did not embrace, guard, and shield us? How would human nature endure the abuse of evil? For, as Job says, "Who can open the doors of his face . . . *with* his terrible teeth all around . . . (who) can come between them. . . . Out of his mouth come fiery torches; sparks of fire shoot out. His nostrils belch smoke, as *from* a boiling cauldron. His breath kindles coals and issues from his mouth like a flame. Strength dwells in his neck, and sorrow dances before him . . . His heart is as hard as stone, unyielding as a *millstone* . . . He churns the depths into a seething cauldron, he makes the sea fume like a scent burner. He leaves a glittering wake behind him . . .

He looks the haughtiest in the eye; of all the sons of pride he is the king" [Job 41:14, 16, 19–22, 24, 31–32, 34].

'This is whom we are up against, brother! These are the words used to describe this tyrant! Yet those who live the solitary life as it should be lived easily achieve victory over him because there is nothing of his evil inside them, because they have renounced the world, because they possess superior virtue, and because we have One who fights on our behalf. For, tell me this: Whose nature has not been transformed by turning to the Lord and by guarding holy fear of Him in his mind? And by illuminating himself with divine laws and works, what man has not clad his soul in light and enabled it to radiate divine wisdom and thoughts? That man will never let his soul be empty, for he has God within himself, Who rouses the mind to reach out insatiably toward the Light. And the Spirit will not permit a soul in such a state of unceasing spiritual activity to waver under the influence of passions; but with a royal authority and a terrible wrath, He will turn on them; and forbidding them to trespass, He then will mercilessly flog them. A man in such a spiritual state will never turn back; but through practicing (the virtues) and praying in his mind with hands uplifted to heaven, he will be victorious in battle.' "

15. The same brother related that among other virtues, Abba Philemon also had the following one:

"He could not abide listening to empty words. If anyone unwittingly discussed something that was not spiritually profitable, he did not respond at all. Likewise, when I went out, he did not ask why I was leaving. And when I returned, he did not ask where I had been or what I had done or how.

"Once I had to sail to Alexandria on important business, and from there I went to Constantinople on some church matter, without informing the starets, this servant of God. After being away a considerable time and visiting the devout local brethren, I finally returned to the skete. The starets was filled with joy to see me; he welcomed me in his customary manner, said a prayer, and sat down. Yet he did not ask anything, but simply continued with his usual spiritual exercises."

16. "Once, I wanted to test him, so for several days I did not bring him any bread to eat. He neither asked for the bread nor said anything about this. I then bowed to him and asked, 'Be so kind, Father, tell me—were you offended because I didn't bring you bread to eat as usual?' He replied, 'Forgive me, brother! If you were to deprive me of bread for twenty days, I would not ask you for it. For as long as my soul endures, so will my body endure as well.' That's how profoundly he was absorbed in the mystical contemplation of true spiritual realities."

17. "He used to say, 'From the time I came to the skete, I never allowed my thoughts to wander outside the confines of my cell. I never permitted any thoughts to enter my mind other than those about the fear of God and the judgment in the next life. I never forgot about the final judgment that awaits sinners, the eternal fire and the darkness of hell; about how the souls of the sinners and the righteous live; about the blessings that await the righteous and how each man is rewarded according to his deeds—one, for a life of valiant spiritual asceticism; another, for honest mercy and love; yet another, for generosity and a life of silent solitude; still another, for extreme obedience or living the life of a pilgrim. In reflecting on all this, I do not allow myself to entertain any other thoughts, and I can no longer be with people or think about them, lest I distance myself from reflecting on the divine."

18. "He added to this a story about a certain solitary ascetic who had achieved dispassion and was receiving the bread he ate from the very hands of an angel. Yet, he became lazy (inattentive) and was deprived of that honor. For when the soul relaxes its scrutiny and intense watchfulness, the night descends upon it. Where God does not shine, every-

thing becomes murky as in darkness, and then the soul can no longer contemplate the One and Only God or tremble at His words. 'Am I God when I am near at hand,' says the Lord, 'and not God when far away? Can man hide in secret places without my seeing him? Do I not fill heaven and earth?' [Jer. 23:23–24]. He also remembered many others who had suffered a similar fate. He gave the example of Solomon, who had lost his fame for a petty lustful pleasure, saying that he had been granted wisdom that brought him fame and renown, because he illumined everyone with the light of his wisdom as dawn lights up a morning sky.

"Thus, it is dangerous to indulge laziness; instead, we must pray unceasingly, so that no encroaching thought draws us away from God and replaces Him in our mind with something else. Only a pure heart, which has become the abode of the Holy Spirit, can clearly see within itself, as in a mirror, the very God of all creation."

19. "After hearing this and seeing how he struggles," said the brother who lived with Abba Philemon, "I understood that the passions of the flesh had completely ceased to act in him, and that he zealously loved all perfection, so that he always appeared transfigured by the Divine Spirit (from glory to glory) and was sighing inexpressible sighs; that he was focused within himself, communing with himself, and checking himself (or striving to preserve a true inner balance, as if using scales); and that he was doing his utmost to prevent anything from entering his mind and obscuring its purity or allowing the slightest filth to attach itself secretly to him.

"Seeing this," said the brother, "I was filled with a zeal to live the same kind of spiritual life, and I earnestly beseeched him, asking, 'How can I attain the purity of mind that you have?' He replied, 'Work hard, for this requires much effort and suffering for the heart. Spiritual blessings, which deserve hard work and to be zealously sought after, will not come to us if we lounge in bed and sleep. He who wants to succeed in the spiritual life must, first of all, renounce all his desires; he must acquire constant tears and must covet nothing. He must ignore the sins of others, focus only on his own and shed endless tears over them day and night; and he must avoid all vain relationships with people. For the soul that grieves over its own wretched state and that is wounded by memories of its own transgressions dies to the world just as the world is dead to it, in other words, no longer are the passions of the flesh active in such a man, and no longer is he under their influence. Moreover, he who has renounced the world, who has united himself to Christ, and who lives in solitary silence, loves God. He preserves the image of God within himself and is enriched by this likeness. For he will he receive the gift of the Spirit from Him on high and will become a home for God, and not for demons; and he will offer up his works of righteousness to God. Thus, the soul that begins to live a pure life that is free of all defilement of the flesh, uncorrupted and without sin, will finally be crowned with the crown of truth and will radiate the beauty of the virtues.

'If at the outset of embarking on a life of asceticism, a person's heart is not filled with sorrow, and he does not shed true tears of contrition; if the thought of eternal torments is not imprinted in his memory; if he does not persevere in true silence, unceasing prayer, psalmodising, and studying divine Scripture; if this rule has not become a habit resulting from constant practice, which would compel his mind to adhere to that practice even against his will; and if the fear of God does not reign sovereign in his soul, this person still has close ties to this world and cannot pray with a pure mind. For only devout reverence and the fear of God purify a soul from passions, and by liberating the intellect, they bring it to its most natural activity of contemplation and thus allow it to partake of the knowledge of God, which it receives in the form of a blessing (*Blessed are the pure in heart, for they shall see God*) [Matt. 5:8]. For him who has been granted this, it will henceforth serve as a pledge (of what is to come) and will preserve (his inner spiritual state) as unshakeable.

'Therefore, with all our strength, let us earnestly strive to practice the rule of living the spiritual life (virtues and ascetic spiritual struggles), which elevates us to a state of devout reverence that is the purity of the mind, and the fruit of this is theological contemplation, which is natural to the intellect. For the practice of this rule is the very ascent toward contemplation, as the perceptive and most divinely illumined intellect (of Gregory the Theologian) states. Therefore, if we neglect to practice the rule of the spiritual life, we become strangers to the love of wisdom. For anyone who attains to the summit of perfection in the virtues will still need to labor assiduously in the ascetic spiritual life, which curbs the unseemly inclinations of the flesh, and to maintain meticulous watchfulness over his thoughts. And even with this, we are just barely able, by force, to take possession of Christ's indwelling in our hearts. For the more righteous we become, the more spiritually mature and strong, until finally, the mind attains perfection, and it undividedly clings to God and is illumined by the divine light, which reveals to it ineffable mysteries. Then will the mind arrive at a true and intimate knowledge of all things—where it is that wisdom resides and where reside power and the faculty for truly knowing all things, where length of years and life itself reside, and where reside the light of the eyes and peace.

'For as long as one still struggles with the passions, he cannot enjoy these delights, since both the virtues and the vices blind the mind—the latter prevent it from seeing the virtues, the former from seeing the vices. But when one finds peace from spiritual warfare and is granted the gifts of the Spirit, he will be under the constant influence of grace, transfigured by the light, and will attain a state of unwavering contemplation of spiritual realities. Such a person is no longer bound to anything of this world, but has passed from death into life. The person who undertakes to follow the excellence of such a life and zealously desires to draw closer to God must have a pure heart and pure lips, so that the pure words that emanate from his pure lips will glorify God in a worthy manner, for the soul that clings to God enjoys constant converse with Him.

'And so, brothers, let us embrace a desire to attain such perfection in virtue, and let us sever our worldly bonds of clinging to the passions. He who struggles and has attained intimacy with God—who has shared in His Holy Light and has been wounded by love for Him—it is he who rejoices in a certain unattainable spiritual delight in the Lord, as the divine psalm states, "Delight also in the Lord, and He will give you what your heart desires. . . . He will make your righteousness clear as the light, and your integrity as bright as noon" [Ps. 37:4, 6]. And what love is so powerful and so irresistible as the one that God pours into a soul that has been purified of all evil? Such a soul speaks from a true and pure state when it says, "For I am lovesick" [Song of Sol. 2:5]. Inexpressible and inexplicable is the brilliant splendor of divine beauty! Our words cannot describe it—our ears cannot contain the sound of it! The light of day, the shining of the moon, the radiance of the sun—all these are insignificant in comparison with that glory; and they are more diminished in the presence of that true light than is the darkest night or the most dense fog in the face of the brightest sun at noon. Marvelous among the teachers, Basil taught us this, having learned it from his own personal experience.' "

20. The brother who lived with the Abba related this and much more. Yet who would not marvel also at the following proof of the Abba's great humility: Although he had long, long ago been ordained as a priest and had with such profound sincerity attained heaven both in his life and with his intellect, he still avoided officiating at liturgical services, for he viewed this as a burden. So that during the many years of living the ascetic spiritual life, not only did he rarely agree to approach the altar (to officiate at the Liturgy as a priest), but despite the life of constant vigilance that he lived, he also refrained from receiving the Communion of the Holy Mysteries if, at the time, he hap-

pened to meet and to speak with people, even though he spoke of nothing worldly, but only what was spiritually beneficial to those who sought to speak with him. But when he did intend to receive the Communion of the Holy Mysteries, he spent a long time persistently entreating God and imploring His good will through prayers, psalmody and confessions. He experienced fear and awe on hearing the priest pronounce the words *the holy things are for the holy*. For he would say that at this moment the entire church was filled with holy angels and that the King Himself mystically officiated at the Liturgy and made the bread and the wine His Body and His Blood—and that through our receiving Holy Communion, He entered and made His dwelling in our hearts. He would add that it is for this reason that we must dare to receive the Communion of the Most-Pure Mysteries of Christ only in purity and chasteness—as if *free from the bonds of the flesh*, so to speak—and without any doubts or hesitation, so that we would participate in the illumination bestowed by these Mysteries. Many of the Holy Fathers saw holy angels who guarded them (from every harm), which is why they remained in a state of profound silence and spoke with no one.

21. And here is yet something else which (that same brother) related: When the starets himself had to go out to sell what he had made with his hands, he would stand silently and pretend to be mentally handicapped, so as to avoid any lies or swearing, or unnecessary words, or any other sinful acts that would occur if he had to engage in conversation and bargaining. Anyone who wanted to buy his wares would simply take them and pay him whatever they wanted. This great man, who so loved wisdom, wove small baskets, and he gratefully accepted whatever he was given for them and never said a word.

A SUMMARY OF THE TEACHINGS OF THE FATHERS

IN CONCLUSION, we would like to offer a summary of the teachings of the Fathers presented in this book.

This is what the Fathers teach us about how to pray and the conditions for effective prayer.

Constancy: the frequent and regular repetition of the Jesus Prayer.

Attention: concentrating the mind on Jesus Christ while resisting all other thoughts.

Variations in praying: reciting the Jesus Prayer either in its entirety or in abbreviated form.

Sequences in a rule of prayer: praying, psalmodising, sitting, standing with uplifted arms, again praying the Jesus Prayer, reading the works of the Fathers after a meal.

Walking in the presence of God: a state of always perceiving the presence of God and preserving a constant remembrance of God, no matter what activity is being performed.

Renunciation of the world: while remembering and reflecting on death and on the sweetness of prayer.

Unceasing invocation of the Name of Jesus Christ: to be done always and at all times—out loud, if you are alone; only with your mind, if you are among people.

Falling asleep: in bed, while praying the Jesus Prayer.

Formal prayers: supplications to attain interior prayer, that is, asking the Lord for His help in zealously and sincerely praying the interior prayer of the heart.

Therefore, you, O, soul, who desires to attain the interior prayer of the heart and who longs for uninterrupted union and exceedingly sweet converse with Jesus Christ—approach! Make your resolve and fulfill the teachings of the Holy Fathers in the following manner:

1. Sit down or, better yet, stand in a dimly lit and quiet corner in a prayerful position.
2. First do a few prostrations, controlling the movement of your arms and legs.
3. Using your imagination, locate the place of the heart under your left nipple and focus your attention on that place.
4. Draw your mind down from your head into the heart and repeat: *Lord Jesus Christ, have mercy on me*. Do this quietly, with your lips, or only in your mind, whichever is more convenient. Pronounce the words slowly and with reverential fear.
5. At the same time, as much as you can, guard your attention and do not allow any thoughts to enter your mind—either bad or good.
6. Be calm and patient and determine to do this for a long time, forgetting everything else.
7. Use moderation in trying to be still, and kneel as often as your strength permits.
8. Be silent.
9. After dinner, read something from the Gospels and from those works of the Fathers that discuss the practice of the interior spiritual life and prayer.
10. Sleep five or six hours a day.
11. Every now and then, verify the progress of your interior prayer by reciting formal prayers.

12. Do not do any kind of work that will distract you.
13. Check your experiences frequently against the instructions of the Fathers.

The Holy Prophet David exclaimed of old: *Lord! Strengthen my resolve*. So you, my soul, must cry out too: *Lord, grant me firm resolve in my intention to be watchful! For both the intention and the doing are from You. After purifying my mind and heart through watchfulness, and with Your help and Your support, may I prepare them as a home for You the Triune God.*

GLOSSARY

akathist A form of Orthodox liturgical hymnology in praise of saints, feasts, and so on. (*See also* kanon)

assignaty A form of paper money in use 1769–c.1840.

barin A member of the land-owning gentry; a gentleman.

bashmaki A special shoe worn over walking shoes or boots.

batyushka "Little father." At the time the pilgrim writes (the nineteenth century), this term of address was still used as a respectful yet affectionate form of address for one's father or other respected men such as teachers, priests, and nobles. Today it is usually used only when addressing priests.

Chet'-Minei A twelve-volume (one for each month) collection of readings from the lives of the saints for every day of the year, arranged in the order in which their feast days occur. It also contains all the books of the Bible along with various other articles on spiritual subjects.

chotki A rosary or prayer rope: a circular string of knots, usually one hundred but often more or less, used to count the number of Jesus Prayers said. Sometimes also used for other prayers as well.

Church Slavonic The language used in the Liturgy of the Russian Orthodox Church. It was devised, along with the Cyrillic alphabet, by the Greek missionaries to the Slavs, Saints Cyril and Methodios, in the ninth century. It remains the liturgical language of the Orthodox Church in Russia and other Slavic countries to this day.

dark water A popular expression for the disease glaucoma.

fool for Christ (Russian *yurodiviy*) A person who takes on an extreme form of asceticism in which even the appearance of sanity is abandoned and madness is feigned for the sake of Christ. "Holy fools" like this were a fairly common sight in Russia right up until Soviet times and can even sometimes be seen today. The pilgrim was thought to be a fool for Christ by the landowner in the Fourth Narrative because he seemed too well educated to be a simple peasant.

kanon A form of Orthodox liturgical hymnology in praise of saints, feasts, and so on. (*See also* akathist)

ksenda A Polish, and thus probably Roman Catholic, priest.

lapti Coarse linen shoes or sandals worn by peasants.

Lyceum High school or law school in pre-revolutionary Russia.

matushka "Little mother." The feminine equivalent of *batyushka*, used similarly in the pilgrim's time as a form of address for women. Today it is used only when addressing a priest's wife or a professed nun.

mir The assembly of all the peasant householders in a village. An ancient institution that endowed peasants with a certain degree of self-government, since the landowner was excluded from its membership.

onoochi Long strips of coarse linen that were wrapped around the feet and legs and worn by Russian peasants instead of stockings.

Philokalia (Greek) "Love of the Beautiful." A collection of mystical and ascetical writings of the Fathers of the Eastern Orthodox Church. In Russian, the book is called *Dobrotolyubie*, "Love of the Good."

prelest Delusion or illusion. Translation from the Greek word that literally means "wandering" or "going astray"; the resulting state in a soul which has wandered away from Truth—hence, error, beguilement, the acceptance of a mirage mistaken for truth.

Presanctified Gifts Reserved Holy Communion, kept in a special container on the altar table and taken for distribution to the sick or dying.

sazhen 1 *sazhen* = 10.7 meters or 2.33 yards.

schima monk/nun (Russian *skhimnik/skhimnitsa*) A fully ordained monk in Orthodox monasticism, living in strict seclusion.

slobody A settlement exempted from normal State obligations; a suburb.

starets (plural *startsi*) "Elder." A monk distinguished for his saintliness, long experience in the spiritual life, and, especially, a unique gift for guiding other souls. Traditionally, the *startsi* were sought out by people for guidance, and entire monastic communities would often grow up around them.

Theotokos (Greek) Birthgiver of God; the Virgin Mary.

versts An old Russian measurement equivalent to approximately 1.06 kilometers or 0.66 miles.

NOTES

1. c. 347–407
2. ? 7th c.
3. Saint John Cassian (c. 560–435). Often called "Cassian the Roman" in Greek sources.
4. Translator's note: *Philokalia, Volume I* (translated from the Greek by G.E.H. Palmer, Philip Sherrard, Kallistos Ware) cites Cassian's work *On the Eight Vices*, which the translator assumes is what the Pilgrim is referring to when he mentions the "eight thoughts."
5. Saint John Climacus
6. The translator understands this to be the Pilgrim's reference to the Kiev-Pechersk Lavra (11th c.), a famous monastery with catacombs that contain the uncorrupted bodies of many saints of ancient Russia and which was and still is highly revered by many pilgrims as a holy place.
7. Literally translated, "the Lord's Law" or, more precisely, "God's Law." These words are also used by the Russian Orthodox to indicate general religious instruction, including Bible studies, akin to what the West calls catechism.
8. Or *raskol'nik* (literally "schismatic"). A sect that broke away from the Russian Orthodox Curch in the 17th century in protest against Patriarch Nikon's liturgical reforms. Factions of this sect are still in existence today.
9. Paissy of Velichkov (1772–1794). A Russian monk who visited Mount Athos and later settled in Moldavia. He was the first to translate a selection of the *Philokalia* texts into Slavonic, which were published under

the title *Dobrotulyubiye (Love of the Good)* in Moscow in 1793 and reprinted in 1822. It was a copy of this translation that the Pilgrim carried on his travels.

10. c. 330–379
11. Early 5th c.; also known as Mark the Monk or Mark the Hermit.
12. c. 300–c. 390
13. Since the *barin* addresses the Pilgrim in the familiar form throughout their conversation, and this phrase switches to the formal "you," the translator understands this to be an insert by the Pilgrim, as a kind of note to the reader.
14. Translator's note: The quote used here by the Pilgrim is a paraphrase of the actual biblical verse.
15. Saint John Chrysostom, called the "Golden-Mouth" because of his divine gift of oration.
16. Hesychius of Jerusalem (5th c.).
17. *Writings from the Philokalia on Prayer of the Heart,* translated by Kadloubovsky, E. and Palmer, G.E.H., part II, page 225.
18. King Solomon
19. Saint Makarios the Great of Egypt (c. 300–c. 390)
20. See "Hesychius of Jerusalem to Theodulus: Texts on Sobriety and Prayer, for the Saving of the Soul" in *Early Fathers from the Philokalia*, page 296, Text 90.
21. Ibid, page 299, Text 102.
22. Ibid.

Shambhala Classics

Appreciate Your Life: The Essence of Zen Practice, by Taizan Maezumi Roshi.

The Art of Peace, by Morihei Ueshiba. Edited by John Stevens.

The Art of War, by Sun Tzu. Translated by the Denma Translation Group.

The Art of Worldly Wisdom, by Baltasar Gracián. Translated by Joseph Jacobs.

Awakening to the Tao, by Liu I-ming. Translated by Thomas Cleary.

Bodhisattva of Compassion: The Mystical Tradition of Kuan Yin, by John Blofeld.

The Book of Five Rings, by Miyamoto Musashi. Translated by Thomas Cleary.

The Book of Tea, by Kakuzo Okakura.

Breath by Breath: The Liberating Practice of Insight Meditation, by Larry Rosenberg.

Cutting Through Spiritual Materialism, by Chögyam Trungpa.

The Diamond Sutra and The Sutra of Hui-neng. Translated by Wong Mou-lam and A. F. Price.

The Essential Teachings of Zen Master Hakuin. Translated by Norman Waddell.

For the Benefit of All Beings, by H.H. the Dalai Lama. Translated by the Padmakara Translation Group.

The Great Path of Awakening, by Jamgön Kongtrül. Translated by Ken McLeod.

Insight Meditation: A Psychology of Freedom, by Joseph Goldstein.

The Japanese Art of War: Understanding the Culture of Strategy, by Thomas Cleary.

Kabbalah: The Way of the Jewish Mystic, by Perle Epstein.

Lovingkindness: The Revolutionary Art of Happiness, by Sharon Salzberg.

Meditations, by J. Krishnamurti.

Monkey: A Journey to the West, by David Kherdian.

The Myth of Freedom and the Way of Meditation, by Chögyam Trungpa.

Narrow Road to the Interior: And Other Writings, by Matsuo Bashō. Translated by Sam Hamill.

The Places That Scare You: A Guide to Fearlessness in Difficult Times, by Pema Chödrön.

The Rumi Collection: An Anthology of Translations of Mevlâna Jalâluddin Rumi. Edited by Kabir Helminski.

Seeking the Heart of Wisdom: The Path of Insight Meditation, by Joseph Goldstein and Jack Kornfield.

Seven Taoist Masters: A Folk Novel of China. Translated by Eva Wong.

Shambhala: The Sacred Path of the Warrior, by Chögyam Trungpa.

Siddhartha, by Hermann Hesse. Translated by Sherab Chödzin Kohn.

The Spiritual Teaching of Ramana Maharshi, by Ramana Maharshi.

Start Where You Are: A Guide to Compassionate Living, by Pema Chödrön.

T'ai Chi Classics. Translated with commentary by Waysun Liao.

Tao Teh Ching, by Lao Tzu. Translated by John C. H. Wu.

The Taoist I Ching, by Liu I-ming. Translated by Thomas Cleary.

The Tibetan Book of the Dead: The Great Liberation through Hearing in the Bardo, translated with commentary by Francesca Fremantle and Chögyam Trungpa.

Training the Mind and Cultivating Loving-Kindness, by Chögyam Trungpa.

The Tree of Yoga, by B. K. S. Iyengar.

The Way of a Pilgrim and The Pilgrim Continues His Way. Translated by Olga Savin.

The Way of the Bodhisattva, by Shantideva. Translated by the Padmakara Translation Group.

When Things Fall Apart: Heart Advice for Difficult Times, by Pema Chödrön.

The Wisdom of No Escape: And the Path of Loving-Kindness, by Pema Chödrön.

The Wisdom of the Prophet: Sayings of Muhammad. Translated by Thomas Cleary.

The Yoga-Sūtra of Patañjali: A New Translation with Commentary. Translated by Chip Hartranft.

Zen Lessons: The Art of Leadership. Translated by Thomas Cleary.

Zen Training: Methods and Philosophy, by Katsuki Sekida.